Literary Treks

Characters on the Move

Mary Ellen Snodgrass

Cartography by Raymond Barrett Jr.

2003
LIBRARIES UNLIMITED
A Division of Greenwood Publishing Group, Inc.
Westport, Connecticut

Copyright © 2003 Mary Ellen Snodgrass
All Rights Reserved
Printed in the United States of America

No part of this publication may be reproduced, stored in a retrieval system, or transmitted, in any form or by any means, electronic, mechanical, photocopying, recording, or otherwise, without the prior written permission of the publisher.

LIBRARIES UNLIMITED
88 Post Road West
Westport, Connecticut
1-800-225-5800
www.lu.com

Library of Congress Cataloging-in-Publication Data

1-56308-953-X
CIP

Contents

Acknowledgments..v
Introduction..vii

Anne Frank: The Diary of a Young Girl.......................1
Bless Me, Ultima...11
Brave New World..19
Dicey's Song...27
Don't Look Behind You......................................33
Go Tell It on the Mountain.................................39
Great Expectations...45
Inherit the Wind...57
The Joy Luck Club..65
Julius Caesar..75
Kindred..83
A Lesson Before Dying......................................89
A Long Way from Chicago....................................97
Macbeth...105
The Midwife's Apprentice..................................113
The Miracle Worker..119
Moby Dick...125
Monster...131
O Pioneers!...137
The Piano Lesson..143
A Prayer for Owen Meany...................................147
Shabanu, Daughter of the Wind.............................153
The Sign of the Beaver....................................161
Snow Falling on Cedars....................................167
Song of Solomon...173
The Things They Carried...................................179
Who Killed My Daughter?...................................187
The Yearling..195

Filmography...201
General Bibliography......................................203
Index...205

Acknowledgments

Anne Frank Museum
Reference Department
Amsterdam, Holland

Dr. Grimes Byerly
MASH surgeon, retired
Hickory, North Carolina

Capitoline Museum
Reference Department
Rome, Italy

Gary Carey
author, editor
Lincoln, Nebraska

Ernest J. Gaines
author
Lafayette, Louisiana

Diana Norman
researcher, novelist
Stevenage, England

Brent Pahde, editor
Perma-Bound
Jacksonville, Illinois

Dr. Laurie Rozakis
author, educator
Farmingdale, New York

Wanda Rozzelle
reference librarian
Catawba County Library
Newton, North Carolina

Mark Schumacher
reference librarian
University of North Carolina
Greensboro, North Carolina

Dr. Elie Wiesel
Boston University
Boston, Massachusetts

I owe a great deal to Raymond Barrett, Jr., cartographer and consultant in Pleasanton, California, for his guidance in the re-creation of character journeys, both real and fictional. Special thanks go to Dan Willis, business manager of Perma-Bound, Jacksonville, Illinois, and his assistant, Roberta Randorf, for allowing me to publish the maps and itineraries that Raym and I sketched to illustrate teacher's guides for the Living Literature Series, edited by Brent Pahde.

Introduction

An understanding of literature demands and promotes a wide knowledge of the world. Because many characters make treks and pilgrimages across known territory, the wise reader can follow along on a map to experience the physical landscape on which events occur. To enhance the reader's journey, the itineraries and maps in *Literary Treks: Characters on the Move* provide the reader, student, teacher, librarian, parent, critic, and historian with details of the terrain and the landmarks that point the way to a destination. Among the twenty-eight titles of novels, drama, diary, and other nonfiction covered in the text are works suited to a varied audience, from middle-school readers to more mature tastes and interests. Each entry covers places visited as well as historical figures, cultures, and sites discussed or referred to, ranging from Mark Antony of republican Rome to Ishmael, fictional survivor of Moby Dick's vengeance in the mid–Pacific Ocean; from an Algonquian Indian village in colonial Maine to a Chinatown crab market in post–World War II San Francisco and a futuristic world where human life takes shape in glass jars on a conveyor belt of Aldous Huxley's *Brave New World*.

The geographic subjects of the chosen works range over many locales, cultures, plants, animals, and historic eras. Plots refer to writers, pioneers, warriors, slaves, apprentices, healers, whalers, conquerors, and prisoners. Examples from classic literature clarify familiar journeys:

- the rise of Macbeth from Scottish general and thane to king, taking him to three castles along the rugged Grampian Mountains and northwest to the highlands along the North Sea in William Shakespeare's stage version of an eleventh-century tyrant. At the end of the duel that kills Macbeth, Malcolm III returns to power with a ceremonial crowning at Scone, Scotland's revered seat of power.

- the journal account of the self-exile of Anne Frank and her family and fellow Jews, who survive in hiding for twenty-five months of World War II in Amsterdam, Holland, before falling into the hands of the Gestapo. Beyond the last sentence, published by Anne's father, Otto Frank, the reader responds to her quiet demise from typhus far from parents and home at Bergen-Belsen, Germany, a notorious Nazi death camp.

- Captain Ahab's manic pursuit of the killer white whale in Herman Melville's *Moby Dick*, a hellish voyage from the whaling ports of New England through the Atlantic and Indian oceans east toward the whale's migratory territory southeast of Japan, from which one man returns to narrate the sinking of the *Pequod*.

In each desperate struggle for survival, a sense of place pervades the literary setting, offering clues to climate, people, governments, and economies that impinge on the outcome.

Some of the geographic travels of characters involve journeys within narrow confines rather than out of familiar territory. For example, biology teacher Bert Cates, the fictional persona of John T. Scopes of Dayton, Tennessee, suffers a jail term for challenging the stifling ignorance of Appalachia. He finds himself supported by a cynical journalist from Baltimore and by the American Civil Liberties Union, a liberal organization headquartered in New York City to promote First Amendment rights. During and after his trial in a hometown courthouse, Bert is publicly damned by a flamboyant Illinois orator, a fictional zealot based on the populist orator William Jennings Bryan. A Chicago radio technician broadcasts to the world the Bible Belt's intent to uphold the Butler Act, state legislation that banned the teaching of Charles Darwin's theory of evolution in favor of biblical creationism. Bert's escape by train with his girlfriend, Rachel Brown, dramatizes the flight of the real John Scopes from the fundamentalist South to the University of Chicago, where he refined his knowledge of geology and the earth's beginnings.

In two entries, *Brave New World* and *Kindred,* fantasy affords an unusual freedom of movement to characters unleashed from the normal constraints of time and place. In Aldous Huxley's dystopian novel, loner Bernard Marx and his conformist date, Lenina Crowne, depart London by rocket ship to vacation among the Zuñi at Malpais Reservation in New Mexico. Far from a technologically controlled environment, they find snake handling, peyote consumption, and kiva worship more pagan and distressing than they imagined. The second work, a sci-fi thriller by Octavia Butler, takes on the style and purpose of historical fiction by chronicling time travel by a black freelance writer from urban California to a Maryland plantation in the antebellum South. Concluding on July 4, 1976, the U.S. bicentennial, the novel comments specifically on the blessings of liberty and democracy. In both literary works, the protagonists' journeys and discoveries about suffering shed light on current attitudes toward human freedoms.

Much of the literature described in *Literary Treks* reflects the history of a particular region and time. In Elizabeth George Speare's *The Sign of the Beaver,* two young boys act out on a limited site the national agony of suspicion and belittlement that European and Native American cultures bore each other as white settlers began pushing Indian tribes off ancestral lands in colonial New England. In *O Pioneers!,* Willa Cather reduces to one community's trials and joys the settlement of the American Midwest by Scandinavian and French immigrant farm families. Within the struggle to tame the shifting Nebraska prairie and its unpredictable weather patterns lies the personal attempt by one woman, Alexandra Bergson, to shuck off the patriarchal tyranny of the old country and create an open environment of ambition and achievement for New World women. In these examples, the authors dramatize actual human choices against realistic backdrops threatening starvation, injury, loss, despair, exhaustion, and financial ruin.

By shadowing fictional and real characters, the reader experiences a variety of cultures characterized by unusual foods, dress, celebrations, beliefs, languages, and labors. Through Karen Cushman's *The Midwife's Apprentice,* the reader can relive the coming of age of an apprenticed beggar child, whose study of English birthing techniques during the time of Edward I reflects the greater culture of the Middle Ages and its superstitions. In *Bless Me, Ultima,* Rudolfo Anaya describes the Hispanic *curandera*'s digging of *yerba buena,* a powerful curative found in the New Mexican desert that creates a climate of distrust in people who confuse natural healing with witchcraft. In *Snow Falling on Cedars*, author David Guterson introduces an insular environment on an offshore island of Washington state. There the post–World War II generation of fishers and laborers ponders the festering prejudices it has harbored since the Japanese sneak attack on Pearl Harbor, Hawaii, on December 7, 1941, and the subsequent incarceration of innocent Asian Americans at internment camps.

Introduction

In each instance, literary characters live out human challenges that are more onerous in fact than they appear in the broad generalizations of history books.

In each of the chosen works, characters encounter elements of nature that require a cautious understanding and appreciation. In Richard Newton Peck's *A Long Way from Chicago*, a brother and sister travel southwest by train each August from the crime-ridden big city to their grandmother's home in rural Illinois, where catfish trapped in a creek become dinner for hungry homeless men battling the Great Depression. Another youth, Jody Baxter, son of a Civil War veteran in Marjorie Kinnan Rawlings's *The Yearling,* abandons boyhood while following his father into the flooded Florida highlands to hunt bears and alligators for meat and skins. Julius Caesar, the title character of William Shakespeare's stage tragedy, exhibits human frailty while swimming the Tiber River in full armor and by ignoring his wife's warning that storms bode ill for political titans. In each example, the players on literary settings learn the limitations that humans accept when braving a wide expanse of nature and its dangers.

The historical events that support these twenty-eight works allow readers a glimpse of real heroes and villains who have influenced the world's peoples. For a Pakistani nomad in Suzanne Fisher Staples's *Shabanu, Daughter of the Wind,* a pilgrimage to an Islamic saint's tomb eases the yearnings of women for positive marital experiences in a land where dominant males limit the choices and aspirations of wives and daughters. In Tim O'Brien's *The Things They Carried,* a movie starring actress Jane Fonda lightens an evening of perimeter patrol in war-torn Vietnam, where a disgruntled soldier torments a guard with a wartime prank that threatens to escalate into murder. From the same era, a teenager's stateside involvement in antiwar protests and an idealistic generation's admiration for President John F. Kennedy color a torturous period of warfare and moral dilemma expressed in John Irving's fictional *A Prayer for Owen Meany.* In each instance, literature describes for the reader the ethical quagmire that the individual character successfully traverses, whether fleeing a feudal marriage, protesting the draft during an unjust war, or maiming a friend to keep him out of combat. From the hazards they encounter, the protagonists acquire a new understanding of self, a greater awareness of society's frailties.

In each work, the accompanying maps specify hard journeys that test the characters' mettle. For Milkman Dead in Toni Morrison's *Song of Solomon,* the search for grandparents in the fictional community of Shalimar, Virginia, parallels the itinerary of his rabid stalker, who joins a clutch of vigilantes that countenances grudge-holding, ambush, and assassination. For visually impaired teacher Annie Sullivan, the test of ambition is a willingness to travel from schools and opportunities for the handicapped in Boston, Massachusetts, by train to rural Alabama, where six-year-old Helen Keller awaits release from a dark and silent prison. For Lois Duncan, author of *Who Killed My Daughter?,* the reality of the unsolved pursuit and assassination of her daughter Kait thrusts Duncan into the milieu of psychics, fraudulent auto accidents, murky criminal dealings, and failed police investigations. Beyond the safety of an affluent home in Albuquerque, New Mexico, Duncan willingly scours the barrios of Martineztown in search of a clue to her daughter's brutal slaying. An eerie chime in the background are the similarity of Kait's death to events and characters in Duncan's young adult novel *Don't Look Behind You,* a fictional flight from a hit man and the allegedly safe harbor of the Federal Witness Protection Program. Just as in Duncan's real experience, government assurances in her teen novel fail to shield a family from recompense for testifying against a powerful drug dealer.

Through these physical, mental, and emotional journeys, characters live out on the page actual human adventures identified on a map. Without risk, readers can vicariously sample bizarre and harrowing experiences—setting up an electric chair in Ernest Gaines's *A Lesson Before Dying,* a religious conversion in James Baldwin's *Go Tell It on the Mountain,* rowing a herdsman from New South Wales toward escape from police down the Thames delta in Charles Dickens's *Great Expectations,* locating lost twin sisters in modern Shanghai in Amy Tan's *The Joy Luck Club,* awaiting a verdict at a murder trial in a New York courtroom in Walter Dean Myers's *Monster,* exorcising a ghost in August Wilson's play *The Piano Lesson,* and the burial of a mother's ashes under a mulberry tree on the Maryland side of the Chesapeake Bay in Cynthia Voigt's *Dicey's Song.* The price of literary travel is available to all—a book, the leisure to read, and the opportunity to pick a character and mentally tag along. For the truly venturesome, the bibliographies at the end of each entry point the way to more data, maps, and pictures in books, newspapers, journals, atlases, online databases, and Internet sites. By following the movements of literary characters, the reader absorbs more of the journey, enjoys greater satisfaction, and acquires a stronger oneness with those who dare.

Teaching with Literary Maps

For the classroom language or social studies teacher, the presentation of literary maps supports multiple applications for extended lessons and activities that pair reading with map study. By examining copies of maps before the reading of a difficult text, students witness on paper the challenges of long journeys such as the rocket flight from London to the rugged American Southwest in *Brave New World.* Maps help students comprehend the geographic scale of action, as with the spread of Roman civil war over the Mediterranean world in *Julius Caesar* after the assassination of the supreme military leader of his day. Disadvantaged readers and students new to the English language can better comprehend complex travels by keeping a map at hand during private reading of a lengthy text such as the meetings between Pip and Abel Magwitch in *Great Expectations.* For visualizing action on unfamiliar territory, as is the case with *Shabanu, Daughter of the Wind,* students can learn more about desert nomads. At the same time, they can apply their lessons to the hardships faced by U.S. Rangers during the search for Al Qaeda insurgents after the surprise attacks on the Pentagon and the World Trade Center on September 11, 2001.

Literary maps offer springboards for detailed reports and individual projects; for example, the background of *Anne Frank: Diary of a Young Girl* or *The Joy Luck Club* serves as adjuncts to units on the plight of Jewish and Chinese refugees, Nazi concentration camps, and battles of World War II. The layout of character treks is a model for additional map drawing for episodes of *A Prayer for Owen Meany* or *The Things They Carried.* By sketching troop movements before and after a significant battle that escalated the U.S. war in Vietnam, readers have a greater awareness of the nation's political involvement in Southeast Asia and the failed attempt to halt the spread of Communism into a rich rice-growing basin. Group mapping on a wall mural can also illuminate a point of view, such as a study of FBI detective work over state lines to rescue an endangered family from a stalker in *Don't Look Behind You* or to solve a contract-style murder in Santa Fe, New Mexico, and its connection to fraudulent auto accidents in California in *Who Killed My Daughter?*

For below-average students struggling to keep up with better readers, classroom study of literary maps expands reading and literature classes with an illustrative visual dimension

Introduction

and a hands-on guide to character actions. For example, a state-by-state coverage of the wanderings of the motherless Tillerman children in *Dicey's Song* enhances an appreciation of their daring in searching for relatives along the Atlantic seaboard. By color-coding important points, students can contrast Dicey's journey south to her grandmother's home with the painful trip north to bid farewell to Dicey's dying mother. A similar cross-country explanation of *The Piano Lesson* along with teacher lectures, videos, or filmstrips on economic differences in South and North expresses the family's loss from sibling separation and characterizes Boy Willie's displacement in a metropolitan area far from the agrarian South. Additional library or online assignments outlining topography and climate in the southwestern United States elucidate for the reader of *Bless Me, Ultima* the lay of the land that Tony travels with the aged *curandera* and the types of weather, waterways, plants, and animals that influence his search for healing herbs and the magical fish of legend.

For teachers presenting background before assigning a new title, display of a map on an overhead projector can circumvent misunderstandings about terrain that crop up in out-of-class reading. By characterizing the distances that separate trial lawyers from rural Tennessee in *Inherit the Wind*, the teacher can point out differences in point of view between Southern religious fundamentalists and the outsiders who clash in the courtroom at the trial of Bert Cates. A pre-reading map of one of the most complicated literary treks, *Moby Dick*, instructs the reader on the demanding, sometimes life-threatening job of the nineteenth-century whaler. By pointing out the lengthy voyage of the *Pequod* as it sails east from New England, the teacher can enlighten the student about the movements of whales over the globe and the hard task of locating and harvesting them to supply markets with whale oil.

Instruction in marking maps with notes and arrows provides valuable preparation of college-preparatory and advanced-placement classes in organizing their work, simplifying confusing elements, outlining chronology, and incorporating marginalia as guides to reading, research, and preparation for tests and exams. For classes studying *Macbeth*, individual copies of maps offer a template for marking act and scene at particular locales and for diagramming the movements of historic figures who vie for the control of medieval Scotland. Likewise, dotted lines and arrows on a literary map of *The Midwife's Apprentice* particularize Alyce's choices of residence in medieval England as she considers what she wants to do with her life. For *The Yearling*, a student copy of the literary map presents a visual study guide of the watery, boggy terrain of central Florida and a basis for sketching Jody's flight from his parents and his intended destination in New England. Additional assignments in applying map legends and estimating distance on land and sea express in miles the unlikelihood that Jody can succeed in abandoning his old life in Florida and begin a new life with Grandma Hutto in Boston.

The applications and extensions of *Literary Treks: Characters on the Move* build numerous skills. For a note-taking exercise, readers can keep a geographic journal to accompany contrasting scenes from *The Miracle Worker* or *Monster*. For a unit on summarizing, the maps accompanying *The Sign of the Beaver, O Pioneers!*, and *Snow Falling on Cedars* provide valuable details of the history of immigrant settlement of New England, the Midwest, and the Pacific Coast. To enhance theme development during an observation of Black History Month, oral presentations based on character treks in *Song of Solomon* and *Go Tell It on the Mountain* consolidate an understanding of the destructive nature of racism. A group project on the importance of railroads to the economic and social growth of America might incorporate a chalk talk on the ease with which the Dowdel parents send their children for annual summer visits with their grandmother in *A Long Way from Chicago*. To assist students opting for extra credit reading, maps offer needed guideposts for an oral analysis of the setting of *A Lesson Before Dying*. For lessons planned by student teachers or substitute teachers, literary maps become valuable handout sheets to orient newcomers to the classroom in the terrain readers will cover as they explore a new title.

Anne Frank: The Diary of a Young Girl
By Anne Frank

Confessional journal, 1993 edition

Geographical Summary

The 1993 edition of *Anne Frank: The Diary of a Young Girl* from Bantam Books reprises the flight of a Jewish family from the Nazi rape of the Netherlands. The geographic focus of the story is Amsterdam, an enclave of 80,000 Jews, the largest gathering in the whole nation. Of that number, 25,000 went into hiding rather than emigrate to escape persecution. Anne's story humanizes the intense hardships of going underground by telling one family's experience with surviving under the noses of Adolf Hitler's S.S.

According to the journal, after the Nazis shut down access to schools, public transportation, the Frank children's grandmother and friends, and purchases of food, books, and other necessities from Amsterdam's markets, the four Franks—father, mother, and two daughters—retreat from sight. They calmly walk up the street with shopping bags and disappear into the annex of Travies N.V., the spice importation business that Otto Frank directs in close relationship with Kolen & Company, which shares the building. The radio informs the tiny cell of world events, bringing to their ears news of D-Day and the Allies' march on Paris. At the nearby Westertoren Tower, the clock chimes the final hours as the victors gradually strip Hitler's forces of power. Nazi storm troopers, obsessed with maximum genocide before they lose the war, arrest and gas more people on their list of undesirables—Jews, homosexuals, political prisoners, the insane and retarded, Seventh Day Adventists, Gypsies.

Within the narrow annex, Anne enlarges her view of the world through romantic fantasy, self-study, reading and schoolwork, and fleeting glimpses out of smudged windows. She identifies her parents and sister by name but conceals the identities of the other inmates. Fritz Pfeffer, a dentist, becomes Dr. Albert Dussel; Hermann, Auguste, and Peter Van Pels become the Van Daan family. Together despite disagreements, they make strawberry jam, peel potatoes, and celebrate Chanuka, St. Nicholas Day, and birthdays. When circumstances permit, they venture below their two upper floors to survey the activities of downstairs office workers.

Infrequent visits from Miep Gies and her husband Henk normalize the environment with news from the neighborhood. To combat stress, Anne drafts royal genealogies and groups on the wall photos of Greta Garbo, Norma Shearer, and Princess Elizabeth of York. As the allies begin their triumphant march over western France toward Aachen, Germany,

Anne and the others monitor British Broadcasting Corporation (BBC) broadcasts by English Prime Minister Winston Churchill and Holland's Queen Wilhelmina and discuss the collapse of fascism and Nazism. The Franks' claustrophobic habitat parallels the stark milieu of hungry, ragged children playing in the street below and a steady march of Jews rounded up and transported to death camps to suffer the Third Reich's "final solution."

Detailed Itinerary

1. Amsterdam, Netherlands

On Sunday, June 14, 1942, Annelies Marie "Anne" Frank begins keeping a daybook, a birthday present from her father, Otto Frank, owner and managing director of Travies, an import office handling pectin, herb, and spice for the sausage and jam trades. A gifted, talkative girl, Anne attended a Montessori school before being forced from public education to a Jewish Lyceum, a secondary school in Amsterdam, the capital and major port of the Netherlands. The city lies on the west side of the Ijesselmeer south of the Wadden Zee, an inlet of the North Sea. A principal trading center built in Roman times on the Amstel River, it comprises ninety distinct land masses separated from the whole by 1,300 bridges and viaducts.

2. Frankfort-on-Main, Germany

Three years younger than her sister Margot, Anne was born on June 12, 1929, in Frankfort-on-Main (Frankfurt on the Main River). Located in Hesse in western Germany, with access to the Rhine River, Frankfurt is a cultural and banking center and a major rail, air, and river hub for Europe, the perfect locale for Otto Frank's spice business. In the summer after Hitler became dictator of Germany in March 1933, the Frank family departed from their five-room flat on Ganghoferstrasse to emigrate to Merwedeplein Square, Amsterdam, where Otto Frank trades in spices. To Kitty, the fictional persona of the diary, Anne indicates that her family worries about pogroms and the anti-Jewish Nuremberg laws, which rescinded Jewish citizenship in 1935 and forced the deportation of Jewish inhabitants from German states and territories to labor camps and death camps.

3. The Jewish State of Israel in Palestine

While still living in Amsterdam like a normal citizen, Anne involves herself in school and social activities and faces regular scoldings from teachers for talking in class. Against her grandparents' wishes, she attends meetings of the Zionist movement, a pro-Jewish faction that originated in eastern and central Europe. After the World Zionist Organization evolved into the Jewish Agency for Palestine, 400,000 European Jews fled oppression by emigrating to Israel by 1936.

European and American strains of Zionism grew politically significant under the rise of the overt and deadly anti-Semitism engineered by Adolf Hitler's Third Reich. It was not until November 29, 1947, that the United Nations General Assembly voted to partition Palestine into Jewish and Arab sectors, a global acknowledgment of an independent Jewish state. By that time, Israel's Jewish population had reached 717,000.

4. Amsterdam, Netherlands

On May 14, 1941, the Netherlands capitulated to the Nazis. According to the diary, in January 1942, Anne's grandmother died about the time the Nazis marked 160,800 Dutch Jews for death. In February, S.S. troops began rounding up Jews. The elite Schutzstaffel, Hitler's bodyguard, consisted of 750,000 criminals and street thugs bearing the blue eyes and blond hair common to people of Aryan descent. An elite commando force, the S.S. received special training, privileges, and advanced weaponry to produce and maintain *judenfrei,* Jew-free cities.

In April, after Jews began identifying themselves with the required yellow star insignia sewn to their outer garments, the S.S. singled out a total of 200,000 Dutch to deport to Germany as slave labor at war industries. As of June 30, 1942, Jews in Holland had to observe an 8:00 P.M.–6:00 A.M. curfew, were not allowed to ride public transportation or use public telephones, and were restricted from entering parks and designated urban sections.

As Anne explains, on July 8, 1942, the call-up of sixteen-year-old Margot Frank for mandatory work and a subsequent summons for Otto Frank to appear at S.S. headquarters force the family into action. They move into hiding ten days earlier than Otto and Mr. Koophuis had planned. They pretend to flee with other Jews emigrating from occupied Holland.

5. Maastricht, Netherlands

For the sake of Mr. Goudsmit, a boarder, Anne's mother, Mrs. Edith Frank-Hollander, leaves behind a false clue—an address in Maastricht, a commune in the Limburg province of southeastern Netherlands. Mr. Van Daan lies to Mr. Goudsmit about the meaning of the incriminating paper and pledges him to keep secret the family's supposed flight from the city. Meanwhile, marked with their yellow stars, the Franks pad their bodies with all the clothes they can wear and walk through the rain to the Travies office on the edge of the Jordaan section west of Damsquare at Amsterdam's city center.

6. Secret Annexe, Prinsengracht Canal

Miep Gies, Otto's trusted secretary, escorts the family past a swinging bookcase and into the Secret Annexe at the rear of the second floor. The two-story hideaway consists of four rooms, a lavatory, a gas stove, a kitchen dresser, and a sink, all of which serve the four Franks and the three Van Daans. As the Franks recede from view behind blackout slats and lace curtains, the Westertoren clock disrupts the peace. The shift in business management leaves Mr. Koophuis in charge of Travies and Mr. Kraler directing Kolen & Company.

A month after disappearing from the Frank home into the annex, Anne describes adjusting to cramped quarters. Limited space ignites frequent quarrels between "Putti" Van Daan, Otto Frank's business partner, and his sulky, materialistic wife Petronella. It appears the forced exile was worth the effort. By December, Nazis troops have executed 2,200 Dutch.

7. Zeeland, Netherlands

The staff of Travies conceals Otto's absence through a fake handwritten message from Zeeland, a heavily diked province of southwestern Netherlands below sea level. Zeeland consists of the Schelde estuary and a cluster of islands on the North Sea.

8. Westerbork, Drenthe, Netherlands

In October, the Gestapo hauls away the Franks' Jewish friends to Westerbork, a transit camp the Dutch built for refugees in 1939 northeast of Amsterdam in the province of Drenthe (or Drente). Before the war, this sandy, boggy area was known for its truck farming, grain and potatoes, dairying and livestock, oil, rope making, and handicrafts.

9. North Africa

By November 9, 1942, BBC (British Broadcasting Corporation) radio brings good news of a British landing in Tunis, Algiers; Casablanca; and Oran, Algeria, on Africa's northwestern coast along the Mediterranean Sea. It is the beginning of the Allied sweep across Sicily and Italy to the heart of Hitler's empire.

The publicly financed BBC is located at Portland Place, Westminster, a borough of London, and operates throughout Great Britain under a royal charter. Until 1972, BBC radio held a public monopoly over other stations.

10. Secret Annexe, Prinsengracht Canal

On November 10, 1942, the seven annex inmates accept an eighth member, Dr. Albert Dussel, Miep Gies's dentist. He arrives five days later and shares Anne's room. On December 7, 1942, the group celebrates Chanuka and St. Nicholas Day and ventures downstairs in the Travies building at 8:00 P.M. to retrieve a basket of holiday gifts.

11. Amsterdam, Netherlands

In the second week of January 1943, Anne Frank reports growing deportation of Jews. From the window, she observes hunger and fear in ragged children on the street below. On March 10, antiaircraft guns disturb the night. For good reason, Otto Frank worries how they will survive under strict food rationing. On March 27, a German official named Rauter gives all Jews three months to depart by ordering them out of Holland by July 1.

The Nazi regime places the Netherlands under martial law. On April 27, British bombers destroy the Carlton Hotel and keep the Annexe group awake with nightly raids. At the window, on May 18, 1943, Anne has a clear view of German and English planes in a midair dogfight.

12. Travies

A July burglary results in the loss of the Travies office cashboxes, postal orders, checkbooks, and sugar coupons. Loss of coupons is particularly dangerous to the two Jewish families, who depend on the clever purchase and delivery of food and other goods by non-Jewish outsiders.

13. Amsterdam, Netherlands

On July 10, 1943, two hundred people perish in the bombing of North Amsterdam. The wounded overrun city hospitals. Two weeks later, nightly bombing resumes.

14. Italy

On July 26, the day after the Fascist Grand Council turns against Italian fascist dictator Benito Mussolini, Annexe inmates rejoice at his resignation, precipitated by the Allied triumph in Sicily, a strategic island southwest of the Italian mainland.

Mussolini enters prison on the Island of Ponza west of Naples in the Tyrrhenian Sea. The Allies transport him briefly to a small landmass off Sardinia, an island northwest of Sicily, and to a hotel in Gran Sasso d'Italia in the Abruzzi Mountains north of Rome. On September 12, 1943, two days after the fall of Italy to the Allies, German commandos swoop down on gliders and release Mussolini. He flees north to Munich, an industrial center in western Germany.

15. Amsterdam, Netherlands

On August 10, 1943, Miep Gies endangers herself by bringing a forbidden book for Dussel. She is bumped by an S.S. car and insults the drivers. As conditions grow more tense in the Annexe, Anne misses her deceased grandmother and thinks about a school friend, Lies Goosens. On January 28, 1944, the inmates long for peace and savor news of the Dutch underground and of people surviving in hiding. In February, they discuss Germany's eventual withdrawal from the Netherlands.

On March 1, a second break-in unnerves the group because the burglar gained entrance with a skeleton key. BBC messages from Winston Churchill on March 27 boost spirits. Two days later, 350 British bombs fall on Ijmuiden on the Dutch coast west of Amsterdam near Haarlem. As the fall of Germany nears, sabotage increases. The Russians fire salvos in celebration of victories over German forces.

16. Secret Annexe, Prinsengracht Canal

On April 11, intruders flee; the Gestapo investigates the premises and rattles the cupboard that conceals the entrance to the Annexe. Otto Frank anticipates a major Allied push by May 20. By May 6, conditions worsen for the Dutch. The inmates slowly starve as prices rise. On May 10, Radio Orange broadcasts over the BBC project hope of liberation from Queen Wilhelmina and Prime Minister Gerbrandy, who live in self-exile in London along with the Dutch royal family and cabinet officials. At the Annexe, Nazis apprehend a deliveryman on May 25 for harboring two Jews.

17. Rome, Italy; Calais, France

On June 5, 1944, the U.S. Fifth Army takes Rome from the Fascists. To Anne and her fellow inmates, the collapse of Hitler's regime seems imminent as the Allies bomb the French coast and Pas de Calais on the Strait of Dover southwest of Amsterdam.

18. Bay of the Seine, France

At 8:00 A.M. on D-Day, June 6, 1944, the BBC announces the successful Allied invasion of northern France on the English Channel. The sea landing started at dawn at Utah, Omaha, and Juno beaches. Around the Bay of Seine, the French coastal cities of Boulogne, Calais, Cherbourg, and Le Havre come under heavy bombardment. Driving the Germans back to their homeland, the Allies press inland over Brittany toward Bayeux and Caen. As the war ends, Winston Churchill, British War Cabinet member Jan Smuts, Allied Commander-in-Chief Dwight D. Eisenhower, and U.S. Army Air Force Chief Henry Arnold extend hope and goodwill by visiting French villages. On June 23, the English occupy Cherbourg on the peninsula northwest of the D-Day beaches.

19. Vitebsk, Russia

The Russians advance to Vitebsk west of Moscow as the Allies begin dismantling Hitler's empire. The Germans evacuate their women and children to the south shortly before an unsuccessful attempt on Hitler's life on July 20, when Colonel Claus von Stauffenberg set a bomb in a briefcase at a meeting at Hitler's headquarters in East Prussia. On August 1, 1944, Anne's diary ends.

20. Secret Annexe, Prinsengracht Canal

At 10:30 A.M. on August 4, 1944, acting on an inside tip from an unidentified Dutch collaborator, the Grüne Polizei (Green Police), led by Inspector Karl Silberbauer, raided the Secret Annexe at Traview. After twenty-five months in hiding, the Jews were arrested. The Amsterdam police chief charged Kraler and Koophuis with conspiring to hide outlaws. Koophuis gained release for medical reasons. Kraler served eight months of forced labor at Zwölle, a Dutch city northeast of Amsterdam. He escaped when Allied planes strafed the camp. To conceal incriminating documents, employee Elli Vossen ran to the drugstore with Koophuis's briefcase. Miep Gies persuaded her interrogator, a fellow native of Vienna, to free her.

The end-of-war turmoil obscured the fate of each refugee. Otto Frank saw Mr. Van Daan depart for the gas chamber. Van Daan's wife Petronella died at Bergen-Belsen. Mr. Dussel perished at Neuengamme Camp on Germany's northern coast near Hamburg, probably in December 1944. Nothing is known about Peter Van Daan, whom German soldiers took with them as they abandoned Auschwitz and fled west.

21. Westerbork, Netherlands

The Germans dispatched the eight detainees by passenger train to Westerbork, where jailers separated the Franks. Nazi staff shaved the heads of convict Jews, confiscated their shoes, and gave them wooden clogs. Under savage Kapos (overseers), inmates labored at digging sod and stripping salvageable parts from discarded batteries.

22. Auschwitz (Oswiecim), Poland

Ten days after the liberation of Paris, the Allies advanced on Aachen in Westphalia, Germany's westernmost city, on the Belgian border southeast of Amsterdam. Meanwhile, as the Allies retook Brussels, Nazis transported the eight Franks by cattle car to the most destructive death camp at Auschwitz-Berkenau, Poland, which opened in March 1942. It was the last convoy of Jews from the Netherlands.

On September 5, 1944, the train arrived at the prison thirty miles from Hindenburg. Guards led the women to Block 29, while the prison staff worked to exterminate Jews in gas chambers and crematories. Guards sent them to the scabies barracks. Anne wept over naked gypsy girls and Hungarian children, who waited a half-day in the rain before being gassed. Edith Frank screamed as she saw her daughters for the last time. On January 6, 1945, withdrawn and demented, she died of malnutrition at the Auschwitz infirmary.

23. Bergen-Belsen, Germany

In October, Nazis deported Margot, Anne, and Petronella Van Daan to Germany. After three days' travel, only Anne and Margot arrived at Bergen-Belsen, a prison in north central Germany near Hannover. Designed for 10,000 inmates, it held 60,000.

Prisoners slept on the ground under tents, suffered starvation and foul water, and stacked corpses for disposal.

Anne, wearing only a shapeless gray garment, reunited with Lies Goosens. Anne survived the experience, but her parents died in camp. Lies tossed supplies across barbed wire fencing, but moiling inmates ripped them from Anne's grasp. Dr. Josef Mengele rejected both Anne and Margot for work at munitions factories.

Shortly after Margot's death from typhus, Anne slipped into a coma and died of the same disease sometime in March 1945. In all, 35,000 died of starvation, exhaustion, and disease at Bergen-Belsen. The British army liberated the camp on April 15, 1945, and later hanged the camp commandant, Josef Kramer. The staff transferred Lies Goosen to Theresienstadt, a preferred treatment camp southeast of Dresden, Germany.

24. Amsterdam, Netherlands

After Canadian troops freed Amsterdam in May 1945, following Germany's surrender to the Western Allies at Rheims, France, Otto Frank, his family's only survivor, returned to Amsterdam via Odessa on the Black Sea and west to Marseilles, a Mediterranean port in southern France. Following his arrival in Amsterdam on June 3, 1945, he learned from the Red Cross of his family's demise. He received Anne's diary along with additional writings, which she had recorded on an office account book and on sheets of colored duplicating paper. Miep Gies had retrieved Anne's journal from a heap of papers when the Nazis tossed it aside. In 1947, Otto decided to publish his daughter's writings as a memorial to the Franks. In June, the book appeared under Anne's title, *Het Achterhuis* (*The Annex*).

25. Secret Annexe, Prinsengracht Canal

Saved from destruction in 1957 by the Anne Frank Foundation, the annex at Prinsengracht became a war museum and shrine. Traveling exhibits about the Franks' wartime experience have reached nine hundred cities in forty-five countries. At Otto's death in 1980, his daughter's writings passed to the Netherlands State Institute for War Documentation. Some thirty million copies of the book circulate in sixty languages.

Further Reading

Adler, David. *Picture Book of Anne Frank*. New York: Holiday House, 1994.

Amdur, Richard. *Anne Frank*. New York: Chelsea House, 1993.

The Anne Frank Center USA. http://www.annefrank.com/.

The Anne Frank House. http://www.annefrank.nl.

The Anne Frank Internet Guide. http://www-th.phys.rug.nl/~ma/annefrank.html.

Anne Frank Online. http://annefrank.com.

Anne Frank: The Life of a Young Girl. New York: A & E Home Video, 1998. Videocassette. Lisa Zeff, producer. 50 min.

Anne Frank Was Not Alone: Holland and the Holocaust. http://www-lib.usc.edu/~anthonya/holo.htm.

Brown, Gene. *Anne Frank, Child of the Holocaust*. New York: Blackbirch Press, 1997.

Corliss, Richard, "Saints in the Neighborhood." *Time* (March 4, 1996): 62.

Covington, Richard, "Forever Young." *Smithsonian* (October 2001): 70–76.

Enzer, Hyman Aaron, and Sandra Solotaroff-Enzer. *Anne Frank: Reflections on Her Life and Legacy*. Urbana: University of Illinois Press, 1999.

Epstein, Rachel. *Anne Frank*. New York: Franklin Watts, 1997.

Gies, Miep, and Alison L. Gold. *Anne Frank Remembered: The Story of the Woman Who Helped Hide the Frank Family*. Boston: G. K. Hall, 1988.

Gilbert, Martin. *Atlas of the Holocaust*. New York: William Morrow, 1993.

Gold, Alison Leslie. *Memories of Anne Frank: Reflections of a Childhood Friend*. New York: Scholastic, 1999.

Goodrich, Frances, and Albert Hackett. *The Diary of Anne Frank*. New York: Harcourt Brace Jovanovich, 1994.

The Holocaust History Project. http://www.holocaust-history.org.

The Holocaust Web Project. http://www.nizkor.netizen.org/hweb.

Hurwitz, Johanna. *Anne Frank: Life in Hiding*. New York: William Morrow, 1993.

I Am Anne Frank. New York: Anne Frank Center USA, 1996.

Immell, Myra H., ed. *Readings on "The Diary of a Young Girl."* New York: Greenhaven Press, 1998.

Israel 1948. http://www.prophesy2000.com/Israel19481.htm.

Kopf, Hedda Rosner. *Understanding Anne Frank: The Diary of a Young Girl*. Westport, Conn.: Greenwood Press, 1997.

Kops, Bernard. *Dreams of Anne Frank: A Play for Young People*. London: Methuen Drama, 1997.

Lee, Carol Ann. *Roses from the Earth: The Biography of Anne Frank*. London: Viking, 1999.

Lindwer, Willy. *The Last Seven Months of Anne Frank*. New York: Anchor, 1992.

Maarsen, Jacqueline van. *My Friend Anne Frank*. New York: Vantage Press, 1996.

McDonough, Yona Zeldis. *Anne Frank*. New York: Henry Holt, 1997.

Menkel, Irma Sonnenberg, "I Saw Anne Frank Die." *Newsweek* (July 21, 1997): 16.

"Miep Gies: Keeping Anne Frank's Story Alive." http://www.msnbc.com/onair/nbc/dateline/MiepGies/.

Muller, Melissa. *Anne Frank: The Biography*. New York: Henry Holt, 1998.

Rittner, Carol, ed. *Anne Frank in the World: Essays and Reflections*. Armonk, N.Y.: M. E. Sharpe, 1997.

Rol, Ruud van der. *Anne Frank, Beyond the Diary: A Photographic Remembrance*. New York: Viking, 1993.

Sheppard, R. Z., "Outside of the Attic." *Time* (September 28, 1998): 1.

Tames, Richard. *Anne Frank: An Unauthorized Biography*. New York: Heinemann, 1998.

Wukovits, John F. *Anne Frank*. San Diego, Calif.: Lucent Books, 1999.

Bless Me, Ultima

By Rudolfo Anaya

Multicultural contemporary fiction, 1972

Geographical Summary

Combining the styles and conventions of the novel of character and the *bildungsroman* with regionalism and elements of myth, Rudolfo Anaya's *Bless Me, Ultima* ties the agrarian Márez family to the cultures of north-central New Mexico's lowlands. Before adapting to community life, the family had computed their household's prosperity in terms of health and harvests. As the story opens outside Guadalupe, they battle unexpected threats by post–World War II upheaval, technological modernization, and the death of folk traditions. Paralleling Tony Márez's loss of innocence, the family undergoes an uprooting from their beloved *llano* (prairie). His father, Gabriel Márez, disdains an unfulfilling job building highways and cultivates utopian reveries of the free-roaming *vaquero* (horseman) and vineyards in California. Similarly, in late 1945, Gabriel's three sons return from World War II bent on adventure and amusement as they cope with battle fatigue. The disintegration of land-based values precedes a postwar adjustment that shames their mother and unsettles Tony as he enters the first grade.

The *llano* throbs with "the hum of the turning earth," Tony's description of positive forces in nature. His love of Ultima, the midwife who delivered him, derives from her wisdom and curative herbs, both antidotes to evil. Through dreams, he relives his father's milieu among *llaneros*, the plainsmen who destroyed offerings of vegetables and fruit around the bed of his mother, María Luna y Márez, when Tony was born. They countered Grandfather Prudencio Luna's blessing of the infant with soil, an agrarian baptism that commits Tony to farming. The acrimonious war of loyalties grows out of this primal scene of conflicting folk values. Cultural strife concludes with Ultima's insistence on peace and on her burial of Tony's afterbirth to settle his destiny.

At the novel's end, at the bridge in El Puerto, nature reclaims Tony as he runs from Tenorio Trementina, a crazed barkeeper at El Puerto, to keep him from murdering Ultima, the boy's protector and mentor. With a benediction, Ultima accepts martyrdom, prepares to merge with earth, and urges Tony to follow her example. Her hand to his forehead, she commits him to "the evenings when the wind is gentle and the owls sing in the hills." A wake and interment in soil satisfies ordinary folk custom. To appease the spirit world, Tony carries out a secret burial when he withdraws to the hills and places her owl near the forked juniper, a reminder that he faces his family's diverging paths.

Detailed Itinerary

1. Farm across the bridge from Guadalupe, New Mexico

At age seven, Antonio "Tony" Márez relives his first acquaintance with Ultima, a midwife and folk healer who lives alone after World War II scatters her patients. Respected as "la Grande," in summer 1945, she comes to his home on a few acres of a yucca-, mesquite,- and juniper-covered hill in sight of Guadalupe, a village on the plains east of Tucumcari in north-central New Mexico and west of Texas. The town, which bears the name of its patron saint, La Virgen de Guadalupe, contains a church, school, and water tank, all visible from the Márez family home.

At first, the family rented a house in town. Gabriel took a job building highways while deciding where to settle. María wanted river-bottom land, but Gabriel, a scion of Spanish *conquistadores* (exploiters), insisted on building on a hill at the edge of the prairie. Far from Guadalupe, Tony's brothers—Léon, Eugenio, and Andrés—are soldiers on active duty. Left at home are Tony and his sisters, Deborah and Theresa, who share two rooms in the attic.

2. Las Pasturas, New Mexico

Gabriel blames his wife for causing the family to emigrate after Tony's birth. The family left the wild prairie at Las Pasturas, the author's homeland, and resettled east across the Pecos River in Guadalupe. Because he lived near town, Gabriel gave up his horse, symbol of the *vaquero*'s freedom. In frustration, he took up alcohol at the Longhorn Saloon on Saturday afternoons, after his despised highway work. Tony eyes the Southern Pacific Railroad tracks in Guadalupe that lead south to the land of his birth.

3. Pecos River

Tony escapes from the house to play with Jasón, who lives in one of only three neighboring homes along the Pecos River, the spiritual watercourse that Tony calls "the River of the Carp." Jasón's mother points past the railroad tracks to the dark hills to the northwest, where the boy seeks Indian burial grounds. In an old cave lives a moody, unpredictable Indian who is given to shouting.

4. Farm across the bridge from Guadalupe, New Mexico

Although superstitious locals think Ultima is a witch, Gabriel fetches her home the next morning. Tony returns from play to work the garden as the truck brings a blue-tin trunk and a wrinkled, brown old lady wrapped in a black shawl. With sincere respect and honor, the family welcomes her to their home, where she intends to die. She is especially close to Tony because she delivered him. He is fascinated by her pet owl, which appears to convey blessing. Ultima perceives Gabriel's longing to resettle in California's vineyards.

5. Bus station café in Guadalupe

One Saturday night, Chávez, brother of Sheriff Reynaldo, demands that Gabriel help local men trail Lupito, a traumatized war veteran. The family learns that Lupito shot Reynaldo while he sipped coffee at the bus depot cafe. Vigil, the New Mexico state patrolman, confirms that the sheriff is dead.

6. Pecos River

While his mother prays for Gabriel's safety, Tony hurries through dense *bosque* (thicket) to the Pecos River bank and locates Lupito crouching in reeds at the water's edge. Gabriel's friend Narciso attempts to halt vigilantism and calm Lupito, whom the searchers locate forty feet away in the beam of their light. Because the angry veteran shoots at the posse's spotlights, they fatally wound him.

Before dying at the river's edge, Lupito asks Tony for a blessing. Too terrified to move, Tony regrets that he isn't a priest and can't confer salvation. In the dark underbrush, Ultima's owl protects him.

7. Farm across the bridge from Guadalupe, New Mexico

After witnessing his first human death, Tony runs home and finds Ultima waiting for him with sympathy and an herbal sedative. She exonerates Lupito of murder because he suffers the "war sickness," her term for psychological trauma caused by combat. That night, Tony dreams he is a priest helping his brothers build the family a home.

8. El Puerto, New Mexico

Tony thinks about the legend of El Puerto, a Mexican land-grant colony led by a priest from the Luna clan on the fifteen-million-acre *Llano Estacado* (Staked Plains), five million of which lie in northeastern New Mexico and the rest in western Texas. The founder's social prominence causes María to long for Tony to become the next Luna priest. Later, Gabriel smirks that the priest broke holy vows of chastity to establish a family. Historically, New Mexico's first colony, the Pueblo of San Juan de Los Caballeros, took shape on the Rio Chama north of Española in 1598.

9. Farm across the bridge from Guadalupe, New Mexico

Early on Sunday morning, Tony worries that Lupito will suffer in the afterlife because he didn't receive absolution. At 6:00 A.M., María sets out for mass with Ultima and Tony following. In the *curandera's* hearing, neighbors whisper "sorcerer" and "witch." Townspeople come to mourn two local men who died while serving the military.

Tony's family lower their heads as they pass Rosie's brothel. Tony and young rowdies from nearby Los Jaros compete at a spitting contest outside the church. Tony rises to the taunts of Horse and tumbles him to the ground in a show of manhood that earns the gang's respect.

10. On the *llano*

As autumn approaches in 1945, with Tony's assistance, la Grande gathers healing roots and herbs from the prairie on both sides of the Pecos River. She reminisces about the arrival of Francisco Coronado at Háwikuh Pueblo in New Mexico in winter of 1539–1540 and the building of the railroad at Las Pasturas after 1878, when the Chicago Rock Island and Pacific line joined the Santa Fe Railway and the Southern Pacific. She tells Tony of plant lore shared with the Indians of the Rio del Norte in El Paso, Texas, and with the Aztec and Maya and the Moors of Spain. After Tony dreams he is a priest mourned by the Virgin Mary, la Grande relieves his anxieties.

11. El Puerto, New Mexico

Ultima recognizes that, within Tony's spirit, a war rages between the restless belligerence of the Márez clan and the serenity of the Lunas. In August, Juan Luna, the boy's maternal uncle, summons the family for the annual pilgrimage to harvest corn, chiles, and apples ten miles south at El Puerto de los Lunas across the El Rito bridge northwest of Fort Sumner. Tony's fatherly Uncle Pedro Luna arrives by truck to escort the family to a reunion with Grandfather Prudencio and Juan Luna.

At the settlement of the Valle de los Lunas, the truck passes Tenorio's Bar and a cluster of tin-roofed mud houses, among which Tony's grandfather's house is the largest. Before beginning the harvest, the family grieves for Lupito and awaits the return of the three Márez brothers from the war. Juan invites Tony to a summer with the Lunas after his confirmation.

12. Guadalupe, New Mexico

The first day of school unsettles Tony. To counter Gabriel's yearning to move west, María emphasizes that the Lunas were New Mexico's first Latino settlers. She refers to Juan de Oñate, who led four hundred expeditioners from Mexico across the Rio Grande to northern New Mexico at the junction of the Rio Chama and Rio Grande. In 1598, he financed San Gabriel del Yunque, the first permanent Hispanic settlement, built opposite the Pueblo of San Juan de los Caballeros. Oñate eventually became governor of the province of New Mexico.

María encourages Tony to enter the priesthood and kneels with the family to receive Ultima's blessing. At school, Tony meets first-grade teacher Miss Maestas and writes his name in crayon. City children deride him for packing a tortilla, chile, and hot beans for lunch. With George and Willy, farm children from rural Delia, he builds a coalition of outsiders.

13. San Diego, California

After World War II, the family prays for Tony's brothers, who return from the Pacific to San Diego, California, a naval hub and the location of U.S. Marine and Navy training centers. During the war, many soldiers were processed in San Diego before shipping out to the Pacific theater. Tony is thrilled by the trio's arrival, which he witnesses in a dream. Gabriel wants them to tell about the vineyards of California.

14. Guadalupe, New Mexico

The three veterans admire their scholarly little brother. Ignoring Gabriel's insistence on a move west to California, they waste their pay at the Eight Ball Pool Hall, incur debts, and dream of cars, women, liquor, and travel. During the winter of 1945–1946, Ultima treats León, who howls with the war sickness. Eugene encourages his brothers to travel to Las Vegas, Santa Fe, or Albuquerque, New Mexico, or beyond the state to Denver or San Francisco.

Tony agonizes that his brothers have become footloose men who can no longer live their parents' settled dreams. They believe Tony will be his mother's farmer and priest, and they ridicule his blessing. In a dream, Tony refuses to follow his brothers to the brothel. The trio reject highway jobs with Gabriel. María blames her husband's ancestry for her sons' yearning to move west. León and Eugene leave home for Las Vegas, New Mexico. While planning to finish high school, Andy works at Allen's Food Market.

On the last day of school, Miss Maestas advances Tony to the third grade. On the walk home, Samuel, a wise third-grader, narrates Jasón's Indian myth about native wanderers who are transformed into carp that live forever. To supervise the river, the gods elevated a golden carp to "lord of all the waters of the valley." The myth challenges Tony to doubt the trinity. He hopes that Cico, a town boy, will introduce him to the magical carp. That summer, Samuel herds sheep on the prairie at the Agua Negra ranch. Tony misses his brothers and Samuel.

15. Farm across the bridge from Guadalupe, New Mexico

Uncle Pedro begs Ultima to remove a curse from Uncle Lucas Luna, mama's youngest brother. He is the victim of Tenorio's three daughters because, in February in the cottonwoods on the Pecos River, Lucas watched them dance at a Black Mass celebrating the devil. After their curse sapped his strength, even the specialist in Las Vegas could not cure him.

16. El Puerto, New Mexico

Ultima takes Tony along because he bears the magical middle name Juan, which confers spiritual power. She passes timorous farmers to confront Tenorio and to charge his three daughters with damning Lucas by gathering and cursing his hair. At the Luna house, she promises Tony that the good she employs for Lucas is more powerful than witchery. She sweats Lucas to rid him of the death spirit. On three clay and wax dolls, she inserts pins. Her elixir of fresh roots forces Lucas to disgorge green bile and a squirming hairball.

As Uncle Lucas languishes, Tony imitates the battle between good and evil with sympathetic physical and emotional symptoms. After three days of treatment, Lucas improves. Because Grandfather Prudencio can never compensate Ultima, she asks that the men of El Puerto save her from future dangers. At the tree in the clearing, she burns the hairball, which emits sulfurous fumes.

17. Pecos River

Cico invites Tony to view the golden carp. As they traverse Narciso's ample garden, Tony gnaws a carrot, which he vomits when Horse demands a magic trick from him. Beyond Blue Lake near the road to Tucumcari, Tony sees the golden carp, which Samuel says can swim upstream to the Hidden Lakes. In proof of enchantment, Cico cites the example of a Mexican shepherd who heard the mermaids sing before he disappeared near the lakes. Cico believes the town sits on a subterranean lake inside a watery moat.

When Tony repeats the myth at home, la Grande is unable to substantiate or refute it. He dreams that Christian beliefs vie with paganism. In the dream, Ultima explains that both extremes form a "great cycle that binds us all." Tony ponders the golden carp all summer.

18. Farm across the bridge from Guadalupe, New Mexico

His sons gone and his dream of westering shattered, Gabriel drinks more heavily. Ultima fears that Tenorio may harm Tony, whom she protects by tying her personal pouch of herbs about his neck. Visitors from Las Pasturas come to buy supplies in Guadalupe and stop by the family's house. They tell of picking cotton in East Texas and of harvesting potatoes in Colorado, where one man died in a tractor accident. They admire their ancestors, the Mexican pioneers.

Bearing news from Jesús Silva that Tenorio's youngest daughter died, Narciso warns Ultima that the old man has instigated a witch-hunt. When vigilantes approach the Márez house and summon the sorceress, Gabriel demands that Tenorio face Ultima. Narciso shames the stalkers for hiding their faces and following a troublemaker. Tenorio vows revenge.

To settle the matter of sorcery, Narciso suggests that Ultima walk under a cross on the door, a test a true witch reputedly cannot pass. Before she accepts the challenge, her owl rips out Tenorio's eye. Ultima steps outside without difficulty. As the men scatter, Tony spies the cross lying shattered on the ground.

19. El Puerto, New Mexico
In August 1946, the family packs to travel south to El Puerto. Gabriel seeks a week's leave to go with them to the Luna family homestead. When Tony accuses Uncle Pedro of failing to support Ultima against vigilantes, Pedro admits he was cowardly. Meanwhile, the priest refuses to bury Tenorio's daughter in hallowed ground. The next day, Tenorio's family carries the reeking cottonwood casket through town and vows vengeance against Ultima.

20. Guadalupe, New Mexico
After the harvest, the Márez family returns north to Guadalupe. The Lunas invite Tony to spend a summer. At school, the boys tease him for living with a witch. After he fights Ernie, they cease their harassment. At Christmas, the children practice for a nativity play, with Tony as a shepherd. When he sets out for school in a blizzard, la Grande warns him of evil in the wind. Along the way, Samuel reports that Tenorio and Narciso fought at the Longhorn Saloon because Tenorio cursed Ultima, Narciso, and the citizens of Las Pasturas.

After the pageant, at 3:00 P.M., Tony walks home through heavy snow. Near the saloon, he witnesses Tenorio fighting Narciso. After Narciso hurries to the brothel to have Andy alert the Márez family, Tenorio ambushes Narciso by the bridge and shoots him. Tony hears Narciso's last confession. At home, Ultima wraps Tony in warm blankets. In delirium, he relives the shooting and dreams of evil people destroying his family. Only the golden carp survives.

21. Santa Fe, New Mexico
During Tony's recovery from pneumonia, a coroner's jury rules Narciso's death accidental or a suicide. Tony anticipates a first communion followed by a summer with the Lunas. The police return the two older brothers from their wrecked car, which burned in a ditch alongside an icy highway. Gabriel regrets that his sons violate family unity. The next day, the three brothers move to Santa Fe.

22. Guadalupe, New Mexico
Tony frets over Tenorio's exoneration for murder. Tony and Cico discuss telling the golden carp the circumstances. At the juniper tree where Narciso died, Tony suffers a curse from Tenorio, whose second daughter is dying. The embittered father blames Ultima for causing the girl's terminal illness. Tony reports all to Ultima, who is unshaken.

In March 1947, as Tony completes catechism, his friend Florence renounces Christianity. Father Byrnes expounds on eternal punishment but fails to soften Florence's hard heart. Samuel proposes introducing Florence to the golden carp. After Ash Wednesday and Good Friday rituals, the gang forces Tony to hear Horse's confession for spying on the girls' bathroom. Tony refuses absolution to Florence, who believes God has wronged him. The gang mocks their first communion, at which Tony sincerely tries to commune with God. At the end of confirmation, he feels empty.

23. Agua Negra Ranch in north-central New Mexico
In August 1947, Téllez seeks an exorcism of a demon that hurls stones at his house and disrupts the kitchen. Ultima blames the curse on the man's grandfather, who hanged three

Comanche. She assumes that their souls wander the ranch. At sunup, she travels to the adobe ranch house on the *llano*.

Gabriel assists Ultima's expert exorcism. As though cremating the dead Indian style, she places bundles on a platform of juniper branches and orders Gabriel to set fire to it. She warns Téllez to avoid Tenorio, who seeks vengeance against Téllez for defending her a month ago at the saloon.

24. Spillway where Blue Lake empties into El Rito Creek

Tony and Cico intend to reveal the carp to Florence. When they arrive at the spillway, they find that Florence has dived in, hit his head on a culvert, and become entangled in rusty barbwire. That night, Tony weeps for his drowned companion and dreams of Narciso, Lupito, and Florence. He envisions Tenorio slaughtering Ultima. She awakens Tony and declares that he has seen too much death. To relieve his fear, she blesses him.

25. El Puerto, New Mexico

In late summer 1947, the family treks south to the Luna farm. Gabriel contracts Tony to work at a sheep camp. Gabriel wishes his son could have grown up on the prairie and acknowledges that the old way of life is almost gone. Tony wonders if a new religion may emerge. To simplify the boy's understanding of evil, his father explains that people comprehend it better after they mature.

During field and orchard work at El Puerto that August, Uncle Pedro reads a letter from María stating that school is starting early and she will soon join them. Juan Luna interrupts the reading with a warning that Tenorio has placed his daughter's corpse on the bar at his saloon in El Puerto. This time, Pedro vows to protect Ultima from Tenorio's vengeance.

At sunset, the family drives from the uncles' fields to the bridge that leads to El Puerto. While Tenorio rages, his horse threatens to trample Tony, who cowers on the bridge. Striking the horse, he escapes. As he runs to save Ultima, from ten miles away she dispatches her owl against Tenorio. After he shoots the bird and aims his rifle at Tony, Pedro draws his pistol and kills Tenorio.

26. Farm across the bridge from Guadalupe, New Mexico

Tony recognizes the owl as Ultima's soul. When he hurries to her, she explains that her approaching death will restore harmony. She instructs him to destroy her herbs at sunrise and bury the owl at a forked juniper tree. He promises to obey; she blesses him with goodness, strength, and beauty and promises that the owl's song will signify her presence. After he buries Ultima's owl, he feels relieved.

Further Reading

"Anaya Mystery Wrapped in Mysticism," *Arizona Republic* (April 4, 1999).

Blair, Linda. "Alienation, Assimilation, and Acculturation—*Bless Me Ultima* by Rudolfo Anaya." *English Journal* (December 1991): 26.

Clark, William, "Rudolfo Anaya: The Chicano Worldview." *Publisher's Weekly* (June 5, 1995): 41–42.

Espinosa, Martha, "A Passion for History." *Hispanic* (September 1, 1999): 64.

Garcia, Rosie, and Brenda Holmes, "Rudolfo Anaya." *Southwestern Literature*, January 1998.

Jones, Margaret, "Bless This Book." *Publishers Weekly* (October 12, 1990): 30.

Olmos, Margarite Fernandez. *Rudolfo A. Anaya: A Critical Companion*. Westport, Conn.: Greenwood Press, 1999.

"Rudolfo Anaya," http://www.unm.edu/~wrtgsw/anaya.html.

Sirias, Silvio, and Bruce Dick, eds. *Conversations with Rudolfo Anaya.* Jackson, Miss.: University Press of Mississippi, 1998.

Snodgrass, Mary Ellen. *Encyclopedia of Frontier Literature*. Santa Barbara, Calif.: ABC-Clio, 1997.

Taylor, Paul Beekman, "The Chicano Translation of Troy: Epic Topoi in the Novels of Rudolfo A. Anaya." *MELUS* (Fall 1994): 19–36.

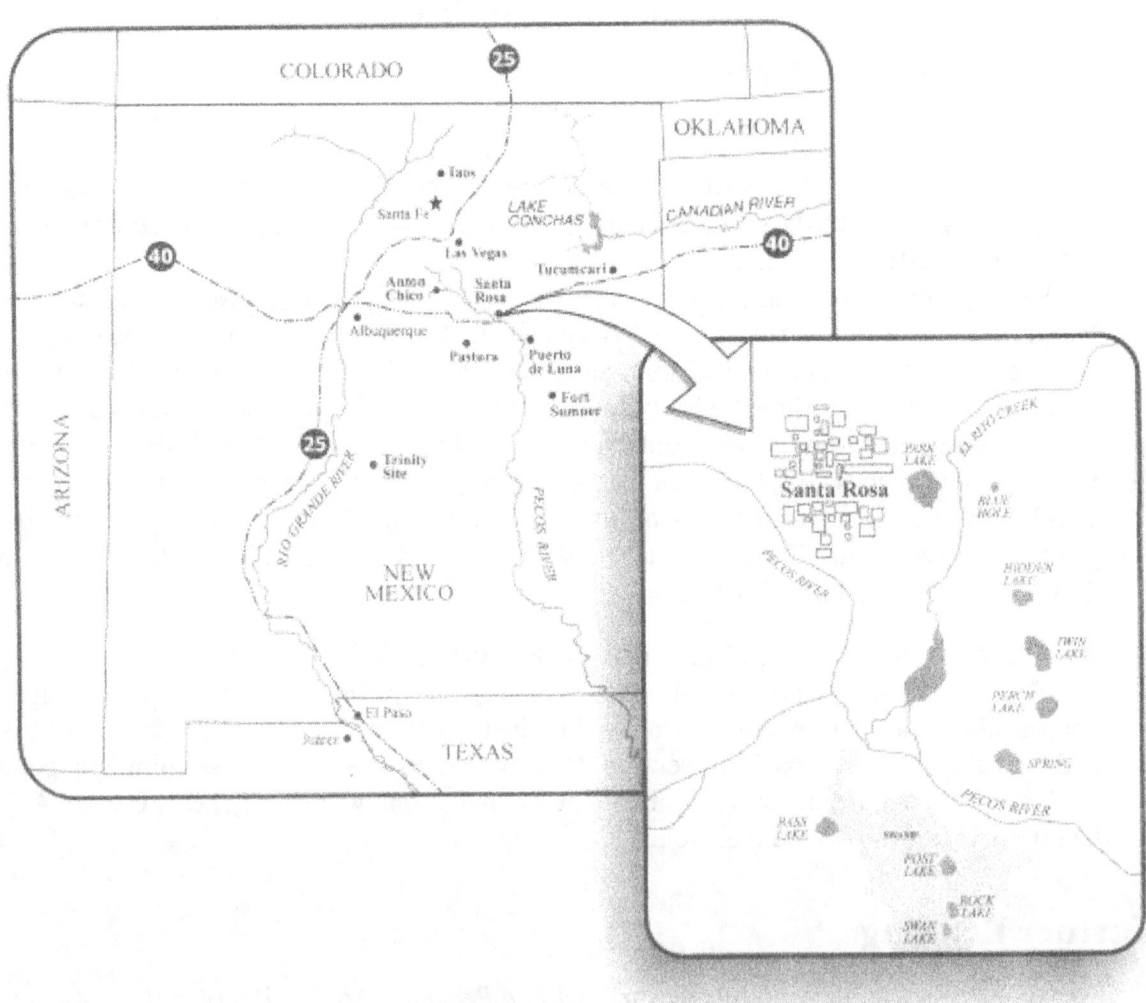

Brave New World
By Aldous Huxley

Science fiction, 1932

Geographical Summary

Aldous Huxley centers his futuristic fiction in a technological haven, but moves his fictional cast over three primary settings—greater London; the Malpais Reservation, New Mexico; and Wey Valley, Surrey, in southwestern England. In west London, Henry Foster and Lenina Crowne travel by helicopter above city streets and familiar landmarks on their way to play obstacle golf at Stoke Poges. Like fingers, the chimneys of the Slough Crematorium stretch upward and belch toxic fumes into the sky as the ovens below reduce corpses to ash. The stalled helicopter flight over the dark English Channel mirrors the ominous emotions in Bernard Marx, an unfulfilled technician living in a repressive, mechanized dystopia. To retreat from the glass and chromium laboratory nightmare with its prefab humans emerging from bottles on conveyor belts, Marx invites Lenina to a getaway in the wilds of the New World.

Rocketed west to New Orleans and across Texas to Santa Fe and a Zuñi pueblo in New Mexico, the two travelers enter a community where people still reproduce, grow old, and die according to outdated human biology. In a fetid, primitive clime, Lenina recoils from a snake ceremony at a Zuñi kiva and from the ritual whipping of John, an Anglo outsider. The obscenities of childbirth, breastfeeding, and mothering counter her experience with a technocratic society that prefers promiscuity and factory-made citizens to old-style family values. To flee the outmoded way of living, Lenina hungers for soma, a common tranquilizer offering an eighteen-hour escape.

Bernard and Lenina's return to London with Linda and her son John as vacation souvenirs forces a harsh face-off between the old world and the new. At the Bloomsbury Centre, Linda bursts into the lab to scream a greeting to the Director, the English lover who fathered John twenty years before. The sight of a New Mexican mother and son upsets not only the staff, but also all of London, where rumors fly about John's savagery and his mother's eccentricities. Unable to live in the pueblo, John denounces the brave new world's pressure to conform and to expect instant gratification. Like a medieval Christian hermit, he withdraws into his apartment and seeks atonement.

The final scenes describe John's flight southwest down the London-to-Portsmouth road into Surrey. At the Wey Valley lighthouse, he recreates an Indian lifestyle as an escape from the city, with its vapid entertainments, sex on demand, and preprogrammed deity. At home in the heather, he doses himself with mustard and warm water to wash disillusion from his gut. Longing for Lenina, he eludes invasive media teams hovering low enough for reporter Primo Mellon to film John's anguish and project it on screens to titillate jaded Londoners. In the end, John hangs himself. Like a pendulum turned at the wind's will, his corpse swings at one with the motion of the universe.

Detailed Itinerary

1. Laboratory, Bloomsbury Centre in central London

In June, 632 years after England's advance under technological control, Henry Foster is assistant to the Director of Hatcheries and Conditioning (D.H.C.) at a squat, thirty-four-story building in the Bloomsbury section of central London. Henry grounds a student tour group in the Bokanovsky Process, a type of cloning or budding that develops a single egg into ninety-six mirror images. The purpose of controlling society is to maintain stability, which will fail if people act on their individual wills. Such liberalism ended after Parliament outlawed it in favor of a comprehensive technological system.

In the bottling room, the godlike Henry Ford's conveyor belt speeds embryos toward a prearranged life in five social castes. Machinery inoculates tissues to make them behave predictably and comply with state-mandated expectations. Rather than a human birth, in the decanting room, newborns undergo ectogenesis, the process that removes them from their glass habitats. They progress to an upstairs nursery, where electric shock and hypnopaedia condition them to follow the prescribed behaviors of their caste. In the garden, the tour group views conditioned play at sex games.

2. Girls' dressing room at the laboratory

When the main laboratory shift ends at 4:00 P.M., a popular girl named Lenina Crowne leaves the Embryo Store and meets coworker Fanny Crowne in the girls' dressing room seventeen stories up from the lab. Wall jets bathe Fanny in warm water, spray her with perfume, and dust her with talcum powder. The two women discuss Lenina's dates with Henry Foster over the last four months and her impressions of Bernard Marx, a bright but eccentric sleep-teaching technician. Fanny shudders at the thought of dating a man who enjoys solitude.

3. Malpais reservation outside Santa Fe, New Mexico

Lenina has a July date with Bernard to sightsee at Malpais, the Savage Reservation west of Santa Fe in northwest New Mexico. Sacred to Acoma, Laguna, Ramah Navajo, and Zuñi, the famed "badlands" carry the Spanish name characterizing their rugged volcanic outcroppings. The preserve is a source of spiritual communion and healing herbs.

The duo will travel by Blue Pacific Rocket either from the station at Hampstead east of Regent's Park or from Charing-T Tower, a satiric name for Charing Cross Station west of Trafalgar Square. Fanny grumbles that Bernard is a nonconformist. Lenina replies that she will risk dating a kook in exchange for a vacation in an exotic Zuñi settlement.

4. Notting Hill to Stoke Poges by air over west London

In the lift, Lenina encounters Bernard as he departs work and accepts his invitation to Malpais. Four minutes late, she joins Henry in his flying machine. They glimpse the Red Rocket returning late from New York, and then fly across the green that rings central London. Near Shepherd's Bush west of Hyde Park, they spy tennis games at courts from Notting Hill to Willesden. Farther west at Ealing Stadium, gymnasts and singers perform. To the south at Hounslow, where workers resurface the Great West Road, a feely studio covers seven and a half hectares. Farther south at Brentford, a television factory the size of a small town stretches near Stoke Poges, where Henry lands near the obstacle golf course.

5. Fleet Street, London

Bernard, a neurotic loner, boards a plane from the roof, flies toward the river, and lands on Propaganda House in Fleet Street, London's financial district. Huxley reshapes the buildings into the "Bureaux of Propaganda," where Bernard asks the porter to summon his friend, Helmholtz Watson, a professor at the College of Emotional Engineering and a critic of Utopia.

Adoring women invite Helmholtz to a picnic supper on Exmoor, Devon, an unspoiled expanse in south central England. Although he will be the only male among them, he is too busy to go. Bernard flies to Helmholtz's house. In private, Helmholtz calms Bernard's jitters.

6. Westminster, London

After the golf course closes at 8:00 P.M., Lenina and Henry fly over the forest of Burnham Beeches and the crematorium chimney at Slough, west of Ealing. With a change of gears, Henry flies back toward London and his forty-two-story apartment roof in Westminster, the historic seat of English government. They go down to the dining hall for dinner and a dose of soma and, at 9:20 P.M., cross the street to the Westminster Abbey Cabaret to five-step around Westminster Abbey, a venerable religious center where early English monarchs are buried.

Meanwhile, Bernard leaves Helmholtz's apartment and takes a flying cab east to a solidarity meeting, which ends at 11:00 P.M. with a mass orgy. A chime emerges from Big Henry, Huxley's version of Big Ben, the bell in the four-faced Westminster clock in a tower rising over the Houses of Parliament.

7. English Channel

Weeks later, Lenina worries about Bernard's odd behavior and considers going to the North Pole with Benito Hoover instead. She looks forward to the rare treat of three days among the Zuñi in Malpais. Before departing, Bernard proposes a hike in the mountainous Lake District, one of northwestern England's main tourist attractions.

Lenina persuades Bernard to fly to Amsterdam, Holland, to view women's heavyweight wrestling. On the flight home, he alarms her when he stops the helicopter over the English Channel to gaze at the dark foam below. As they fly back to his apartment, Lenina is further disturbed by Bernard's abnormal thinking. He yearns for genuine passion and regrets intimacy with a woman who is his intellectual inferior.

8. Iceland

Bernard requests a vacation pass to New Mexico, an area the director visited twenty years earlier. Before replying, the director muses on the Beta female he took with him, who got lost in the mountains. He threatens to exile Bernard to a "sub-centre of the lowest order" in Iceland if he rejects Utopian policies. That evening, Bernard gives Helmholtz a macho account of his conference with the director. Realizing Bernard's need to conceal humiliation, Helmholtz can only stare at the floor.

9. New Orleans to Santa Fe

Although Lenina is uncomfortable with her date, she boards the trans-Atlantic Blue Pacific Rocket from London and travels from New Orleans through a tornado over Texas to a hotel in Santa Fe. The next morning, the reservation warden signs their permits and warns them of the deadly electrified fence around the area. He embarrasses Lenina with a salacious reference to native births.

Remembering that he left the cologne tap running in his apartment, Bernard phones Helmholtz to turn it off. Helmholtz informs him that the director has begun looking for Bernard's replacement. After Bernard swallows four soma tablets, he and Lenina take a plane from the hotel roof to Malpais. The topography below consists of forests, salt or sand deserts, crags and peaks, and a mesa. They land at a small, square resthouse near the pueblo of Malpais.

10. Zuñi Pueblo, Malpais Reservation, New Mexico

In the zigzagging gully below, the sight of disease, breastfeeding, old age, filth, and smells of pueblo life repulse Lenina. Located in McKinley and Valencia counties of western New Mexico to the south and east of Gallup, historically, the natives have lived in the same locale for more than eight centuries. In 1500, their population was around 20,000. Erected from stone and plaster, pueblo villages in the Zuñi Valley had deteriorated by the time Huxley wrote his novel.

On the mesa, Lenina regrets leaving her tranquilizer behind after viewing a snake ritual and a coyote-man whipping John, whom the Zuñi consider an outsider because of his light skin and hair. Afterward, John greets Lenina and Bernard in Shakespearean English and introduces Linda, his fat, unkempt mother, who is missing two front teeth. A former native of Utopia, she lost her way on the mesa during a visit with a man named Tomakin twenty years before and reluctantly adopted the Zuñi culture.

Living in squalor on the outskirts of the pueblo and reeking of alcohol, Linda contrasts southwestern ways with habits and Utopian attitudes she learned while working in the London lab. Because she practices promiscuity and escapism via mescal and peyote, she has alienated herself on the reservation, especially among native women. To Lenina, she fondly recalls the abortion center in Chelsea southwest of London.

John was just a boy when pueblo women burst in on Linda to lash her with whips for seducing their men. While she retreated into alcohol, her son lived on cold tortillas. When she was sober, she taught him to read. When John was twelve, her native lover Popé brought him a copy of William Shakespeare's plays. At fifteen, Mitsima taught John to mold clay by the river. At the Antelope Kiva, John underwent manhood training.

Intrigued with John, Bernard invites him to return to London with him. John brightens and recites "O brave new world," the words of Miranda, an innocent island maid in Shakespeare's *The Tempest*. John accepts the invitation and insists that Linda come with them.

11. Resthouse, Malpais Reservation, New Mexico

That evening, Lenina retreats into soma for eighteen hours, but Bernard is sleepless. At 10:00 the next morning, he flies to the post office. At 10:37 A.M., he calls Mustapha Mond,

Resident Controller for Western Europe, to announce a scientifically valuable find—a Utopian woman and her son who have reverted to primitive ways. After making arrangements with the warden for the rocket to London, at 2:30 P.M., he returns to Malpais. Meanwhile, John enters Lenina's room to rifle her suitcase and watch her sleep.

12. Laboratory, Bloomsbury Centre in central London

The day after the foursome arrives in London, the Director's reunion with Linda prevents Bernard's exile to Iceland. She embraces the Director, calls him Tomakin, and informs him of the birth of their baby. John recognizes Thomas as his father. The hatchery staff laugh at the idea of the Director taking part in viviparous reproduction. Embarrassed, he resigns from the hatchery.

13. Bernard's apartment

Aged, fat, and sick, Linda is an obscenity to the technologically advanced Londoners. She swallows too much soma, and in her little room on the thirty-seventh floor of Bernard's apartment house, recedes into television. After Dr. Shaw examines her, he predicts that the drug will paralyze her respiratory system in a month or two.

14. John's apartment, London

In subsequent days, Bernard becomes a hero. John follows him on a guided city tour and looks out on the Bombay Green Rocket from Charing-T Tower. He visits Eton, a boy's preparatory school, and the television factory at Brentford. Lenina escorts John to the Alhambra Theatre in the center of London to view *Three Weeks in a Helicopter*, then invites him to her apartment to seduce him. Outraged, he spouts lines from Shakespeare and reads drama alone in his apartment. He broods over London's shallow pleasures and refuses to attend a party with Bernard and Lenina.

The next morning, Bernard is annoyed that John befriends Helmholtz, a rebel against Utopia who teaches subversive poetry. Helmholtz thrills to John's reading from *Romeo and Juliet*. After John proposes marriage, Lenina retreats to the bathroom.

15. Park Lane Hospital, London

John receives a message that Linda is rapidly expiring at the Park Lane Hospital for the Dying. Inundated with sounds, smells, colors, and light, she barely acknowledges reality while losing herself in a televised tennis championship. He angrily ousts children on a death-conditioning tour. Linda clutches at her throat and dies as the children gape and ask questions. On the way out of the hospital vestibule at 6:00 P.M., John starts a riot among menial employees by tossing their soma rations out the window. Police officers play soothing taped music and spray soma and aerosol anesthesia before arresting John and his rescuers, Bernard and Helmholtz.

16. Falkland Islands

John is excited to find that his judge, Mustapha Mond, has read Shakespeare. Bernard and Helmholtz suffer exile to the Falkland Islands, a strategic British colony off the southeastern tip of South America. John debates Utopian principles with Mond, who states that God and mechanization are mutually exclusive. John ripostes that consumerism will doom Utopia and boldly embraces God, literature, freedom, goodness, and the right to sin.

17. John's apartment, London

The day before banishment to the Falklands, Helmholtz and Bernard enter John's apartment to say goodbye. They find him regurgitating mustard and warm water. Mond refuses to let John accompany the exiles and retains him as an experiment. John chooses not to be the subject of scientific inquiry.

18. Wey Valley between Puttenham and Elstead, Surrey

The next day, John hides for the winter in a nonfunctioning lighthouse in the Wey Valley. He intends to become self-supporting by spring. He rids himself of lust for Lenina by drinking mustard water, whipping his naked flesh, and collapsing into juniper brambles. Three workers driving from Puttenham to Elstead spy his bizarre self-whipping on naked flesh.

Three days later, while gawkers crowd around, the media covers John's masochism. He shoots an arrow into their helicopter. Twelve days later, after reporter Primo Mellon publicizes John's agonies on screen as *The Savage of Surrey,* voyeurs pressure John to lay on the whip. When Lenina appears at the aircraft door with tears in her eyes, he calls her a strumpet. After midnight, fun-seeking intruders leave him asleep in the heather. The next morning, he hangs himself in the lighthouse. That evening, his corpse dangles in the breeze.

Further Reading

Bloom, Harold, intro. *Aldous Huxley's Brave New World.* New York: Chelsea House, 1999.

De Koster, Katie. *Readings on Brave New World.* Westport, Conn.: Greenhaven Press, 1999.

Dunaway, David King. *Aldous Huxley Recollected: An Oral History.* Matawan, N.J.: Altamira Press, 1998.

"El Malpais National Monument," http://www.nps.gov/elma/.

Golding, William, ed. *Aldous Huxley's "Brave New World."* New York: Chelsea House, 1996.

"Huxley Hotlinks," http://www.huxley.net/hotlinks.htm.

Huxley, Laura Archers. *This Timeless Moment: A Personal View of Aldous Huxley.* Berkeley, Calif.: Celestial Arts, 2000.

Meckier, Jerome, ed. *Critical Essays on Aldous Huxley.* Westport, Conn.: Greenwood, 1996.

Pritzker, Barry M. *A Native American Encyclopedia: History, Culture, and Peoples.* Oxford: Oxford University Press, 2000.

Snodgrass, Mary Ellen. *Encyclopedia of Utopian Literature.* Santa Barbara, Calif.: ABC-Clio, 1994.

Tedlock, Barbara. *The Beautiful and the Dangerous: Encounters with the Zuni Indians.* Albuquerque, N.M.: University of New Mexico Press, 2001.

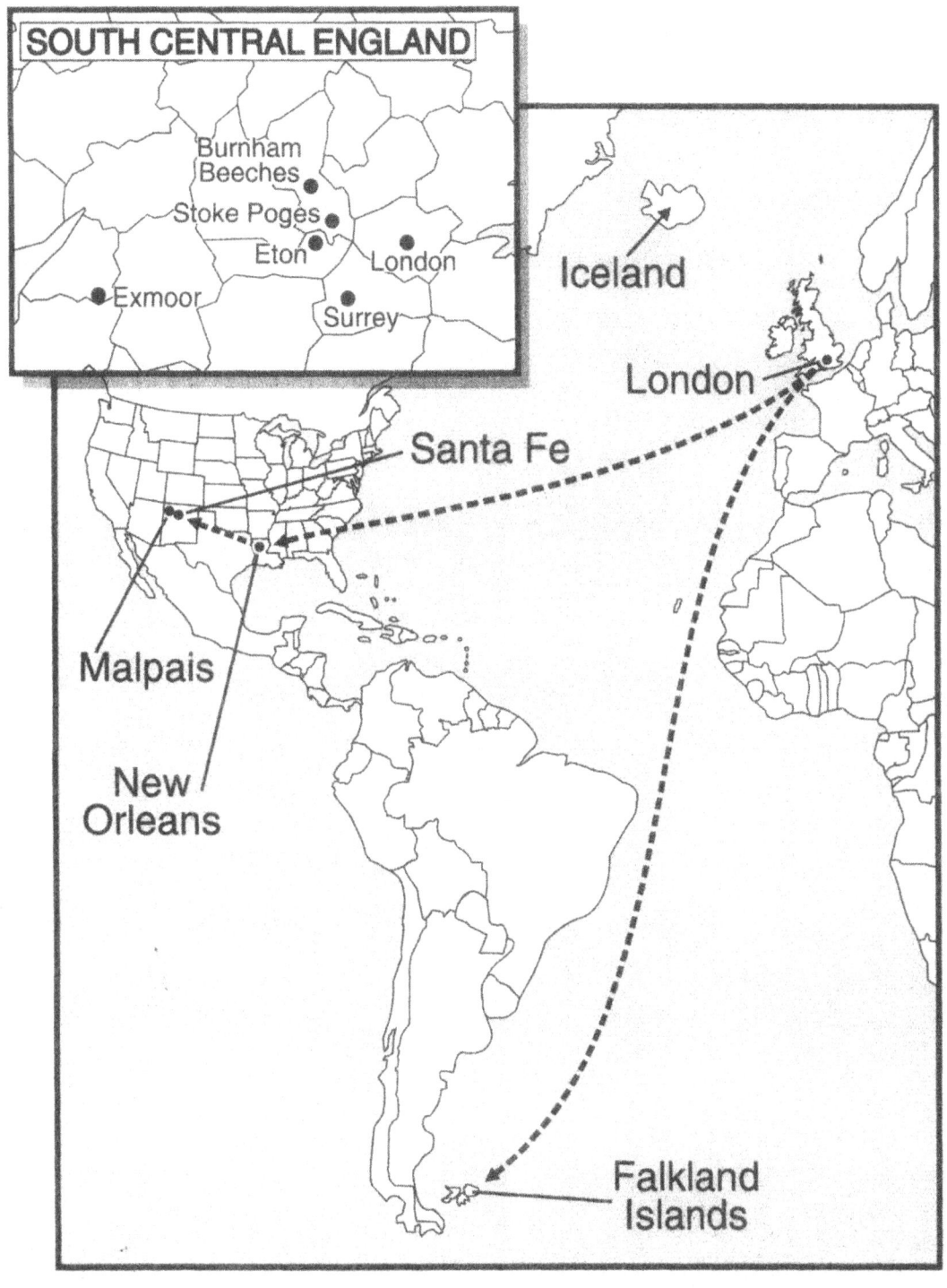

Dicey's Song

By Cynthia Voigt

Contemporary mainstream fiction, 1982

Geographical Summary

Written by Bostonian Cynthia Irving Voigt, *Dicey's Song* is part two of a five-part family saga that links two landmarks of the four orphaned Tillerman children. In the past lay their childhood beach house amid the windy dunes outside Provincetown, Massachusetts. Their mother, Liza Tillerman, deserted them at a shopping mall in action covered by *Homecoming* (1981). After Dicey identified her mother's photo for the police in Bridgeport, Maryland, she realized that she was now head of the family.

In *Dicey's Song,* the Tillerman children's future depends on their ability to make a new home. After a period of wandering, the four children settle with their Gram, Abigail Tillerman, at her rundown farm in fictional Crisfield, within driving distance of Salisbury, Maryland, on the shores of Chesapeake Bay.

Before Dicey, the heroine, achieves closure with the past, she must journey with her grandmother more than three hundred miles by plane without knowing the cause of their trek. They travel northeast to Boston, Massachusetts, and find their mother's room at a hospital. While Dicey enjoys a taste of independence, Gram holds an overnight vigil as Liza's life slips away. They must make what arrangements they can afford to return her remains to Crisfield.

The homeward journey by plane to Wilmington, Delaware, and by train south across Delaware to Crisfield, Maryland, gives Dicey a chance to cherish her mother's ashes. She prepares to inform the three younger children of their mother's death. The family buries the ashes in Gram's yard under a mulberry tree.

A young adult classic, *Dicey's Song* won a Newbery Medal in 1983. Voigt continued the Tillerman series with *In a Solitary Blue,* a 1984 Newbery Honor book, followed by *Sons from Afar* (1987) and *Seventeen Against the Dealer* (1989).

Detailed Itinerary

1. Crisfield, Maryland, on the Chesapeake Bay

Thirteen-year-old Dicey and her brothers James and Sammy and little sister Maybeth end a hard summer after their mother deserts them. The four children have little choice but to live with their crusty Gram Tillerman. She owns shore property near Crisfield, a fictional town somewhere west of Salisbury, Maryland, on the Chesapeake Bay, the nation's largest estuary. The old house and barn are set back from the road; the dock and motorboat once served the Tillerman family's bootleggers.

In late summer, the children traverse the sand and swim in the warm waters. Gram travels to town by boat to buy groceries and to take James to the library, where he locates books on repairing and maintaining wood boats. Indoors, the children play checkers and read. Dicey anticipates the first day of school and after-school time with a rebuilt boat that she will sail.

2. Bridgeport, Maryland

Dicey recalls an unpleasant stay in Bridgeport, a major city in northwest Maryland just south of the Pennsylvania state line, where the four motherless Tillermans had lived temporarily with Cousin Eunice. The Bridgeport police showed Dicey a picture of a faraway face, which she identified as their mother. Dicey carries the heavy sadness of their mother's mental decline and the necessity for the long journey to Gram, their closest living relative.

3. Provincetown, Massachusetts

Dicey says little in class and thinks of her former home in a rickety seaside cabin among the dunes outside Provincetown, Cape Cod. The area is now one of the Western Hemisphere's most cherished vacation spots for its dunes and long beach fronting the Atlantic Ocean and the protected inner shore of the hook-shaped peninsula, which curls around Cape Cod Bay. Dicey recalls, "The ocean rolled up toward her rickety cabin, like it wanted to swallow it up; but it never did. . . . The wind was always blowing around the cabin, like it too wanted to have that little building gone" (Chapter 7, p. 118).

Gram, once more a mother to young children, begins adoption proceedings. Dicey clings to a frail hope that her mother will get well and claim them. James worries how the family will cope financially and fears he will never fit in with his peers. Gram forces herself to request welfare assistance. To help out, Dicey clerks in a local grocery store. Feeling a duty to her siblings, she has difficulty freeing herself from the burden. Gram urges her to let go.

4. Boston, Massachusetts

Gram maintains no contact with Dicey's mother since she left home and never mentions her name. Gram conceals letters that arrive sporadically from the hospital in Boston. Because her daughter can never function as a parent, Gram doggedly pursues adopting the children.

5. Plymouth, Massachusetts

While Gram sews a dress for Maybeth, James writes a paper on "the Mayflower people," who settled Plymouth Colony at Plymouth Bay in southeastern Massachusetts, on December 21, 1620. The site of the first permanent settlement by Europeans in New England, Plymouth produced a history similar to the Tillerman children. The new colony sheltered people who were unwelcome in England and who cherished the New World wilderness, where they could practice their religion unhampered. Similarly, the Tillermans are glad to arrive at Crisfield, where they can live free of disapproving relatives under the protection of their grandmother, who is adept at boating and fishing.

6. Crisfield, Maryland

When Mr. Chappelle assigns Dicey's English class a character sketch, Dicey writes fondly about Momma, a character she identifies as Mrs. Eliza. After Gram has a telephone installed as a safeguard for the family, Dicey realizes how much her grandmother has sacrificed to take them in.

7. Salisbury, Maryland

In November, Gram realizes that Dicey has reached womanhood and needs clothes that suit a mature body. She takes Dicey by bus to Salisbury, a "scraggly city" in southeastern Maryland. They walk through an arched gateway at the Salisbury Mall at Civic and Glen avenues, where they shop for clothes, shoes, and underwear and dine on club sandwiches. Gram speaks plainly about the problem of supporting the family. She urges Dicey to hold on to people.

8. Provincetown, Massachusetts

Dicey recalls how their father deserted them before Sammy's birth. She realizes that Sammy blames himself. He is unable to get along with friends who provoke fights by ridiculing Gram. In English class, Mr. Chappelle selects two essays to read aloud. He praises the first one. After reading the second, he accuses Dicey, the author, of plagiarizing a sketch on her mother and their life in Provincetown.

To protect her inner self, Dicey offers no defense of the false accusation. It is her friend Wilhemina who disproves the teacher's charge. Realizing Dicey's gift for writing, Mr. Chappelle changes the grade to A+. After Gram reads the essay, she tells Dicey about feeling alone after her husband died. Dicey telephones Wilhemina to thank her for interceding with Mr. Chappelle.

9. Easton, Maryland

Mr. Lingerle, Maybeth's music teacher, helps out by babysitting and sometimes stays for meals. He proposes that Gram sell her long-handled silver stuffing spoon at an antique store at Easton.

10. From Salisbury to Baltimore, Maryland

When Gram asks Dicey to pack for a journey to Boston shortly before Christmas, she offers no other information about the purpose of their abrupt departure. From Salisbury Airport, they fly to the Baltimore/Washington International Airport to connect with the 8:45 P.M. plane to Boston's Logan Airport. On the tense plane trip, paid for by the proceeds from Gram's heirloom spoon, Dicey anticipates that they will see her mother.

11. Boston, Massachusetts

Gram and Dicey take a cab to a two-story motel. The next morning at the hospital, Gram insists that Dicey accompany her. Because family funds are limited, Gram chooses to have Liza's remains cremated rather than to transport her body in a casket. The toy shop owner gives them a black walnut box to hold the ashes.

12. Wilmington, Delaware

Bringing Momma's ashes home that snowy morning requires a long train ride from the Boston station. Following the same path that the children followed on their way to Gram's house, the train crosses the Connecticut River. Dicey clings to the wooden box, realizing that Momma really died the previous summer.

Gram and Dicey arrive at Salisbury before breakfast. Mr. Lingerle escorts the three younger children to meet the train, sparing Gram and Dicey the bus ride to Crisfield. The children ask Dicey about the box and weep when they learn that it holds their mother's remains.

13. Crisfield, Maryland

Because Maryland law allows the family to choose any spot for interring Momma's ashes, the Tillermans bury her under the mulberry tree in the front yard, with each child helping with the digging. Dicey believes that Momma is really gone forever and yet finally home. While Mr. Lingerle supplies pizza for dinner, Gram retrieves family albums from the attic. Through photos and stories, she brings the children up to date and fills the gaps in their family knowledge. They form a loving household.

Further Reading

Albritton, Tom, "Teaching, Learning, and Archetypes: Images of Instruction in Cynthia Voigt's 'Dicey's Song.' " *ALAN Review* (Spring 1994): 56–59.

"Awards Announced at Midwinter." *School Library Journal* (March 1983): 80.

Cart, Michael, "Top Children's Authors, Artists Warm to Candlelit Banquet: Association for Library Service to Children, Newbery-Caldecott-Wilder Awards Presentation." *American Libraries* (September 1983): 532.

"Cynthia Voigt," http://www.psnw.com/~grammaj/voigt.html.

"Cynthia Voigt, Marcia Brown Win Newbery, Caldecott." *Publishers Weekly* (January 28, 1983): 32.

"Cynthia Voigt's Biography," http://teacher.scholastic.com/authorsandbooks/authors/voigt/bio.htm.

"Dicey's Song." *School Library Journal* (January 1983): 89.

Donelson, Ken, and Alleen Pace Nilsen, "1994 Honor Listing: Some Standard Writers, Some New Writers, and a Few Surprises." *English Journal* (November 1995): 95–98.

Hammond, Nancy C., "Dicey's Song." *Horn Book* (December 1982): 653–54.

"History of Chesapeake Bay," http://clab.cecil.cc.md.us/faculty/Biology/Chesapeake/history.html.

Irving, Elsie K., "Cynthia Voigt." *Horn Book* (August 1983): 410–12.

Kaye, Marilyn, "Dicey's Song." *New York Times Book Review* (March 6, 1983): 30.

Maples, Mary Louise, and Betty Dean Newman, "Choosing Books for Today's Women." *ALAN Review* (Fall 1995): 24–27.

McCray, Nancy, "Dicey's Song." *Booklist* (December 15, 1992): 757.

Mengers, Susan, "Self-Sacrifice or Self-Development? Choices Made by Characters in the Novels of Cynthia Voigt." *Journal of Youth Services in Libraries* (Spring 1989): 250–55.

Patner, Myra Mensh, "Making Book on a Very Dicey Situation." *The Washington Post* (August 12, 1993): C5.

Saunders, Laura S., "Lingering with Dicey: Robin's Song." *Journal of Adolescent & Adult Literacy* (April 1997): 548–57.

"Scholastic Announces '200 FOR 2000'; Children's Publishing Company Releases List of Top 200 Children's Books for the Millennium." *PR Newswire* (November 23, 1999).

Shadiow, Linda K., "Recommended: Cynthia Voigt." *English Journal* (April 1987): 71–72.

Shaw-Eagle, Joanna, "Cynthia Voigt: Family Comes First." *Christian Science Monitor* (May 13, 1983): B2.

Sullivan, Emilie P., "Three Good Juvenile Books with Literacy Models." *Journal of Reading* (September 1994): 95.

Sutton, Roger, "A Solitary View." *School Library Journal* (June 1995): 28–32.

Voigt, Cynthia, "Newbery Medal Acceptance." *Horn Book* (August 1983): 410–13.

"Wilmington, Delaware, and the Brandywine Valley," http://www.wilmcvb.org/.

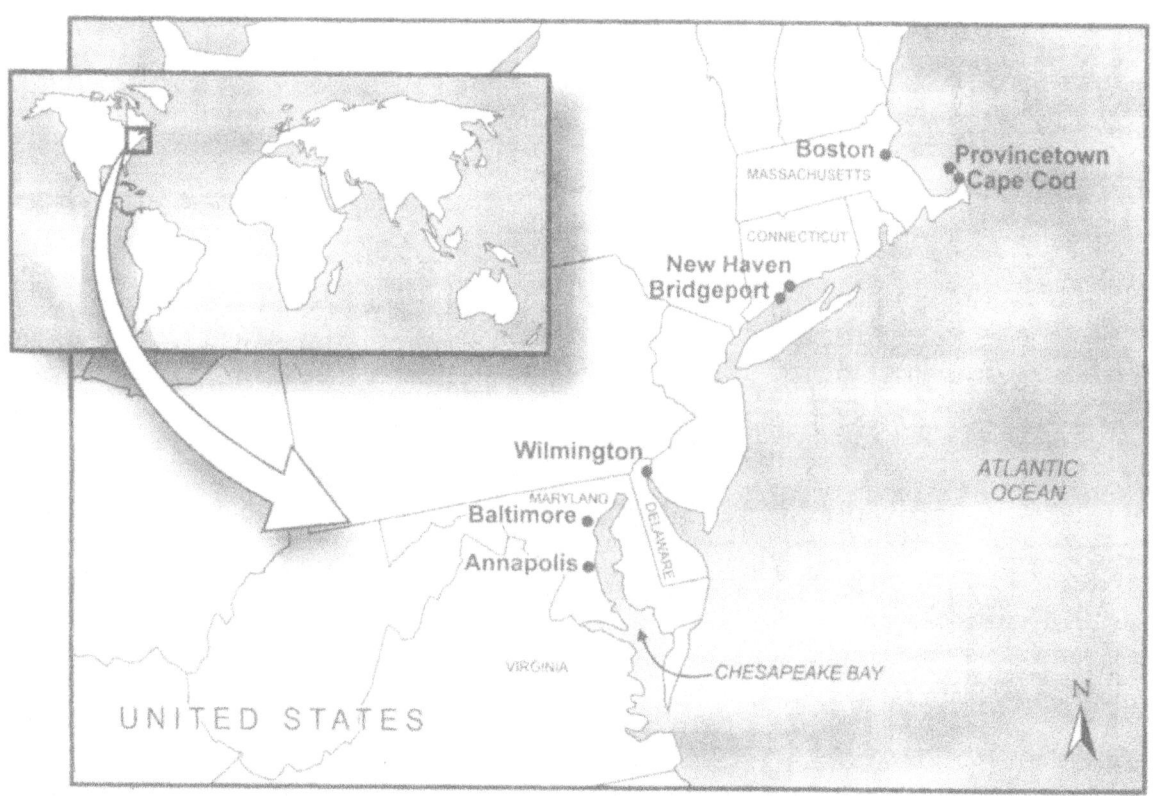

Don't Look Behind You

By Lois Duncan

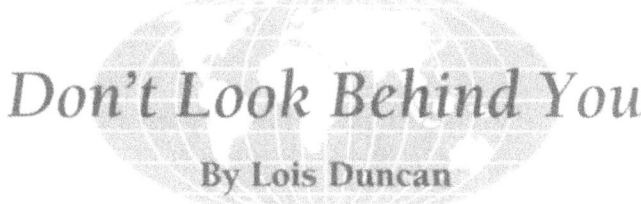

Mystery/suspense fiction, 1989

Geographical Summary

The suspenseful story of a family in flight from a hit man takes the foursome—April Corrigan and her parents and little brother Bram—on a desperate flight from home on the outskirts of Washington, D.C. The family takes part in the Federal Witness Security Program, which protects people who jeopardize themselves by testifying against dangerous criminals. Under armed guard, they first travel northwest to Richmond, Virginia, then southeast to Williamsburg where they assume new identities. They proceed to Florida's west coast and a rundown house in a fictional town in the citrus-growing section of the state.

The new setting upsets April, who misses her friends and lively high school activities. After she runs away from home, she returns from Florida by bus and plane to the original Virginia setting. She and her grandmother Lorelei, realizing they are in danger from a pursuer, move rapidly south to Grove City, Florida, with April driving her grandmother's Porsche. April knows they must reunite with her parents and little brother to prevent the Corrigans' execution. She speeds south from a pursuing gunman driving a black Camaro, whom she eventually kills in the family's driveway. The story concludes mysteriously in an undisclosed location with the Corrigans once more facing new identities as they opt to remain together as a family.

The author, Lois Duncan, suffered the loss of her daughter, nineteen-year-old Kaitlyn Arquette, whom stalkers chased in Santa Fe, New Mexico, on July 16, 1989. As a result of precognition, a form of prophecy, Duncan discovered that April's journeys in the fictional *Don't Look Behind You* predicted some of the events in her daughter's murder. Like April, Kait fled a hired gunman who looked like the drawing of the fictional Mike Vamp that appeared on the cover of a British paperback edition of *Don't Look Behind You*. Duncan, who consulted frequently with psychics for details and direction, reprised the terrible era in her family's life in *Who Killed My Daughter?: The True Story of a Mother's Search for Her Daughter's Murderer* (1992). Moved by the inexplicable commonalities between fictional and real events, Duncan also coauthored a book on ESP with William Roll, *Psychic Connections: A Journey into the Mysterious World of Psi* (2000), and initiated a sequel to *Who Killed My Daughter?*

Detailed Itinerary

1. Outskirts of eastern Virginia, south of Washington, D.C.

On a Tuesday in May, two weeks after her birthday, seventeen-year-old April Corrigan, a junior and tennis champ at Springside Academy, leaves her home in the fictional town of Norwood, Virginia, south of Washington, D.C. When boyfriend Steve picks her up before school, she confirms that her father, George, an employee of Southern Skyways, has been involved in a trial for three and a half weeks. He testifies as a witness against Richard Loftin, with whom he had traveled on business trips to South America. Later that day, April is in typing class when she receives a summons from the counselor's office. Without knowing why, she must depart from school with her maternal grandmother, Lorelei Gilbert.

To her dismay, April learns that an FBI agent they know as Uncle Max has arranged for protective custody of the Corrigans because someone shot at George in the courtroom. April, her brother, and their mother leave their residence immediately and switch vehicles at the Federal Building. They arrive at a Richmond hotel, where they must remain incommunicado.

2. Richmond, Virginia

At the Mayflower, a fictional hotel on the outskirts of Richmond, the Corrigans chafe at confinement to their room and the annoyance of each other's company. Jim Peterson, a pro at witness protection, stays with them as bodyguard. April's mother Liz confides that George has been spying on Loftin's illegal activities for the FBI.

April quarrels with Jim after he forbids her to phone Steve. While sulking in her room, she picks up on a phone conversation between Jim and Max and learns that anonymous letters have targeted the family with death threats. She realizes that the family's hotel-style house arrest may extend longer than she expected.

3. South America

On Wednesday, George phones to announce that the family can't return home until the trial ends. A newspaper article discloses that, over the past eight months, he had accompanied Loftin on two flights to an undisclosed locale in South America, the source of an illicit drug trade. Loftin used his airline staff to help him import illegal substances. Liz accuses George of enjoying playing spy.

4. Richmond, Virginia

Over the next eighteen days, the family orders food, sends out laundry, and receives extra clothing and amusements from Jim, who shops at a nearby mall. News of a guilty verdict against Loftin does not end the hotel stay. April, angry that she missed the prom, writes a letter to Steve, seals it in a Columbia Records envelope, and sneaks out during the night to drop it down the hotel postal chute.

While the bodyguard goes to the mall for board games, April opens the door to a tall woman from the hotel staff. When the worker turns out to be a male hit man in disguise, April presses on the door as Jim drops his packages and runs up the hall drawing his gun. She hears shots but remains out of sight. Liz phones Max, who arrives at 3:00 A.M. and spirits the family out the service elevator, then drives them away from the gunman, Mike Vamp.

5. Williamsburg, Virginia

The family flees to a motel on the edge of Williamsburg where they reunite with George. He explains their enrollment in the Federal Witness Security Program, managed by the U.S. Marshals Service. Max relates that Vamp hit Jim in the head at the shootout in the Mayflower hall and stuffed his body into a linen closet. To maintain anonymity, the family moves from motel to motel. On the third night, Agent Rita Green assigns them new identities.

6. Pittsburgh and the Catskills

April's father recalls that he grew up in Pittsburgh. He met his wife Liz while he worked at a resort in the Catskills, a tourist haven in the Allegheny Plateau of the Appalachian Mountains. Liz predicts that she will have difficulty around librarians and English teachers, who might recognize her as an author and winner of the California Young Readers Medal. Rita liquidates the family's investments and property and supplies contact lenses to Bram, to cover his mismatched eyes. Five days later, Rita renames the family Ellen and Philip Weber and their children Jason and Valerie.

7. Sarasota-Bradenton Airport, Florida

At 6:00 P.M., the family splits up at an unidentified airport to fly under false names to the Sarasota-Bradenton Airport on the west coast of Florida. On the flight south, April, traveling as "Val Weber," meets Abby Keller, an intrusive girl who asks personal questions. Momentarily frozen by the girl's inquisitiveness, April introduces herself as April Gross.

At the airport parking lot, the "Webers" drive away in a dented Plymouth. In an hour, they approach their new home in fictional Grove City, a small town in the citrus-growing section of Florida. They locate Lemon Lane and a driveway that carries them away from the main road through undergrowth and over a drainage ditch. Their house is hot, cramped, and ludicrously shabby.

8. Durham, North Carolina

At the Grove City Secondary School, the newly named "Val Weber" meets Kim Stanfield playing tennis with her cousin Larry Bushnell, who is captain of the school tennis team. "Val" claims to be from Durham, the location of Duke University. On a subsequent movie date with Larry, she encounters Kim and Larry's guest, Abby Keller, who recognizes her as April Gross. "Val" accidentally identifies her home state as Virginia. She lies about her identity by claiming that her family moved to Florida to escape financial difficulties.

9. Disney World, Orlando, Florida

The next day, the "Weber" family drives to Walt Disney World and Epcot Center at Orlando in east central Florida. The family shares lunch at two, then splits up. "Val's" parents proceed to Epcot. While watching her brother enjoy the teacup ride, "Val" unexpectedly encounters Jodi Simmons, her former tennis partner, and cannot avoid her. "Val" explains to Jodi that she is unable to account for the family's sudden disappearance from their Virginia home. "Val" weeps when she learns that Steve is dating her old friend Sherry.

10. Grove City, Florida

That evening, "Val" fights with Larry over the phone. When they reunite four days later, Larry's friend Amy invites them to a party on Saturday. "Val" drinks too much punch and fumbles her cover story. Larry accuses her of lying about meeting Abby on the plane.

The next day, "Philip" announces that someone shot Loftin after he was released on bail. "Philip" is still on the hit list. He gives a handful of $50 bills to "Val," but deflates her with the news that she can't go to Duke University as planned. Instead, to avoid encounters with old friends from Norwood, she must attend New College of Florida in Sarasota, a small liberal arts school established in 1960.

11. Sarasota-Bradenton Airport, Florida

The next morning, three months after the family's flight from Williamsburg to Florida, "Val" lies to her parents about spending the weekend with Kim. Instead, she books a flight to Norwood, Virginia. She sneaks away with her bags and phones Steve from Sarasota's city hall bus terminal. Before boarding a bus, she mails a note to her parents explaining the sudden departure, then journeys to the Sarasota-Bradenton Airport.

After landing in Virginia, April rushes to embrace Steve, who is less affectionate than she expected. At her grandmother's residence, Pat, the security guard, calls before admitting April. Lorelei is in a cast with a broken arm from an attack by an intruder posing as a deliveryman. She convinces April to return to Florida. They plan to leave that night in Lorelei's Porsche. She identifies her attacker as a dark-eyed man whom April assumes is the hit man Mike Vamp.

12. Petersburg, Virginia, to South Carolina

On the way out of Lorelei's apartment complex, the two travelers pretend to be vacationing in New England, but April drives them to a motel in Petersburg south of Richmond. During the night, April fears that the driver of a black Camaro is following them and begins driving erratically the next morning to outrun him. A police officer warns her about speeding and gives her a ticket. She leaves the highway in the fictional town of Tutterville, South Carolina. Lorelei realizes that her phone was tapped and that the stalker heard April's call from Sarasota.

13. St. Augustine, Florida

April drives north on Interstate 95 to St. George in south central South Carolina, then travels southeast toward Florida. She and Lorelei stop for the night at St. Augustine. Lorelei realizes that the stalker stole their marked route map and knows they are driving to Grove City. April tries to warn her unsuspecting parents, but no one answers the phone.

14. Grove City, Florida

When April and Lorelei traverse central Florida and arrive at the "Weber" home in Grove City, they find the family's Plymouth nose down in a drainage ditch. Vamp captures April and Lorelei. He recounts how he traced her letter to Steve and brags that he killed Jim before he could draw his gun. Regretting the kind, fatherly bodyguard's demise, April blames herself for disobeying.

Armed with a flashlight, April escapes captivity in a bedroom closet by climbing through the attic to Bram's room. She flees through the kitchen and into the Plymouth. When Vamp brandishes a pistol, she opens the door and strikes him with a tennis racket, knocking him into the ditch. Her parents return home.

After recovering Vamp's body, George blames himself for the chaos in the family's lives and offers to pose as a corpse to rid them of the need to hide. His wife insists that they start a new life together. Liz understands that they are on their own: they can no longer depend on the federal government to bankroll the move.

15. Unidentified location

In December, April, using the identity she adopted in September, shops with her brother at an undisclosed locale while her mother works as a secretary at an insurance agency and her grandmother sells upscale clothes at a boutique. Her father temporarily sells sporting goods. April, who tends the counter at Burger King, meets someone new, who invites her to a holiday party.

Further Reading

"Blockbuster, Inc. to Distribute Miracle Entertainment's 'Held for Ransom.'" *PR Newswire* (November 17, 2000).

"Children of Eve: The Lois Duncan Fan Club," http://www.geocities.com/Athens/Parthenon/8033/ld.html.

Graham, Fred. *The Alias Program*. Boston: Little, Brown, 1977.

"Interview with Lois Duncan," http://www.travers.com/educ/erms/EighthGrade.html.

Kies, Cosette. *Presenting Lois Duncan*. New York: Twayne, 1994.

"The Murder of Miss Kaitlyn C. Arquette," http://www.netzone.com/~holmes/wall/kca.html.

"New College of Florida," http://www.ncf.edu/index.html.

Office of Enforcement Operations. http://www.usdoj.gov/criminal/oeo.html.

Overstreet, Deborah Wilson, "Help! Help! An Analysis of Female Victims in the Novels of Lois Duncan." *ALAN Review* (Spring 1994): 43–45.

"Who Killed My Daughter?," *People Weekly* (November 24, 1997).
   See also *Who Killed My Daughter?* entry, this volume.

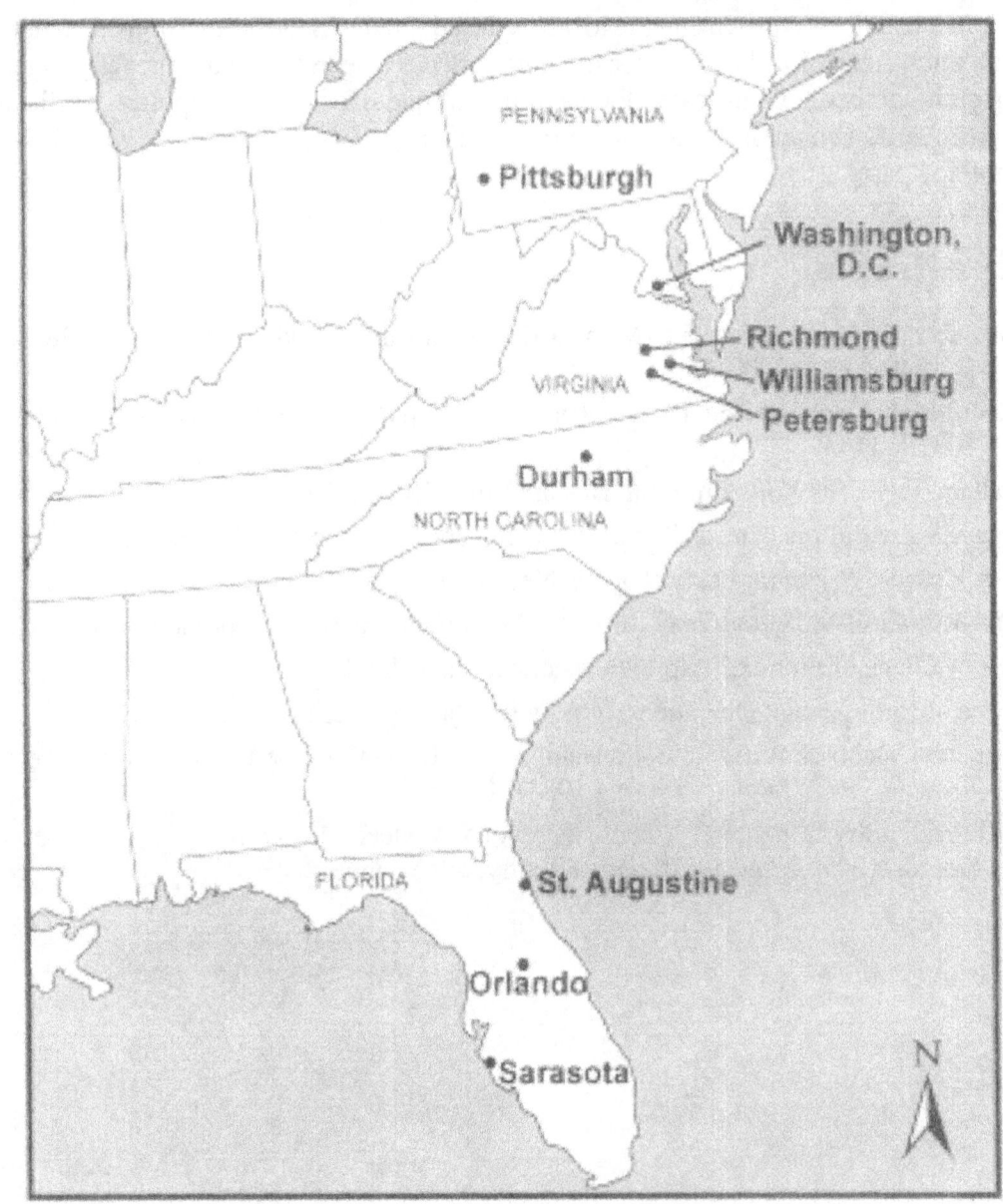

Go Tell It on the Mountain
By James Baldwin

Classic literary fiction, 1953

Geographical Summary

With his landmark novel about the young John Grimes, an autobiographical protagonist, James Baldwin characterizes the black diaspora of the 1920s and 1930s. He contrasts the squalor and wretchedness of black people both in the South and in the urban ghettoes of Chicago and Harlem, New York, where Baldwin was born. Without naming a place, he describes the Grimes' home during Florence and Gabriel's youth and characterizes the miserable existence of blacks in Southern neighborhoods threatened by evil white men. Uprooted to Maryland to live with an unloving aunt, Elizabeth, who later gives birth to John out of wedlock, awaits reunion with her father, who manages a bordello away from his motherless daughter.

In the North, Florence Grimes hopes to improve her life, yet exists on the rim of defeat without money or her husband Frank's support. When he arrives home drunk, she sinks to the parlor floor in despair at his waste of a paycheck that could have alleviated their grim lifestyle. Elizabeth, another immigrant from the South, boards in Harlem with Madame Williams, a spiritualist who wants the girl out of the way during weekend séances. At work in a hotel, Elizabeth meets Richard, the elevator operator. When the police arrest Richard at the subway platform and take him to the Tombs, a city prison north of City Hall Park and Centre and White streets, he fears a place where black men are beaten without having the chance to prove themselves innocent.

Dominating the novel is the Temple of the Fire Baptized, a storefront Pentecostal church four blocks up Lenox Avenue in Harlem, where young John cleans the premises in preparation for the Saturday night tarry service that precedes Sunday morning worship. The church is part of a growing gospel-based religion found in Philadelphia, Georgia, Florida, Boston, Chicago, and Brooklyn. In the dusty, unwholesome atmosphere, his wrestling with the spirit produces a dawn conversion. Baldwin balances the intensity of John's spiritual awakening with his emergence on the sin-filled street for the walk home with his aunt and father. The sounds of sirens that greet their ears presage more suffering and loss in a dark and threatening metropolis where black people do little more than survive and pray for deliverance.

Detailed Itinerary

1. Harlem, New York, 1935

Born in March 1921, fourteen-year-old John must emulate Head Deacon Gabriel Grimes, his hostile, pious father. Grimes preaches to youth at the Temple of the Fire Baptized, a storefront Pentecostal church four blocks up Lenox Avenue at a corner, probably near Harlem Hospital on West 136th Street. John, already a promising student, resolves not to behave like Gabriel, who bans friends, movies, and street games for John and John's half-brother Roy, Gabriel's favorite child.

Gabriel's hypercritical brand of Pentecostalism is an early-twentieth-century phenomenon of foot washing, charismatic healing, and glossolalia, or speaking in tongues as evidence of an individual's receipt of sanctity. On January 1, 1901, during a service led by Holiness preacher Charles F. Parham in Topeka, Kansas, Agnes Ozman, a student at Bethel Bible College, entered an ecstasy that caused her to speak in tongues. Worshippers interpreted her effusive and indecipherable utterance as a sign of Godliness. From 1905 to 1913, the phenomenon inspired black evangelist William J. Seymour, whose Azusa Street Revival at a warehouse in Los Angeles preceded the emergence of Pentecostalism in the rural South. In the grip of spiritual ecstasy, worshippers evolved individual theologies and fragmented themselves into independent assemblies. Criticism of Pentecostal strictness stereotyped followers as mean-spirited, narrow-minded, critical of outsiders, and abusive of women and children. Mainline Christians disdained the extreme piety among Pentecostals, as displayed by their denunciation of jewelry, makeup, women's slacks and short hairstyles, card playing, dancing, movies and sporting events, and television.

2. Central Park and Fifth Avenue, New York City

At 11:00 A.M. on Saturday morning, Elizabeth, Grimes's second wife, releases John from scrubbing woodwork and gives him money for a birthday present. He recognizes a prevailing sadness on her face. On the way south through unmelted snow in Central Park, beyond Broadway, and down Fifth Avenue into view of lower Manhattan's skyline, he wonders why his father despises whites, especially racist Southerners. John passes the Sixth Street Automat, a self-service diner, and admires the public library on 42nd Street and the candy in Woolworth's. He retreats into a movie theater to immerse himself in *Of Human Bondage*. Afterward, he sees his sister Sarah searching for him at the drugstore. He expects trouble at home.

3. Harlem, New York

When John arrives at the family's flat, his mother and Aunt Florence are treating a knife gash in Roy's head. Gabriel blames John for being gone, slaps Elizabeth for negligence, and beats Roy with his belt. Roy threatens to kill Gabriel for abusing his mother. Florence accuses her brother of piety and innate wildness. At 6:00 P.M., two hours early for the tarry service, Gabriel escorts John to church. Elisha, another church member, wrestles with John for sassing him and exhorts him to examine the condition of his soul.

4. The Jim Crow South

Nearing death at age sixty, Florence resents the exhibitionism that Pentecostal congregations expect of members. She relives the terminal illness of her mother, a former slave and washwoman. Most grievous is her mother's preference for Gabriel, an illegitimate son who attends a one-room school and receives religious instruction denied to Florence. He drinks and carouses, then undergoes a conversion at age twelve at a camp meeting. During a twelve-day revival, he preaches at the Twenty-Four Elders Revival Meeting with pulpit ministers arriving from as far north as Chicago and as far south as Florida.

At the closing Sunday night dinner, Gabriel recoils from Elder Peters's vulgar jokes about Deborah's rape by white men. To end her isolation and rejection, he proposes marriage, but later regrets having a childless wife and passionless home life. While working in a white household, he eyes Esther, a flirtatious fellow servant. She comes to church to hear one of his sermons. Unmoved by his preaching, she walks out during the closing hymn. While their employers are gone for three days, Gabriel seduces Esther on the kitchen floor and continues their affair for nine days.

5. Chicago

Six weeks after discovering her pregnancy, Esther reports her shame to Gabriel. He refuses to marry her and claims that he owes allegiance to his pulpit calling. On the savings he stole a week earlier from Deborah's tin box in the cupboard, Esther travels north to Chicago. That winter, she dies. Shortly after Christmas, her parents retrieve her body and bring their infant grandson Royal south to raise.

6. The South

Gabriel preaches in the mission field for three months before returning home to Deborah and replacing the stolen cash. Without admitting fatherhood, he watches Esther's son, who grows up spoiled and undisciplined. At the beginning of World War I, Gabriel prays that the boy will be spared the draft and warns him away from the sight of a black soldier murdered by whites. In 1921, according to Esther's mother, Royal dies from a knife wound to the throat among gamblers in a Chicago tavern. Revealing her knowledge of the family's history, Deborah relates to Gabriel that Royal was buried beyond Lincoln Park in potter's field, the city cemetery for the homeless and poor.

7. New York City

Leaving her mother for Gabriel to tend, in 1900, twenty-six-year-old Florence makes her way to New York alone. Five years later, she marries Frank, a heavy drinker who causes her grief for ten years. Florence receives a letter from Deborah describing Esther's death and revealing that Esther died after bearing Gabriel's illegitimate child. In 1915 Frank abandons Florence for another woman and dies two years later in France during World War I.

8. Maryland

Gabriel's second wife, Elizabeth Grimes, was born in 1901. After her mother dies in 1909, she travels northeast to Maryland by train to reside with a complaining, pious aunt who makes fun of the child's dark coloring. Unaware that her father pimps at a bordello, Elizabeth awaits their reunion in vain. At age eighteen, while shopping at a grocery store for lemons before a church picnic, she meets Richard, a bold grocery clerk four years her senior.

9. Harlem, New York

In 1920, Elizabeth follows Richard to Harlem to board at an ugly back room with a relative, a spiritualist named Madame Williams. Richard lives apart from Elizabeth and on occasion, escorts her to the Museum of Natural History and the Metropolitan Museum of Art. Their intimacy grows, but they delay marriage while he completes school.

After the robbery of a white man's store, police arrest Richard and two black boys at the subway platform. They jail Richard at the Tombs, a dismal prison in lower Manhattan near City Hall. By refusing to sign a confession, he gains his freedom but returns covered in welts from a beating. Elizabeth conceals her pregnancy until Richard shakes his despair. Without knowing about the impending birth, he slits his wrists with a razor. His landlady discovers his body.

10. Wall Street, New York City

Elizabeth supports her infant son by cleaning a "high, vast, stony office-building" on Wall Street, America's most powerful financial district, which extends from Broadway to the East River and encompasses major banks and the New York Stock Exchange. At her job, Elizabeth encounters Florence, a fellow worker who invites her for coffee at an all-night coffee shop. After Florence's twenty-year separation from Gabriel, they reunite. In September 1922, to retrieve herself and her six-month-old son John from the stigma of illegitimacy, Elizabeth marries Gabriel. Mourning Royal's death in secret, Gabriel considers his stepson John a second chance at fatherhood.

11. The Temple of the Fire Baptized, Lenox Avenue, Harlem

After John experiences a religious transformation at the altar, Florence accompanies him and his father home. She confronts Gabriel for abandoning Esther and for refusing to acknowledge fathering Royal. On the way up Lenox Avenue, she gives him the source of her information—Deborah's letter, which she has carried for thirty years. Gabriel wards off blame by declaring himself "the Lord's anointed." Florence predicts that Roy will cause him pain and that Gabriel is trying to escape hurt by tormenting Elizabeth and John. Elisha honors John's conversion with a holy kiss.

Further Reading

Balfour, Katharine Lawrence. *The Evidence of Things Not Said: James Baldwin and the Promise of American Democracy*. New York: Cornell University Press, 2000.

Cantor, George. *Historic Landmarks of Black America*. Detroit: Gale Research, 1991.

Champion, Ernest A. *Mr. Baldwin, I Presume*. New York: University Press of America, 1995.

Clegg, Roger, "Go Tell It on the Mountain." *The American Enterprise*, January 1, 1999.

Gottfried, Ted. *James Baldwin: Voice from Harlem*. New York: Franklin Watts, 1997.

Grady, J. Lee, "The Other Pentecostals." *Charisma* (June 1997).

Harris, Trudier. *New Essays on 'Go Tell It on the Mountain.'* Cambridge: Cambridge University Press, 1996.

Hudson, Barbara, "Beneath the Black Aesthetic: James Baldwin's Primer of Black American Masculinity." *African American Review* (June 22, 1998).

"James Arthur Baldwin," http://www.bridgesweb.com/baldwin.html.

"James Arthur Baldwin," http://www.kirjasto.sci.fi/jbaldwin.htm.

"James Baldwin, Writer," http://www.HomeToHarlem.com/Harlem/hthcult.nsf/notables/6985f4c8d890f25f852565cf001dbca1.

McBride, Dwight A. *James Baldwin Now*. New York: New York University Press, 1999.

Miller, D. Quentin. *Re-Viewing James Baldwin: Things Not Seen.* Philadelphia: Temple University Press, 2000.

Noll, Mark A. *American Evangelical Christianity: An Introduction.* Newburyport, Mass.: Blackwell, 2000.

Shaw, Stephanie J. *What a Woman Ought to Be and to Do: Black Professional Women Workers During the Jim Crow Era.* Chicago: University of Chicago Press, 1996.

Stevenson, John, "James Baldwin: An Appreciation." *Boston Book Review* (December 1995).

Tackach, James. *James Baldwin.* New York: Lucent Books, 1997.

Teachout, Terry. "James Baldwin: Early Novels and Stories." *National Review* (February 9, 1998).

Tomlinson, Robert. "Payin' One's Dues." *African American Review* (March 22, 1999).

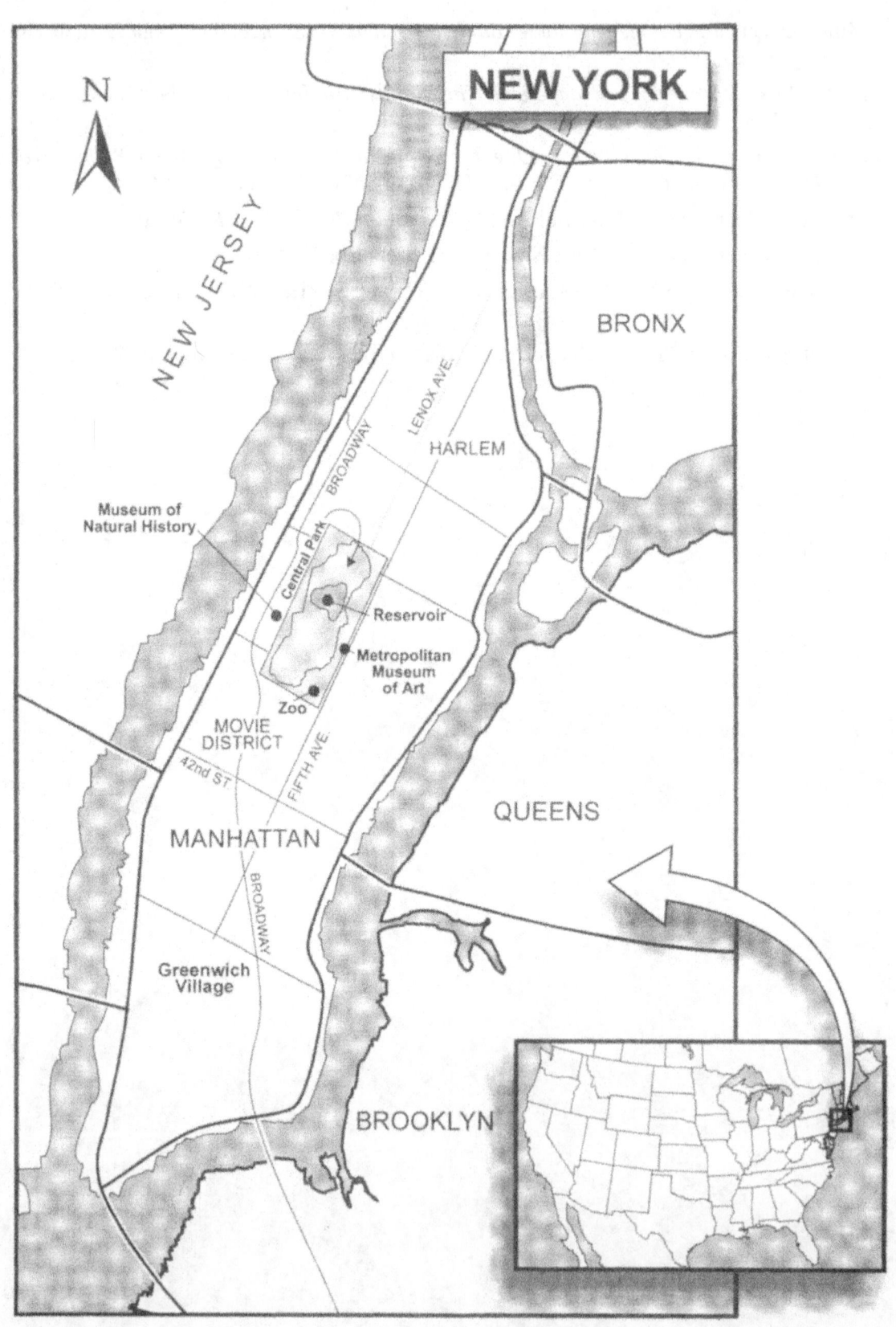

Great Expectations
By Charles Dickens

Classic literary fiction, 1861

Geographical Summary

In setting *Great Expectations* in England during the first quarter of the nineteenth-century, Dickens relies on indoor and outdoor locales and lifestyles he knew from personal experience during his childhood on the marshlands east end of the Thames and subsequent years reporting on London's legal sector. He contrasted village folk life and Londoners and their relationships, beliefs, ambitions, and values. Significant to his comparisons of social classes are the inner workings of poverty and gentrification, of privilege and exclusion, and of the dangers from felons and wayside predators.

The story opens on a dreary, misty Christmas Eve in a churchyard as Pip visits the graves of his parents and five brothers. Set on boggy coastal land, the area suggests Gad's Hill, the scene of highway robberies, and also Cooling near Chatham, Kent, where Dickens saw thirteen graves of children. The novel stresses the child's imagined fears of cemeteries and the real menace of England's criminal element. Dramatizing both is the boy's surprise graveyard encounter with Abel Magwitch, a runaway felon from the Hulks, the recycled ships that were—and still are—England's relief for overcrowded jails. Terrified by the convict's threats, Pip raids the pantry of his hostile sister, Georgiana Maria Gargery, and treats Abel to pork pie and brandy. For his compassion, Pip unknowingly stores up treasure for his future.

In his teens, Pip apprentices with Joe Gargery, his brother-in-law/foster father, who works at a forge similar to the one Dickens knew at Chalk, east of Gravesend. The emotional battle between hatred of grime and the rough smithy's apron and the need to thank his sister's husband for job training eats at the tender-hearted boy. Worsening his longing for a better life are his visits to the decaying Satis House mansion, based on Restoration House at Rochester. In murky chambers, he entertains Miss Havisham by conversing with Estella, her young daughter. Pip naturally assumes that he owes his sudden wealth and advancement to Miss Havisham.

In a short span, Pip acquires a gentleman's clothes, moves to London, and studies at a cram school in Hammersmith. Pip imitates a gentility and style he thought he had witnessed at Satis House. The sudden upgrade to urbanism allows him to fraternize with peers at a men's club in Covent Garden and to squire Estella at the Assembly Ball in Richmond. A bizarre turn of events reveals that his funds come from a sheepherder exiled to Botany Bay, the notorious prison settlement in New South Wales, Australia.

The novel's falling action rattles Pip's complacency with a nightmarish return to Satis House, the rescue of Miss Havisham from flames at her hearthside, and a warning letter at midnight from a stranger lurking at his lodgings. Without time to recover, Pip plots to get Abel out of the country by packet boat. The old convict dies, believing that his bulging pocketbook passed to Pip and will guarantee financial security. Facing imprisonment for debts, Pip collapses and slowly regains his health through Joe, who quietly pays outstanding debts before returning to the village. Pip realizes that snobbery robs rather than enriches.

Detailed Itinerary

1. Woolwich Marsh on the Thames River estuary

On Christmas Eve in the early 1800s, Philip "Pip" Pirrip, a seven-year-old orphan, visits a churchyard at the edge of Woolwich marsh on the south side of the Thames estuary east of Gravesend. He surveys the graves of his parents and "five stone lozenges" above his five brothers—Alexander, Bartholomew, Abraham, Tobias, and Roger—who died in infancy. Beyond the sanctuary, dikes, mounds, and gates command the boggy ground all the way to the river and the sea beyond. Pip's eyes fix on the harbor beacon and a gibbet where a pirate was hanged.

An escapee from the Hulks, a prison ship anchored in the nearby harbor, suddenly looms from behind a gravestone and seizes the "small bundle of shivers." The convict, bemired and lacerated by briars, snatches at Pip's bread. He threatens the boy with cannibal dismemberment if he does not locate a file and more "wittles." Terrified, Pip runs home.

2. Gargery home near Chatham, Kent

Since being orphaned, Pip has lived with his sister, twenty-seven-year-old Mrs. Joe Gargery. As his unwilling guardian, she has reared him grudgingly and at times violently. His brother-in-law, blacksmith Joe Gargery, is a humble, compassionate surrogate parent who seems to suffer his wife's rampages as often as Pip. The family lives in a wood dwelling that adjoins Joe's forge. The sound of the "after sunset-gun" announces the search for the convict, who fled the previous night. Pip steals brandy, cheese and bread, a jar of mincemeat, a meaty bone, and a holiday pork pie from the Gargery pantry and a file from the forge.

3. Marshes on the Thames River estuary

Pip runs a mile toward the river to the convict's hiding place. Pip crosses a ditch on the battery, a defunct fortification at Cliffe Creek that once protected London for attack on the east. On the way, he passes a scar-faced convict. On reuniting with the first felon, who suffers a touch of fever, Pip learns that the man is unaware of the second escapee's whereabouts.

4. Gargery home near Chatham, Kent

The Christmas Day dinner Pip's sister cooks is intended to impress Mr. Wopsle, the church clerk; Mr. Hubble, the village wheelwright, and his wife; and Mr. Pumblechook, a prosperous corn merchant who is Joe's uncle. Pip clings to the table in anticipation of being caught for theft. Just as his sister discovers the pie missing at 2:30 P.M., soldiers interrupt and demand that Joe repair the lock on their irons, which they plan to clamp onto two escaped convicts. Carrying Pip on his back, Joe follows the soldiers through the mist toward the old battery.

The soldiers apprehend the two felons, who fight in a ditch. Pip's acquaintance, who calls the other man a villain, claims that the scar-faced man was a traitor at their trial. Piercing the gloom are torches, musket fire, and the sound of three cannons. After 3:30 P.M., the party arrives at the soldiers' outpost. Pip comes under no suspicion for taking the missing items because his convict confesses to stealing them. In irons, the prisoner returns to the Hulk by boat from the landing.

5. Gargery home and village school

Returned home on Joe's back, Pip is warming himself by the kitchen fire when his sister hustles him to bed. He attends an evening dame school at Mr. Wopsle's great-aunt's cottage, which doubles as a shop. On market day, Mrs. Joe returns in the chaise-cart from shopping for Uncle Pumblechook at an unspecified town, probably Chatham and Rochester south of the marshes on the Medway River. She reports that the boy is to play at Satis House, a grim building inhabited by Miss Havisham, a wealthy recluse.

6. Satis House

Traveling four miles from the forge, Pip arrives at Pumblechook's residence on High Street for an 8:00 A.M. breakfast and the ride to Satis House at 10:00. In a quarter hour, they reach the dismal brick estate alongside an old brewery. Estella unlocks the gate without identifying herself and, by candlelight, leads Pip upstairs.

Inside, Pip sees a large dressing room, and at the mirrored dressing table, an old woman clad in a yellowed wedding gown. She requests diversion from her broken heart. He summons Estella to a game of cards. Although she is pretty, he thinks her insulting and proud. Miss Havisham invites him to return after six days.

7. Village near the marshes

On return to the forge, Pip makes up lies about playing with flags, but confesses to Joe the truth about Miss Havisham's peculiar residence. After school, Pip calls for Joe at the village pub, the Three Jolly Bargemen, and sees a stranger carrying the file Pip stole from the forge. The man slips the boy a shilling and two one-pound notes.

8. Satis House

On the second visit to Satis House, Estella ushers Pip into a room near the courtyard. Miss Havisham's greedy relatives—Camilla, Cousin Raymond, and Sarah Pocket—and an unidentified burly man attend a birthday celebration at a sumptuous but dusty table decked in spider webs and covered with moldy wedding refreshments. Pip walks Miss Havisham around the perimeter, then plays cards with Estella. In the walled garden, a pale young gentleman challenges him to a fistfight, which Pip wins. Estella offers Pip her cheek to kiss.

On subsequent visits, Pip pushes Miss Havisham in her garden chair and hears her urge Estella to break men's hearts. Pumblechook discusses with Mrs. Joe Pip's indenture. At noon the next day, Joe accompanies Pip to Satis House, where Miss Havisham allots Joe twenty-five guineas for Pip's apprenticeship. After a celebratory dinner at the Blue Boar, Pip goes to bed wretched at the thought of becoming a blacksmith.

9. Forge

Pip despairs at the blacksmith's trade. He fears that Estella will see his dirty, humble work. At the old battery, he tries to educate Joe, who is illiterate. Pip requests a half holiday. Joe agrees and also extends time off to Dolge Orlick, Pip's fellow forge worker. Orlick lives with the sluice-keeper, who regulates water flowing onto the marsh.

10. Satis House

To express his thanks, Pip visits Miss Havisham, who invites him to return only on his birthday.

11. Gargery home near Chatham, Kent

While passing the Three Jolly Bargemen at 11:00 P.M., Pip learns that between 8:00 and 9:45 P.M., an unknown assailant struck his sister on the head, leaving her semi-paralyzed. A month later, Biddy comes to keep house for the family. The only clues to the assault are a convict's leg-iron filed in two and the T that Mrs. Joe draws. Biddy concludes that the letter represents Orlick's hammer.

12. Satis House

A year later, Pip receives a guinea on his next birthday visit to Miss Havisham at her home.

13. Gargery house

Biddy loves Pip, who confesses that he wants to be a gentleman to impress Estella. Biddy confides her fear that Orlick likes her. Pip begins watching the journeyman.

14. Village

On a Saturday evening in Pip's fourth year of apprenticeship, at the Three Jolly Bargemen, he recognizes Jaggers, Miss Havisham's portly attorney. Walking toward the forge, Jaggers informs Pip and Joe that a secret benefactor wants the boy educated as a gentleman in London and tutored by Matthew Pocket. Jaggers offers twenty guineas for Pip's new clothes and instructs him to take a hackney coach from the stagecoach office in London to Jaggers's office.

The windfall causes mixed feelings in Pip. When he withdraws to bed after announcing his good fortune, he feels uncommonly lonely. He makes a final tour of the churchyard and longs to head for London and greatness. In the village, he buys a fashionable suit from Trabb the tailor and accessories from other tradesmen.

15. Satis House

On Friday, Pip dresses at Pumblechook's house for a visit to Miss Havisham. He assumes that she is his benefactor; she neither denies nor confirms his surmise.

16. Gargery house

Dressed in finery, Pip takes an evening meal with his family before departing the next day at 5:00 A.M. After a restless night's sleep and a hurried breakfast, he walks up High Street and leaves the village in tears.

17. Jaggers's office near Smithfield Street, London

Following a five-hour trip to London, Pip travels into heavy traffic at Wood Street and Cross Keys—an inn and coach terminal at the major intersection of Cornhill, Lombard, Threadneedle, and King William streets. He travels north to Cheapside, a street near St. Paul's Cathedral. Somewhat cowed by the city's size, Pip takes a hackney to Jaggers's office at Little Britain near Smithfield.

18. Barnard's Inn, London

In an office lit only by a skylight, Pip becomes Jaggers's ward and receives money and directions to his lodgings at Barnard's Inn, a medieval townhouse serving the legal community and law students. John Wemmick, the trusted law clerk, escorts Pip northwest up Holborn Hill, an area where the Dickens family lived during the author's rise to fame. Pip is disappointed on reaching his destination. At the sooty complex, he climbs stairs to the top floor, where he recognizes Herbert Pocket as the pale young man he fought at Satis House.

After a waiter serves dinner, Herbert scorns the proud Estella and renames Pip "Handel." Herbert explains that Miss Havisham was the daughter of a country brewer. Twenty-five years earlier, her fiancé jilted her with a letter ending their relationship. Herbert knows little about Estella's adoption. From the inn, Herbert and Pip walk the streets, visit parks, and attend church at Westminster Abbey, an imposing cathedral opposite the Houses of Parliament. On Monday, Pip follows Herbert to his accounting office.

19. Matthew Pocket's house, Hammersmith

After lunch, Herbert and Pip return to their rooms to get Pip's luggage and board a coach. At Hammersmith, five miles west of Westminster and Chelsea and north of a loop of the Thames, Pip meets Belinda and Matthew Pocket, Miss Havisham's relative and the harried father of six small Pockets. Matthew works as a grinder or tutor at his cram school. He shows Pip to his room and introduces the boys' fellow students, Startop and Bentley Drummle, a nasty-tempered, snobbish youth from Shropshire, a western English county bordering Wales.

20. Jaggers's office and police court in the city

Several days later, Pip requests twenty pounds from Jaggers, who complies and takes him on a tour of the city and police court.

21. The Hammersmith road east to Barnard's Inn

Herbert and Pip frequent the road between their permanent quarters and Matthew Pocket's house in Hammersmith. Herbert shares a half interest in Pip's boat, which he keeps on the Thames River at Hammersmith.

22. Walworth, London

Several weeks later, Pip walks home with Wemmick to Walworth, an unassuming residential section two miles south of London Bridge. Withdrawn into a private realm far from Jaggers's law practice, Wemmick has fitted out his domain like a fortress with flagstaff, bridge, moat, guns, and battery. Wemmick cares for his aged parent, a former wine cooper who is nearly deaf. At 8:30 the next morning, Pip and Wemmick walk back toward the office.

23. Soho, London

Jaggers invites Pip, Herbert, Startop, and Bentley Drummle to dinner in Soho. At Jaggers's home on the south side of Gerrard Street west of Charing Cross Road, he introduces his guests to Molly, a housekeeper whom he saved from a murder charge. At 9:30 P.M., the boys walk west to Hammersmith, with Drummle lagging behind his three companions in the shadows.

24. Barnard's Inn, London

The following Tuesday, Joe arrives in London at 9:00 on a drizzly morning. His social unease in Pip's lodgings ruins the visit. He informs Pip that Estella has returned to Satis House and that Miss Havisham wants to see Pip. Joe asserts that he will not return again to embarrass Pip.

25. Satis House

The next day at 2:00 P.M., Pip takes the coach from Cross Keys, London, sharing the ride with the convict who gave him money at the Three Jolly Bargemen. At the village, Pip rooms at the Blue Boar instead of returning to Joe's house. At Satis House, Pip finds Orlick securing the gate. Estella has become a heartbreaker whom her foster mother wants Pip to love. Later, he dines with Jaggers and stays at the inn that night exulting in his love for the haughty Estella. The next morning, Pip warns Jaggers that Miss Havisham should not trust Orlick.

26. Barnard's Inn, London

Pip takes the noon stage back to London and sends a penitential codfish and cask of oysters to Joe. Pip confesses his adoration of Estella; Herbert expresses his love of a motherless girl, Clara Barley, but is too poor to marry her.

27. Newgate Prison, London

When Estella visits London, Pip paces in anticipation of meeting her coach at Wood Street near Cheapside in central London. Wemmick encounters him and gives him a tour of Newgate Prison, a two-story stone facility. London's chief lockup, it was established by Henry II in 1188 and became the most loathsome and feared jail for foul odors, epidemics, and the overcrowding of a motley population of felons, debtors, traitors, spies, and religious heretics. Newcomers depended on a system of bribes to supply them with such minimal comforts as blankets and decent food. In addition to regular public hangings before a jeering crowd, the jail hosted pressings, pillorying, whippings, and stocks.

28. Richmond, Surrey

Estella plans for Pip to escort her to Richmond, Surrey, a residential borough and art and culture center ten miles away in southwestern London. On the way out of town, she shudders at the sight of Newgate Prison. At a staid old house in Richmond, Estella intends to enter society with the help of Mrs. Brandley, a great lady. Pip returns to Hammersmith heavy of heart. He joins the Finches of the Grove and attends meetings at a hotel in Covent Garden. At other times, he haunts Richmond and goes into debt.

29. Gargery home near Chatham, Kent

A letter arrives from Trabb & Company stating that Pip's sister Georgiana has died. A week after her death, Pip attends the funeral and has supper with Joe and Biddy, who wants to teach at a new school. Pip learns that Orlick is working at the quarries. Pip leaves immediately with a promise to come back to visit. Biddy doubts his sincerity.

30. Jaggers's office near Smithfield Street, London
At their London quarters, Pip and Herbert grow extravagant and incur debts. At age twenty-one, Pip hears from Jaggers that Pip's annual income will be five hundred pounds. Pip still doesn't learn his benefactor's name.

31. Walworth, London
The next Sunday, Wemmick gives Pip money to buy Herbert a post at Clarriker & Company. Pip pays 250 pounds down and sets up a payment schedule. The arrangement gives him a warm feeling and delights Herbert, who is not aware of having a benefactor.

32. Satis House
At Estella's request, Pip escorts her to Satis House, where she quarrels with Miss Havisham about Estella's coldness. Meanwhile, Drummle courts Estella and toasts her at a gathering of the Finches.

33. Assembly Ball in Richmond
At the Assembly Ball in Richmond, Pip is dismayed to see Drummle hanging on Estella, the most beautiful woman in attendance. She continues to discourage Pip's love. The fashionable event may have occurred at the Castle Inn, an entertainment center in Richmond.

34. Barnard's Inn, London
Pip celebrates his twenty-third birthday alone on a rainy night while Herbert travels to Marseilles, France. At 11:00 P.M., the old convict, Abel Magwitch, surfaces unexpectedly at Pip and Herbert's quarters and reveals that he is Pip's anonymous benefactor.

35. Botany Bay, Australia
After working for years as a sheep farmer at Botany Bay, a port city and settlement of transported criminals in New South Wales, Australia, Abel has come to think of Pip as his son. Upon arrival at Portsmouth, Abel has come to see Pip even if the visit results in recapture and hanging at Newgate Prison. Pip protects Abel on the second floor of a residence close by in Essex Street between the Strand and the Thames. When Herbert arrives back from France, Pip tells him the whole story of his relationship with Abel and swears Herbert to secrecy.

36. Epsom races
The next morning, Pip questions Abel about his fellow convict and learns that he met Compeyson twenty years earlier at Epsom Downs, a derby course southeast of London. Compeyson manipulated and deceived Abel, who was incarcerated at the Kingston Jail on a vagrancy charge. Pip recognizes that Compeyson's friend Arthur was Miss Havisham's half-brother.

Arthur suffers incriminating hallucinations as a result of their plot to defraud Miss Havisham, to whom Compeyson was engaged. Compeyson used his polish and educated speech to lighten his sentence to seven years, while Abel was sentenced to 14 years on the same prison ship. At a subsequent court appearance, Abel drew a life sentence.

37. Satis House

On his way to reunite with Estella at Satis House, Pip encounters Drummle at the Blue Boar and initiates a shoving match. Pip realizes that Miss Havisham used him to taunt greedy relatives and never intended to educate him to marry Estella. He learns that Estalla is engaged to Drummle and urges her not to marry such a brute.

38. Barnard's Inn, London

Past midnight, Pip returns to London. At Whitefriars Gate, he receives a handwritten warning from Wemmick to avoid home. Pip spends the night at Hummums Hotel at Covent Garden and Russell Street. The next morning, he travels to Walworth and learns from Wemmick that Abel is in danger. Wemmick confirms that Compeyson is in London and tells Pip how to locate Herbert at Clara's residence.

39. Clara's house

An hour later, Pip travels east five miles along the Thames and over the Pool, the name of the segment of the river between London Bridge and Greenwich, to Clara's riverside house between Limehouse, a dock and ferry crossing south of Bow Street on the Thames, and Greenwich, a town on the river's south bank southeast of London. At Mill Pond Bank on Chinks's Basin, he locates Mrs. Whimple's boardinghouse at the Old Green Copper Rope-Walk. Although Abel is safely resettled upstairs, under the name Provis, near the growly invalid Bill Barley, Pip remains on edge. Herbert suggests that he and Pip keep a boat at the Temple stairs and row regularly on the river to establish a pattern of activity.

40. Barnard's Inn, London

Pip finds his quarters quiet and Provis's former rooms dark. Pip begins rowing west above Blackfriars Bridge and east toward London Bridge. He travels as far as Erith, a port in Kent twelve miles below London on the river's south bank. Meanwhile, he sinks further into debt and tries not to think of Estella's marriage. At a restaurant, Wopsle observes one of the convicts following Pip.

41. Gerrard Street, London

At Jaggers's home on Gerrard Street, Pip surmises that Molly is Estella's mother. Wemmick narrates how she was acquitted of a murder charge at the Old Bailey, London's Central Criminal Court. The murdered woman, found near Hounslow Heath, a woodland scored with footpaths west of London, had inflamed Molly with jealousy. At the time, Molly had a three-year-old daughter.

42. Satis House

Traveling by coach, Pip arrives at the village and begs Miss Havisham to give Herbert nine hundred pounds to buy a partnership at Clarriker & Company. She agrees to send that amount by Jaggers and kneels to demonstrate her regret for manipulating Estella and Pip. He asks nothing for himself. On questioning Miss Havisham, Pip learns that Jaggers brought Estella to her when the child was two or three and that he arranged the adoption. After departing, Pip is drawn back to Miss Havisham's room and rescues her from flames at the hearth. He burns his hands and arms. Rolled in his cloak, she lapses into unconsciousness. He summons a surgeon. At six the next morning, he kisses Miss Havisham, who asks him to write, "I forgive her."

43. Barnard's Inn, London
Herbert reports the accident to Matthew, then tends Pip's dressings. The previous evening, Herbert learned from Abel that he and Molly are Estella's parents and Compeyson blackmailed Abel with threats involving Estella.

44. Jaggers's office near Smithfield Street, London
The next morning, Pip visits Jaggers's office to divulge that Abel is Estella's father. Jaggers explains indirectly the circumstances of Estella's adoption. Pip concludes the purchase of Herbert's position at Clarriker & Company through Miss Skiffins's brother, an accountant. The partnership earns Herbert a post in Cairo, Egypt. Herbert later offers Pip a position as clerk. Pip and Herbert decide to send Abel aboard the Hamburg steamer the next Wednesday.

45. Limekiln on the marshes
A mysterious letter mentions Uncle Provis by name and urges Pip to come to the limekiln. After dark, Orlick captures Pip, binds his sore arms to his side, and holds him at gunpoint for costing Orlick the job at Satis House. He intends to burn Pip's body in the kiln and boasts of assaulting Mrs. Joe. Herbert, guided by Trabb's boy, rescues Pip, who faints from pain and trauma.

46. River to Gravesend
Aided by Startop, Pip and Herbert intend to row below Gravesend, a major departure point for seagoing ships exiting the Thames estuary between Kent and Essex. Past London Bridge, they move steadily east and reunite with Abel, who is cloaked like a river pilot. The foursome breakfast at a public house called the Ship and take rooms for the night. Jack, the innkeeper, reports seeing two men in a galley and fears they are customhouse inspectors. From the window, Pip spies two suspicious men walking toward Nore, a sandbank near Steerness on the Thames estuary.

As the foursome row out to the steamer on Thursday morning, a police galley carrying the informer Compeyson rams the rowboat. Abel pulls his old adversary into the water in a deadly tussle. Compeyson drowns and is located downriver horribly disfigured. Abel, manacled and taken on board the galley, is seriously injured. A police officer claims Abel's pocketbook.

47. Jail, London
Pip visits Abel daily at the prison infirmary. Abel suffers broken ribs and an injured lung. By April, he has healed enough to sit in a chair at the trial, at which he is condemned to death. After Pip confesses that he loves Estella, Abel dies in his infirmary cot content that Pip will inherit his money. Pip conceals the fact that the pocketbook is in the hands of the police.

48. Barnard's Inn, London
After Herbert leaves for Cairo, Pip falls so ill that he can't comply with two agents, who arrest him for nonpayment of debt to the jeweler. Joe nurses and feeds Pip in May and early June and then informs him that Miss Havisham is dead and that Orlick is in the county jail after robbing and assaulting Pumblechook. Pip is pleased to see that Biddy has taught Joe to read and write. Without a good-bye, Joe leaves a farewell note and a receipt for payment of Pip's debts.

49. Village

Pip returns to the village on a June day, stays at the Blue Boar, and visits Satis House and the new school where Biddy is mistress. He learns that Joe has married Biddy. Pip promises to repay the loan and departs to Cairo to work for Herbert. Pip rises as manager of the eastern branch of Clarriker & Company and lives contentedly with Herbert and his wife Clara. Eleven years later, Pip meets his namesake, little Pip.

50. Satis House

After an absence of eleven years, Pip visits Satis House and encounters Estella. She admits she suffered during her marriage to Drummle, who died while mistreating a horse. Leaving the garden together, Pip and Estella realize they must live as friends. An earlier ending to the novel has Pip meeting Estella in London and learning that she had married a Shropshire doctor.

Further Reading

Ash, Russell. *Charles Dickens*. London: Aurum Press, 1995.

Besant, Walter, "Medieval London: City of Palaces," http://www.britannia.com/history/londonhistory/lon-pal1.html.

"Charles Dickens," http://65.107.211.206/victorian/dickens/dickensov.html.

Connor, Steve. *Charles Dickens*. New York: Longman, 1996.

Davis, Paul. *Charles Dickens A to Z*. New York: Facts on File, 1998.

"Dickens' London," http://www.fidnet.com/~dap1955/dickens/dickens_london_map.html.

"Dickens Page," http://ernie.lang.nagoya-u.ac.jp/~matsuoka/Dickens.htm.

"Dickens Project: University of California," http://hum.ucsc.edu/dickens/Dickens.Project.Home.html.

Eagle, Dorothy, and Hilary Carnell, eds. *The Oxford Illustrated Literary Guide to Great Britain and Ireland*. New York: Oxford University Press, 1992.

Giuliano, Edward, and Philip Collins, eds. *The Annotated Dickens*, two vols. New York: Clarkson N. Potter, 1986.

Hardwick, Michael, and Mollie Hardwick, comp. *The Charles Dickens Encyclopedia*. New York: Citadel Press, 1993.

Hitchens, Christopher. *American Notes: Charles Dickens*. New York: Modern Library, 1996.

Kappel, Lawrence, ed. *Readings on Great Expectations*. Westport, Conn.: Greenhaven, 1999.

Like the Dickens (CD-ROM). Parsippany, N.J.: Bureau of Electronic Publishing, 1995.

Long, Richard W., "The England of Charles Dickens." *National Geographic* (April 1974): 443–81.

Moynahan, J. M., and Troy R. Burke, "London's Famous Newgate Gaol," http://www.class.ewu.edu/class/CJ/newgate.html.

Newlin, George, ed. *Everyone in Dickens*. Westport, Conn.: Greenwood, 1995.

———. *Everything in Dickens*. Westport, Conn.: Greenwood, 1996.

Smith, Graham. *Charles Dickens: A Literary Life*. New York: St. Martin's Press, 1995.

Stanley, Diane, and Peter Vennema. *Charles Dickens: The Man Who Had Great Expectations*. New York: William Morrow, 1993.

Great Expectations

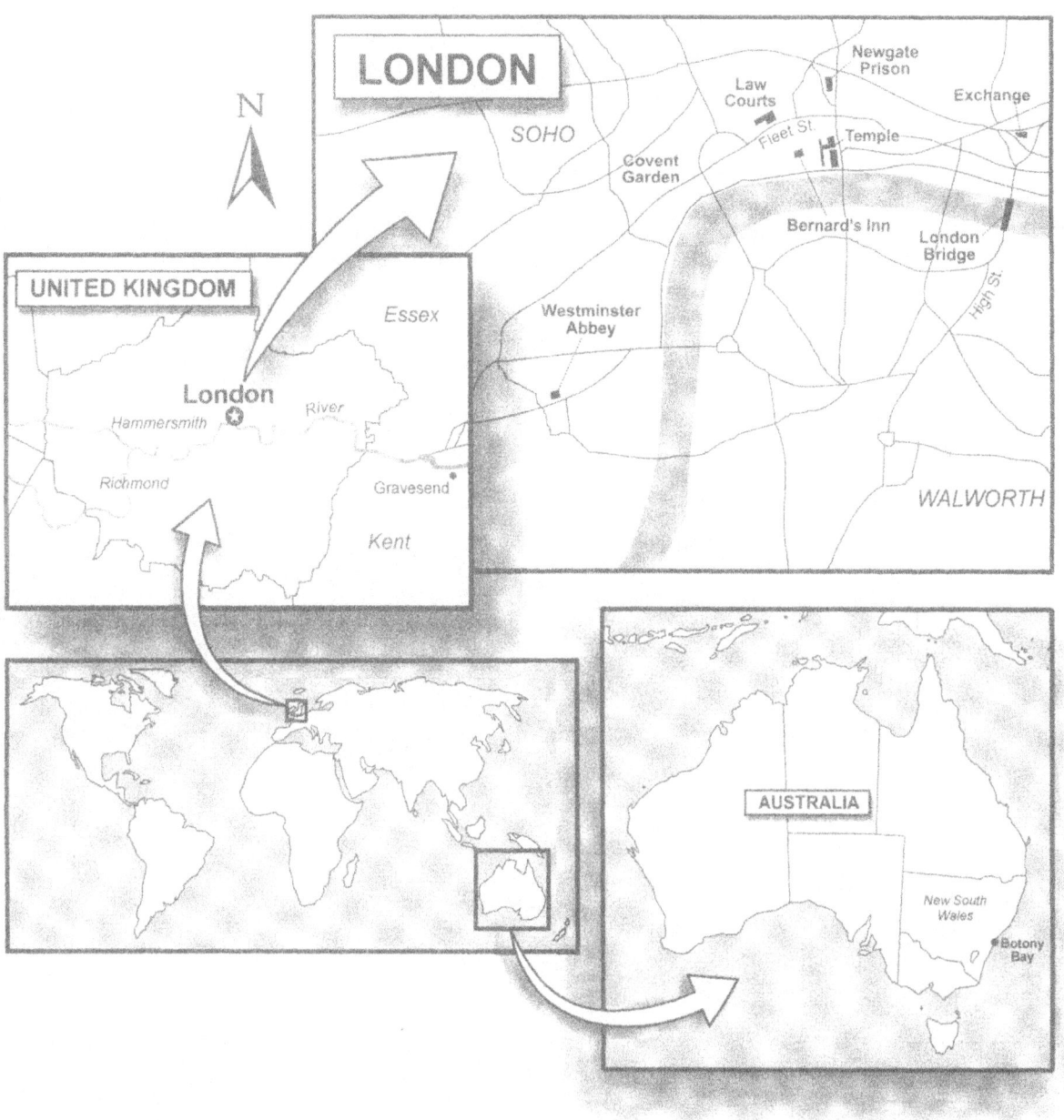

Inherit the Wind

By Jerome Lawrence and Robert E. Lee

Historical drama, 1955

Geographical Summary

Playwrights Jerome Lawrence and Robert E. Lee set *Inherit the Wind* in the fictional milieu of Hillsboro, Tennessee. Composed during the McCarthy era, the dynamic text becomes a microcosm of the undereducated South and of the Bible Belt, rife with narrow-mindedness, suspicion, and unquestioned religious dogma. The characters remain in town throughout the play yet express the clash between Southern principle and cosmopolitan views from the outside world—Baltimore, New York City, Washington, D.C., even Reuters news agency in London.

Newly arrived in Tennessee, the cynical journalist E. K. Hornbeck and attorney Henry Drummond observe the Scopes Monkey Trial from the liberal, urbane point of view of sophisticated and well-educated northerners. They actively challenge traditions long accepted in Appalachia, including the Reverend Brown's condemnation of Tommy Stebbins, an unbaptized drowning victim, and Brown's assertion that the defense attorney is Satan. At the center of the dramatic conflict is Tennessee's antievolution law, defended by Matthew Harrison Brady, a famed orator and failed candidate for the U.S. presidency. The public at large maintains enough interest in the trial of the local high school biology teacher to warrant a direct radio hookup with Chicago.

To demonstrate the Tennessee attitude toward outsiders arriving from the urban North, Hillsboro's religious fundamentalists display their opinions and principles through supportive hymn sings, sloganeering, a community picnic, and religious unanimity. During a prayer meeting on the courthouse lawn on a hot July evening, their call and response to the Reverend Jeremiah Brown's old-style preaching seems dated and naive. Their single-mindedness heightens tension as a handful of intruders threatens a Tennessee legal system that challenges a teacher who openly defies a law banning dissemination of Darwinism in public schools.

Set early in American experience with electronic media, the small-town drama surrounding Bert Cates's trial becomes headline news. The setting discloses an antediluvian mountain mindset as selection of an all-male jury takes place in the stifling, claustrophobic courtroom. The playwrights focus on the pro-fundamentalist judge and his token punishment of science teacher Bertram Cates. The jury's guilty verdict prefaces an eruption of national involvement after Harry Y. Esterbrook begins broadcasting the outcome of the trial to Chicago over WGN radio.

At the play's end, an ambiguous conclusion leaves unsettled the matter of Cates's classroom lectures on humankind's physical beginnings. After Matthew Brady collapses, onlookers mill about distractedly. Because the Baltimore *Herald* pays Bert Cates's bond, he is free to join Rachel and Drummond in boarding a train out of Hillsboro and, more to the point, out of the South. The playwrights imply that justice and free thought are not likely to flourish among religious fundamentalists in a milieu as complacent and backward as the Tennessee hills.

Detailed Itinerary

1. Main Street, courthouse square, Hillsboro, Tennessee

An hour after dawn on a hot July day, Rachel Brown, daughter of the Reverend Jeremiah Brown and teacher of the second grade at Hillsboro Consolidated School, slips into town with a suitcase. She asks bailiff Meeker for permission to talk with high school biology teacher Bertram Cates, a fictional name for John Thomas Scopes, a twenty-four-year-old science and math teacher and football coach in Dayton, Tennessee. For defying a state law by educating biology students in a public high school about Charles Darwin's theory of evolution, Cates, like Scopes, goes to jail. The real teacher was arrested on May 7, 1925, for violating the Butler Act, a law passed the previous January 28 stating that it was unlawful to teach any theory denying the Divine Creation of man as revealed in the book of Genesis. In particular, the law bans the teaching of any theory that humankind descended from a lower order of animals.

2. New York City; Washington, D.C.

After passage of the Butler Act, the American Civil Liberties Union (ACLU), a nonprofit, nonpartisan organization dedicated to preserving and defending the Bill of Rights, promised free legal counsel to anyone testing the legality of the Tennessee law. Founded in 1917, the ACLU is headquartered in New York City and maintains a lobbying effort in Washington, D.C., on behalf of individual freedoms. Chief among the organization's battles is an ongoing defense of the First Amendment right to freedom of speech.

3. Courthouse, Hillsboro, Tennessee

The play develops romantic interest as Bailiff Meeker allows Rachel private visitation with the prisoner in the courtroom. Caught between Cates's scholarly lesson from G. W. Hunter's *A Civic Biology* (1914) and her father's narrow, simplistic pulpit bluster, Rachel is uncertain how to support her boyfriend. She urges him to plead guilty rather than face Matthew Harrison Brady, a powerful populist and crowd pleaser. Cates asks for her love.

4. Washington, D.C.

The playwrights mask the identity of the real Bible spokesman at the Scopes Monkey Trial, William Jennings Bryan, a pompous American orator and Democratic congressman from Salem, Illinois, who lost an initial presidential race against William McKinley. Bryan ran for president a second time two years after serving as colonel of a Nebraska infantry regiment during the Spanish-American War. He established the *Commoner,* a populist newspaper, and, in

1908, lost a third presidential campaign against William Howard Taft. After a four-year term as secretary of state, he resigned in 1916 to protest Woodrow Wilson's decision to plunge the United States into World War I.

5. Courthouse, Hillsboro, Tennessee

Cates admits that he presented lessons drawn from English naturalist Charles Darwin's *On the Origin of Species* (1859). The treatise was an instant best-seller that stirred the clergy to loud protests but found favor with the international scientific community. Cates's stand on pure science challenges the Reverend Brown's conservatism, which is based on biblical inerrancy.

6. Baltimore, Maryland

Cates has sought the backing of the Baltimore *Sun*, an influential U.S. newspaper. It once employed writer H. L. Mencken, a brilliant, sharp-tongued essayist and social analyst who subsequently joined the staff of the *Baltimore Sun* in 1906. An outspoken critic of Southern fundamentalism, Mencken satirized Bible Belt theology for its fear of scientific inquiry in his own publication, *The American Mercury,* a monthly literary journal he and George Jean Nathan founded to examine the content and future of American thought.

7. Main Street, courthouse square, Hillsboro, Tennessee

On a hot morning, the Reverend Brown exhorts the Bible League to obey a banner slogan advocating Bible reading. The banner is a copy of an actual Dayton, Tennessee, courthouse sign commanding "Read Your Bible." Brown makes a public display of piety to impress sixty-five-year-old Brady, a self-righteous, melodramatic rabble-rouser who is traveling to Hillsboro aboard "old 94," a special train from Chattanooga. While Mrs. Krebs organizes a picnic lunch, Ted Finney sports his bass drum, residents decorate downspouts with ribbons, and onlookers purchase "red-hots," Bibles, and 35¢ paper fans advertising Maley's Funeral Home. News reporter E. K. Hornbeck, an urbane, provocative egotist representing the Baltimore *Herald,* derides the pretrial hoopla. As the train approaches, the Reverend Brown leads the Bible league in singing "Marching to Zion" and "Old-Time Religion."

Into this expectant atmosphere, Brady and his wife Sarah grandly approach Hillsboro. He describes Cates as arrogant for challenging the "Revealed Word." Hillsboro's mayor praises the former presidential candidate for championing women's suffrage and for supporting President Woodrow Wilson, a backer of American involvement in World War I. The mayor awards Brady an honorary title—colonel in the state militia. Brady predicts that he and circuit district attorney Tom Davenport will suppress Cates's blasphemy against the book of Genesis, which contains the biblical account of creation. Before attendees of the Ladies' Aid picnic, Rachel exonerates her boyfriend of criminal intent. Brady takes her aside to talk in private.

8. Chicago, Illinois

To townsman Bannister's query about who will defend Cates, the reporter relates that the Baltimore *Herald* is dispatching Henry Drummond, the era's most able attorney. Drummond is the fictional persona of Clarence Darrow, a well-read, Ohio-born trial lawyer who established a Chicago practice that championed the weak underclass and supported labor unions as well as railroads. In 1911, he reached a height of notoriety as the nation's prime criminal lawyer. John Scopes selected Darrow to defend him on June 8, 1925. On July

9, after William Jennings Bryan made a media splash by addressing the Dayton board of education, Darrow arrived in town with little fanfare.

9. Main Street, courthouse square, Hillsboro, Tennessee

In the play, the Reverend Brown retorts that Drummond is a vicious atheist. Bannister states that Drummond successfully defended two child killers. The comment refers to a historical event the year before the Scopes Monkey Trial, when Clarence Darrow represented Nathan Leopold and Richard Loeb, reprieving them from the death penalty for kidnap and murder by pleading their insanity. To the mayor and preacher's conspiracy to oust Drummond from Hillsboro, Brady prefers to welcome the outsider and challenge him as a bullying Goliath. Before departing to Mansion House for a nap, Brady thanks his hostesses.

Public supposition darts into dark corners. Rachel wonders why a big-city reporter would support a biology teacher in Tennessee. Hornbeck, who claims that Baltimore is a "wicked modern Sodom and Gomorrah," replies that he takes no one's side. He accuses Brady of seizing the public rostrum to gain credibility from Hillsboro's churchgoers. That night, no one welcomes Henry Drummond to town. After Melinda shrieks that he is the devil, Hornbeck welcomes the lawyer to Hell.

10. Courtroom, Hillsboro, Tennessee

A few days later in an overheated courtroom packed with onlookers, the judge oversees jury empanelment much as Judge John Tate Raulston of Marion County, Tennessee, supervised the real grand jury selection in Dayton. For the eleventh seat, Drummond accepts Bannister, an illiterate. At the real trial, the twelve venire men sworn in on July 10 consisted entirely of farmers, one of whom was illiterate. After a recess until 10:00 A.M. the following day, Drummond objects to the judge's announcement of prayer meeting on the courthouse lawn that evening. Drummond also demands that the pro-Bible banner be removed. At the actual trial, Clarence Darrow opposed the custom of beginning a trial with prayer.

11. Main Street, courthouse square, Hillsboro, Tennessee

That night at a press conference on the courthouse lawn, Brady maligns Cates for challenging conservative tenets and accuses the Baltimore reporter of bias. At the community prayer meeting, attendees respond antiphonally to Brown's comments on the creation story in Genesis. He calls down hellfire on Cates and on his own daughter if she defends an apostate teacher. Facing Brady at the end of the service, Drummond accuses his adversary of "standing still."

12. Courtroom, Hillsboro, Tennessee

Two days later at noon in the courtroom, Brady cross-examines thirteen-year-old Howard Blair, a student who heard Cates lecture on evolution. The boy depicts actual testimony by fourteen-year-old Howard Morgan, a student of John Scopes. The fictional Howard states that Cates made no classroom reference to God. Brady lambastes Cates for teaching "Godless science." Drummond declares that Brady challenges the right to think. Drummond establishes that Howard is capable of independent thought.

Drummond calls for the defense zoologist, Dr. Amos Keller from the University of Chicago; Dr. Allen Page, a Congregational minister and teacher of geology and archeology at Oberlin College in Ohio; and anthropologist Walter Aaronson. At Brady's objection to expert witnesses, the judge concurs. In a surprise maneuver, Drummond chooses Brady as a biblical scholar, a reenactment of Clarence Darrow's actual courtroom strategy on July 20. Brady anticipates a public forum for his opinions. In response to questions from the defense, he states that he has not read Darwin's *Origin of Species* and that he believes the Bible is literally true. To questions about a fossil found in the county, he cites Bishop James Usher (1581–1656), Archbishop of Armagh, Ireland, who established that the earth was created on October 23, 4004 B.C. at 9:00 A.M. At the Scopes trial, the judge struck the July 20 testimony of William Jennings Bryan the following day. The next day, while the jury deliberates, Cates fears he will lose and go to prison. The actual jury deliberation required only ten minutes.

13. Chicago, Illinois

Harry Y. Esterbrook, a radio technician for WGN, Chicago, begins broadcasting preliminaries to the verdict in the "Hillsboro Monkey Trial." He comments that the proceedings are the first public event ever broadcast. At the real trial, the admission of journalists produced a media circus amid temperatures reaching more than one hundred degrees. The miserable atmosphere caused Judge Raulston to move the proceedings to the courthouse lawn. Of considerable levity among his fellow reporters, H. L. Mencken warned, "Let no one mistake it for comedy, farcical though it may be in all its details. It serves notice on the country that Neanderthal man is organizing in these forlorn backwaters of the land, led by a fanatic, rid of sense and devoid of conscience."

14. Courtroom, Hillsboro, Tennessee

When court reconvenes, the jury unanimously condemns Cates for breaking the law. Drummond insists that Cates respond before the judge passes sentence. Cates promises to fight suppression of truth in the classroom. Because he has no previous violations, the judge fines him $100, the actual amount levied against John Scopes on July 24. Spectators are shocked that Cates receives so light a fine; Brady demands more stringent punishment. Drummond interjects that, because Cates will appeal, he will not pay his fine. The judge grants Drummond's request and sets bond at $500, which Hornbeck pays.

While Brady attempts to claim victory, Esterbrook returns the radio station to "Matinee Musicale." Brady stiffens and collapses. While Meeker directs onlookers to carry Brady across the street to a doctor, Brady delivers a rambling acceptance speech for the U.S. presidency. Cates is uncertain of his status. Drummond insists that he has bravely "smashed a bad law." After the actual trial, local people crowded around Darrow to thank him for defeating a law that caused outsiders to think all Tennesseans were ignorant rubes.

Rachel fears she contributed to Cates's conviction. Before she can join him at the depot to catch the 5:13 train, the judge announces that Brady is dead. Historically, William Jennings Bryan addressed eight thousand fundamentalists at Jasper, Tennessee, then returned to Dayton, Ohio, and died in his sleep on July 26, 1925. At the play's conclusion, Drummond upbraids Hornbeck for belittling a great orator. As a biblical comeuppance, Drummond surprises the reporter by quoting from Proverbs 11:25 that troublemakers "inherit the wind." After stowing Darwin's book and the Bible in his briefcase, Drummond exits. John Scopes eventually earned a Ph.D. in geology from the University of Chicago.

15. Washington, D.C.

Tennessee's Butler Act remained a law, influencing the enactment of similar educational strictures in Mississippi and Arkansas in 1926. In 1927, John Scopes won an appeal to the Tennessee Supreme Court, which ruled that only a jury can impose a fine greater than

$50. After an Arkansas teacher challenged the ban on teaching evolution in a public classroom in 1966, Tennessee repealed the Butler Act the following year. Arkansas's creationism law remained on the books until 1968, when the U.S. Supreme Court, convened in Washington, D.C., overturned it in the case of *Epperson v. Arkansas*.

Further Reading

"About the Scopes Trial Play and Festival," http://www.concentric.net/~paulvon/festinfo.htm.

Allen, Robert. *William Jennings Bryan*. Milford, Mich.: Mott Media, 1992.

Beaudoin, Jack, "Evolution on Trial." *New York Times Upfront* (October 4, 1999).

"Between the Wars: The Scopes Trial," http://chnm.gmu.edu/courses/hist409/scopes.html.

"Bishop Usher's Biblical Chronology," http://www.commsalv.org/biblstdy/biblchrn.html.

Charen, Mona, "Scopes Trial Replayed in Kansas." *Omaha World-Herald* (August 14, 1999).

Cornelius, R. M., *William Jennings Bryan: The Scopes Trial and Inherit the Wind*, http://www.concentric.net/~paulvon/wjbinfo.htm.

Donaghue, John W., "Of Many Things." *America* (December 28, 1996).

Ellenbogen, Charles M., "Introducing Censorship: One Teacher's Approach." *English Journal* (February 1997) 65–66.

Folsom, Burt, "Two Scopes Trial Myths Debunked." *Human Events* (November 20, 1998).

"Hunter's Civic Biology," http://www.law.umkc.edu/faculty/projects/ftrials/scopes/hunt196.htm.

"An Introduction to John Scopes' Trial," http://www.law.umkc.edu/faculty/ projects/ftrials/scopes/evolut.htm.

"Mencken's Coverage of Scopes Trial Revisited." *Topeka Capital-Journal* (August 15, 1999).

Menton, Dr. David, N., *Inherit the Wind: A Hollywood History of the 1925 Scopes "Monkey" Trial*, http://www.gennet.org/SCOPES.HTM, July 21, 1994.

Michael Miller, "Religion Beat: Have We Inherited a Warped View of the Scopes Trial?" *Peoria Journal Star* (May 29, 1999).

Schermer, Michael, "75 Years and Still No Peace." *The Humanist* (September 2000).

Scopes Trial Activity, http://outcast.gene.com/ae/AE/AEPC/WWC/1991/scopes_activity.html.

"The Scopes Trial, Play and Festival," http://www.bryan.edu/Scopes/Default%20scopes.htm.

"The Trial of John Scopes," http://www.interact-simulations.com/Titles/TrialScopes.html.

Vitullo-Martin, Julia, "Monkey Business: What Really Happened in Tennessee." *Commonweal* (October 8, 1999).

The Joy Luck Club

By Amy Tan

Multicultural contemporary fiction, 1989

Geographical Summary

Amy Tan distributes a large but tightly interwoven cast of characters and events over two continents, from China to northern California with a concluding reunion scene in Shanghai. From flashes of China's shell-pocked countryside during World War II and Japanese bombs falling on the innocent below, the author contrasts the emotion-torn internal landscapes of affluent Chinese Americans living in safety in California during the second half of the twentieth century. Using historic times and places in Asia, she enhances the predicament of Chinese women living in feudal Chinese households and submitting to patriarchal marriages. In the United States, the women, freed of male and family dominance, rear daughters in leisure, plenty, and educational and career opportunity. Without fear of coercion or gender stereotypes, the second generation of girls learns piano, composition, cooking, decorating, art, and chess; yet they still echo their mothers' self-doubts and misjudgments.

Peers in Tan's fiction live unusually disparate lives. In the home of a vituperative mother-in-law, twelve-year-old Lindo Jong enters a traditional marriage to a spoiled darling whose immaturity and willfulness destroy her hopes for contentment. A contemporary named Ying-ying innocently expects entertainment at a Moon Festival, but she encounters instead boys tormenting a diving bird and a cross-dresser posing as the Moon Lady. Another contemporary, An-mei Hsu, is burned by a splash of hot soup from a tabletop brazier. She leaves the home of unforgiving relatives and reunites with her stylish mother. Unfortunately for An-mei, the mother has no security to offer. In desperation, the mother kills herself with an overdose of opium because she lives the ignominy of a third wife and has no son to elevate her lowly status. The misery of An-mei's life in China parallels the insecurity of her daughter, Lena St. Clair, whose unstable marriage resembles a wobbly marble table. As An-mei predicts, the shaky foundation is not strong enough to anchor Lena's relationship to her husband.

The final scenario, "A Pair of Tickets," contrasts June's family life in San Francisco with her reunion with twin half-sisters left behind in south central China while their mother recovered from dysentery in a Chungking hospital. Before June sets out on her journey, her father, Canning Woo, reveals how June's mother, Suyuan, and her two infants joined refugees fleeing a Japanese invasion of Kweilin. On the way, as disease, fatigue, and terror weakened her, she abandoned the infants with her jewelry to pay for the infants' care. Among tourists at the terminal in China, June encounters the girls, now grown and grieving for the mother who left them behind. Born on opposite sides of the Pacific, the three women embrace and celebrate the resemblance to their mother, which they see in each other's faces.

Detailed Itinerary

1. Leavenworth, San Francisco, California

After a cerebral aneurysm kills Suyuan Woo of Leavenworth, her daughter, Jing-mei "June" Woo, takes her mother's corner at the mah jong table of the Joy Luck Club, a group of Chinese American women whom Suyuan organized in 1949 in San Francisco. Within the bounds of Portsmouth Square, Grant Avenue, Bush Street, and Columbus Avenue, the city's Chinatown comprises the largest Chinese settlement outside China. A warren of markets, temples, shops, newspapers, tenements, and restaurants, the original Chinese district grew from Asian newcomers seeking their fortunes during the 1849 Gold Rush. Immigrants created a milieu perpetuating their language, religions, and way of life.

2. Kweilin, China

As Chinese citizens fled Japanese invaders, Suyuan left the two-story house in Kweilin, China, while her husband Wang, a military officer, returned to fight for the Kuomintang in the northwest at Chungking. People poured into the Kweilin area from Shanghai, Nanking, and Burma. As the situation worsened, Suyuan kept busy playing mah jong with three women friends.

After the Japanese captured the Wuchang-Canton railway, Suyuan's husband summoned her to Chungking. She knew that his message meant for her to escape the doomed city of Kweilin. For four days, as bombs fell, she pushed her twin daughters in a wheelbarrow along the roads to the northwest in sight of a row of mountain peaks. When the wheel broke, she carried the infant girls in cloth slings. She halts the story without telling June how it ended or what happened to the two babies.

3. San Francisco, California

At the home of George and An-mei Hsu in the Sunset District of San Francisco, June hears the remaining three members of the Joy Luck Club trade news as they cook and eat. She recalls that, three years before, the Hsus saved $2,000 to spend on candy and gaudy American clothes when they visited relatives in Hangzhau. In one day's visit, the rapacious relatives and guests forced the Hsus to go into debt for another $9,000.

Auntie Ying-Ying St. Clair informs June of Suyuan's dying wish to find her lost daughters, whom she lost in China in 1939, long before June was conceived. At the time of their parting, Suyuan had been desperate and ill. Weakness kept her from returning immediately to reclaim the babies. The three older Joy Luck Club members collect $1,200 in mah jong winnings to send June to China for a reunion with her half-sisters.

4. Ningpo, China

In 1923, nine-year-old An-mei Hsu lives at her uncle's house in Ningpo, a coastal industrial center sixteen miles inland from the Yung River delta. An-mei suffers the scorn of Grandmother Popo, who denigrates the child's mother, a scholar's widow now remarried.

The mother dishonored her family by becoming the third wife of Wu Tsing, a wealthy carpet maker living far to the northwest in the commercial city of Tientsin.

Five years later, An-mei's mother returns to Grandmother Popo. After the long separation, the mother identifies her daughter by the scar on her neck from a splash of hot soup. At Grandmother Popo's bedside, An-mei's mother dutifully slices flesh from her arm to add to soup meant to heal Popo. The sacrifice, an ancient folk custom, comes too late to save the embittered old grandmother.

5. Taiyuan, China

Lindo Jong grows up in Taiyuan in Shansi Province of northeastern China southwest of Peking. Pledged at age two by the village matchmaker to wed Huang Tyan-yu, Lindo Jong moves in with the Huangs, her future in-laws, a decade after the flooding Fen River destroys her own family's wheat and forces them to move in with relatives at Wushi outside Shanghai. Lindo comes under the control of Taitai Huang, her snoopy mother-in-law. On the unlucky day the Japanese invade Shansi Province, sixteen-year-old Lindo weds Tyan-yu, an immature mama's boy. He is incapable of consummating the marriage and forces her to sleep on the sofa for months.

To cover the shame of her childish son, Taitai Huang accuses Lindo of refusing to sleep with her new husband. Lindo defeats the Huangs by faking a prophetic nightmare. She interprets the vision, which predicts that Tyan-yu will die if he remains with her. If he leaves Lindo, he will sire a child by a servant who has imperial blood. The ambitious Huangs prefer the servant as their daughter-in-law. They reward Lindo with a ticket to Peking and enough money for passage to America.

6. Wushi, China

In 1918, four-year-old Ying-ying attends the Moon Festival in Wushi at Tai Lake, one of China's largest bodies of water. The festival unites families for storytelling of traditional holiday legends, public gatherings, and the distribution of moon cakes, pastries filled with red bean paste, dates, lotus seeds, or nuts. In San Francisco, visitors to Chinatown celebrate the Moon Festival with puppet shows, drummers, acrobats, martial arts demonstrations, music, banners, lantern-lit processions, and a parade of children costumed like lion dancers.

Instead of finding fun and entertainment, Ying-ying observes boys tormenting a diving bird by constricting its throat with a ring to keep it from swallowing fish. She gets blood on her clothing from the scaling and gutting of fish. When the moon rises, net fishers rescue her after she tumbles into the water at the sound of firecrackers. Left on the dock, she intrudes on the Moon Lady's shadow play. After the Moon Lady promises to grant a wish, Ying-ying moves closer and discovers that the actor is a male. The Ying-ying who reunites with her parents has lost her little-girl innocence.

7. Chinatown, San Francisco, California

Waverly Jong and her older brothers, Vincent and Winston, live at Waverly Place, a back street in San Francisco's Chinatown. At a Christmas party in 1958 at the First Chinese Baptist Church, the Jong children receive used toys from Santa Claus, including a model World War II airplane to put together. Although the mother scorns cast-off toys from white donors, Vincent's chess set suits Waverly better than the twelve packs of Lifesavers she receives and arranges in order of preference.

After learning to play chess, Waverly beats the Chinatown chess master. She becomes a national champion featured with a photo in *Life* magazine. Because Lindo Jong boasts to passersby of her daughter's prowess, the child becomes rude to her mother. Waverly runs away from Lindo in the market and stays gone for two hours until mealtime. Lindo retaliates by locking the front door and serving dinner without waiting for Waverly. Her brother warns that she comes home to a plate of fish bones while the family eats and pretends not to notice her discomfort.

8. Oakland, California

Lena recalls how Clifford St. Clair, her English-Irish father, rescued Gu Ying-ying and altered her name on immigration papers from Gu Ying-Ying to Betty St. Clair, his war bride. Immigration officials labeled her an official displaced person after she passed through Angel Island Immigration Station in San Francisco Bay. Ying-ying and Clifford settled among Oakland's Italians. During her mother's pregnancy when Lena was ten years old, Ying-ying began moving furniture to balance her home. She showed no interest in bearing another child as she steadily went insane. At the hospital, Lena, who spoke both Chinese and English, translated Ying-ying's babbling for Clifford. She realized that her father was unaware of her mother's mental instability. Ying-ying delivered an anacephalic son who died at birth. She considered his death her punishment for aborting a son during her first marriage in China.

9. Ashbury Heights, San Francisco

Rose Hsu Jordan, a liberal arts major at the University of California at Berkeley, must explain to her mother the collapse of her marriage to Ted Jordan, a dermatologist. Rose met him while he was in medical school at the University of California at San Francisco. Although his social-climbing mother disapproved of an Asian wife for Ted, he moved in with Rose within a month. They married and settled in San Francisco's Ashbury Heights. After losing a lawsuit against a patient whom he disfigured and paralyzed by unintentionally slicing into a facial nerve, he began shifting blame to Rose, whom he accused of being weak and indecisive.

10. Devil's Slide, San Francisco

Rose recalls how her four-year-old brother Bing drowned in the ocean at Devil's Slide south of San Francisco, where her parents and their seven children lived in the Sunset district. Rose, who took charge of the younger siblings at the beach, blames herself for allowing him to edge out on the reef to where his father was fishing. She relives her mother's loss of religious faith and their drive to the site the next day to search for Bing's body. Rose later discovered that her mother recorded Bing's death in the Bible.

11. Chinatown, San Francisco

In an unhealthy competition against Waverly Jong, Suyuan Woo tries to manipulate her daughter June into mastering the piano. At a talent show, Waverly taunts June for her poor performance of German composer Robert Schumann's "Pleading Child," taken from his suite *Scenes from Childhood* (1849). Unable to best Waverly at anything, June wishes that she, like her twin half-sisters, had died in early childhood. Years later, Suyuan passes the piano to June. After Suyuan's sudden death, June has the instrument tuned and performs Schumann's "Pleading Child" and a companion piece, "Perfectly Contented," two contrasting pieces that form a whole.

12. Woodside, California

Lena St. Clair, who majors in Asian American studies, joins her husband Harold Livotny in remodeling a barn at Woodside, southeast of San Francisco. She helps him open Livotny & Associates, an avant-garde restaurant design firm. He discounts her contribution as project coordinator and pays her little. To strengthen marital sharing, they balance duties and finances. When Ying-ying visits, Harold and Lena quarrel over the minute separation of expenses, which Ying-ying notices posted in two columns of figures on the refrigerator door. In Ying-ying's room, the collapse of a marble table symbolizes the shaky marriage.

13. Leavenworth, San Francisco, California

With her friend Marlene, Waverly Jong discusses her wish to marry Rich Schields, a tax attorney at Price Waterhouse, a global investment conglomerate. As she anticipates, her mother Lindo disdains the couple's lavish lifestyle and Waverly's pretentious fur coat. Lindo also scorned her daughter's elopement with a first husband, the father of their daughter Shoshana. Waverly recalls giving up chess after her mother took credit for her success. Waverly returned to chess, but as her mother taunted, she had lost the ability to play competitively.

To trick Lindo, in December Waverly dines at Suyuan's house in Leavenworth, where Rich compliments the meal as the best Chinese food he has ever eaten. Word of Suyuan's success reaches the envious Lindo. After she insists on cooking for Rich, he insults her by putting soy sauce on a platter of steamed pork and vegetables to flavor the meal and mispronounces the couple's names as Linda and Tim. Later, Lindo identifies her daughter's weaknesses. Waverly and Rich decide to marry in the fall and consider taking Lindo with them on a Chinese honeymoon.

14. Chinatown, San Francisco, California

At the funeral of China Mary at the First Chinese Baptist Church in Chinatown, Rose Hsu Jordan tells her mother An-mei that she is divorcing Ted. An-mei replies that she knows her daughter better than any psychiatrist. Rose takes An-mei's advice to remain strong during divorce negotiations. Ted mails Rose a check for $10,000. When he arrives to finalize the paperwork giving him their property so he can remarry, he finds the garden overrun with weeds. She surprises him by refusing to give up the house.

15. Leavenworth, San Francisco

At Chinese New Year, June helps her mother Suyuan select eleven crabs for a gala group dinner at a market on Stockton Street in Chinatown. A World War II refugee from Chungking in 1938, Suyuan fled to Shanghai and Hong Kong. She emigrated from China and has lived in San Francisco since 1949. At dinner, she refuses to eat a defective, lifeless crab.

In the presence of old family friends, June tries to humiliate Waverly by stating that she owes June payment for composing advertising copy the previous month. With a condescending air, Waverly claims that the work was inferior and that she assigned June the project out of pity. Later, as June and Suyuan discuss Waverly's ruthless competitiveness, Suyuan reminds her daughter that she bought a low-quality crab at the market because she doesn't demand high standards. Suyuan gives June a light jade necklace, a family heirloom, to prove how important June is to her.

16. Tientsin, China

After her Grandmother Popo's death, An-mei Hsu accompanied her mother to live in Wu Tsing's household. Following a seven-day rail and boat journey, they arrived in Tientsin at Wu Tsing's residence in the British Concession. Two weeks later, Wu Tsing further devalued An-mei's mother by taking a fourth concubine.

After the second wife pretended to commit suicide, Wu Tsing withdrew his promise to give An-mei's mother a private dwelling at the charming seaside resort of Petaiho, an enclave of widows. During Chinese New Year, she deliberately overdoses on opium stuffed into sweet dumplings. Because the holiday is a time of settling old debts, An-mei states that her mother's spirit will haunt Wu Tsing for mistreating her. In terror of avenging ghosts, he accepts An-mei and her brother Syaudi as his honored children. For the first time, An-mei confronts the devious second wife, causing her hair to turn white.

17. Wushi, China

While visiting her daughter Lena and son-in-law Harold Livotny at their modern house in Woodside, California, Ying-ying St. Clair criticizes the oddly shaped guest bedroom, which is badly out of balance. She recalls her adulterous first husband, a man she refuses to name. He cloaked his philandering by making many business trips to the north. She remembers the infant boy she aborted to punish her husband for taking up with an opera singer.

After leaving her mother-in-law's house ten years after separating from her husband, Ying-ying worked as a shopgirl. Clifford St. Clair courted her for four years. When a relative wrote in 1946 to report that her first husband had died, Ying-ying married Clifford without enthusiasm and settled in Oakland, California. She believes that her immoral actions have compromised her daughter's life and marriage.

18. San Francisco

When Waverly plans a second honeymoon in China, she wonders if she will blend in with local people so well that the Communists will never let her out of the country. Lindo knows that her daughter will display American traits because of her posture and facial expression. In Lindo's opinion, Waverly lacks native Chinese obedience, emotional control, perseverance, and self-worth.

At a San Francisco beauty salon, Waverly patronizes her mother as the hairdresser, Mr. Rory, tries to conceal her mother's Chinese qualities. After twelve years as a telephone operator, Lindo traveled through Hong Kong, Vietnam, the Philippines, and Hawaii on her way to San Francisco. Using advice from an insider, she located a cheap apartment on Washington Street and worked in sales, as a hostess, and in a factory making fortune cookies. She met Tin Jong, a Cantonese immigrant, in an English class. They married after one month's courtship and produced Winston, Vincent, and Waverly.

19. Shanghai, China

With her seventy-two-year-old father, Canning Woo, June travels to Shanghai to meet Chwun Yu Wang and Chwun Hwa Wang, her twin half-sisters. Before the long-anticipated reunion, June and her father discuss the difficult situation that Chinese refugees faced at the time of the children's abandonment. Suyuan left them with family photographs and a Shanghai address, 9 Weichang Lu. After the death of their father, Wang Fuchi, she met Canning Woo at the hospital in Chungking, where she was recuperating. In 1949, they married and settled in the Leavenworth section of San Francisco.

Mei Ching, the kind Muslim woman who rescued the babies, lived outside Kweilin in a stone cave with her husband, Mei Han. He died in 1952, seven years after Suyuan and Canning Woo had begun a hunt for the children. In search of relatives, Mei Ching found a factory built on the address in Shanghai, but located no one who remembered the former residents. Suyuan's schoolmate encountered the twins while shopping at Number One Department Store on Nanjing Dong Road. After Suyuan's death, Lindo locates the twin girls as a kindness to her departed friend. In Shanghai at last, June and the twins recognize each other by their resemblance to their mother, a face the abandoned girls knew only from pictures.

Further Reading

"Amy Tan," http://www.mountmedia.de/verlage/bertlgrp/wlg96/autor04.html.

"Amy Tan Argues Against Ethnic Literary Label," http://kwaziwai.cc.columbia.edu/cu/record/record2004.19.html.

Baker, John F., "Fresh Voices, New Audiences." *Publishers Weekly* (August 9, 1993).

Benjamin, Susan J., "Recommended Fiction of the 1980s: The Joy Luck Club." *English Journal* (October 1990).

Bloom, Harold. *Amy Tan*. New York: Chelsea House, 2000.

Chambers, Vernica, "Surprised by Joy." *Premiere* (October 1993).

"Chinatown Walking Tour," http://www.consumer-information.org/sftraveltour4.asp.

Do, Thuan Thi, "Chinese-American Women in American Culture," http://www.ics.uci.edu/~tdo/ea/chinese.html, 1992.

Feldman, Gayle, "Spring's Five Fictional Encounters of the Chinese American Kind." *Publishers Weekly* (February 8, 1991).

"A Fiery Mother-Daughter Relationship." *USA Today* (October 5, 1993).

Gates, David, "The Joy Luck Club." *Newsweek* (April 17, 1989).

Goodavage, Maria, "The Joy Luck Club Is Born from Her Life of Hardship." *USA Today* (October 5, 1993).

Greenfield, Larry, "Calamity at Kweilin," http://www.comcar.org/1st_ComCar/4th_Crew_Stories/l_greenfield_calamity_at_kweilin.htm.

"Hall of Arts: Amy Tan," http://www.achievement.org/autodoc/page/tan0bio-1.

Hansen, Janet, et al., "Selected from 'The Joy Luck Club.'" *Library Journal* (September 1, 1992).

Haskell, Molly, "Movie of the Month: 'The Joy Luck Club.'" *Ladies' Home Journal* (October 1993).

Hubbard, Kim, "The Joy Luck Club Has Brought Writer Amy Tan a Bit of Both," *People Weekly* (April 10, 1989).

Huntley, E. D. *Amy Tan*. Westport, Conn.: Greenwood, 1998.

Iyer, Pico, "Review." *Time* (June 3, 1991).

Jokinen, Anniina, "Anniina's Amy Tan Page," http://www.luminarium.org/contemporary/amytan, 1998.

"The Joy Luck Club," http://roella.tripod.com/AmyTan/JoyLuck.html." 'Joy Luck Club' Home Page," http://www.cwrl.utexas.edu/~sbowen/314fall/novels/.

Law-Yone, Wendy, "Review." *Washington Post Book World* (June 16, 1991).

Liu, Ping, "Chinese-American Women in the United States," http://www.ics.uci.edu/~tdo/ea/chineseWomen.html, 1997.

Marbella, Jean, "Amy Tan: Luck but Not Joy." *Baltimore Sun* (June 30, 1991).

Maslin, Janet, "Intimate Generational Lessons, Available to All." *New York Times* (September 8, 1993).

Mathews, Laura, "Books: 'Joy Luck Club.' " *Glamour* (September 1992).

Maynard, Joyce, "The Joy Luck Club." *Mademoiselle* (July 1989).

Merina, Anita, "Joy, Luck, and Literature." *NEA Today* (October 1991).

"The Moon Festival," http://www.chinavista.com/experience/moon/moon.html.

Needham, Nancy R., "By Their First Lines You Shall Know Them." *NEA Today* (May 1993).

"Racially Mixed People in America," http://www.sagepub.uk/books/details/b003595.html.

"The Salon Interview: Amy Tan," http://www.salon1999.com/12nov1995/feature/tan.htm.

Schleier, Curt, "The Joy Luck Lady," http://detnews.com/menu/stories/23098.htm.

Shapiro, Laura, "From China, with Love." *Newsweek* (June 24, 1991): 63–64.

Shields, Charles J. *Amy Tan*. New York: Chelsea House, 2001.

Simpson, Janice C., "Fresh Voices above the Noisy Din." *Time* (June 3, 1991).

"Tan Welcomes the Unusual," http://www.pub.umich.edu/daily/1995/12-05-95/Arts/amytan.html.

Tavernise, Pete, "Mother Tradition and Sacred Systems in 'The Joy Luck Club,' " http://www.duke.edu/~ptavern/Pete.Tan.html.

Taylor, Joan Chatfield, "Cosmo Talks to Amy Tan." *Cosmopolitan* (November 1989).

"Voices from the Gap: Amy Tan," http://www-engl.cla.umn.edu/lkd/vfg/Authors/AmyTan.

Young, Pamela, "Mother with a Past." *Maclean's* (July 15, 1991).

The Joy Luck Club

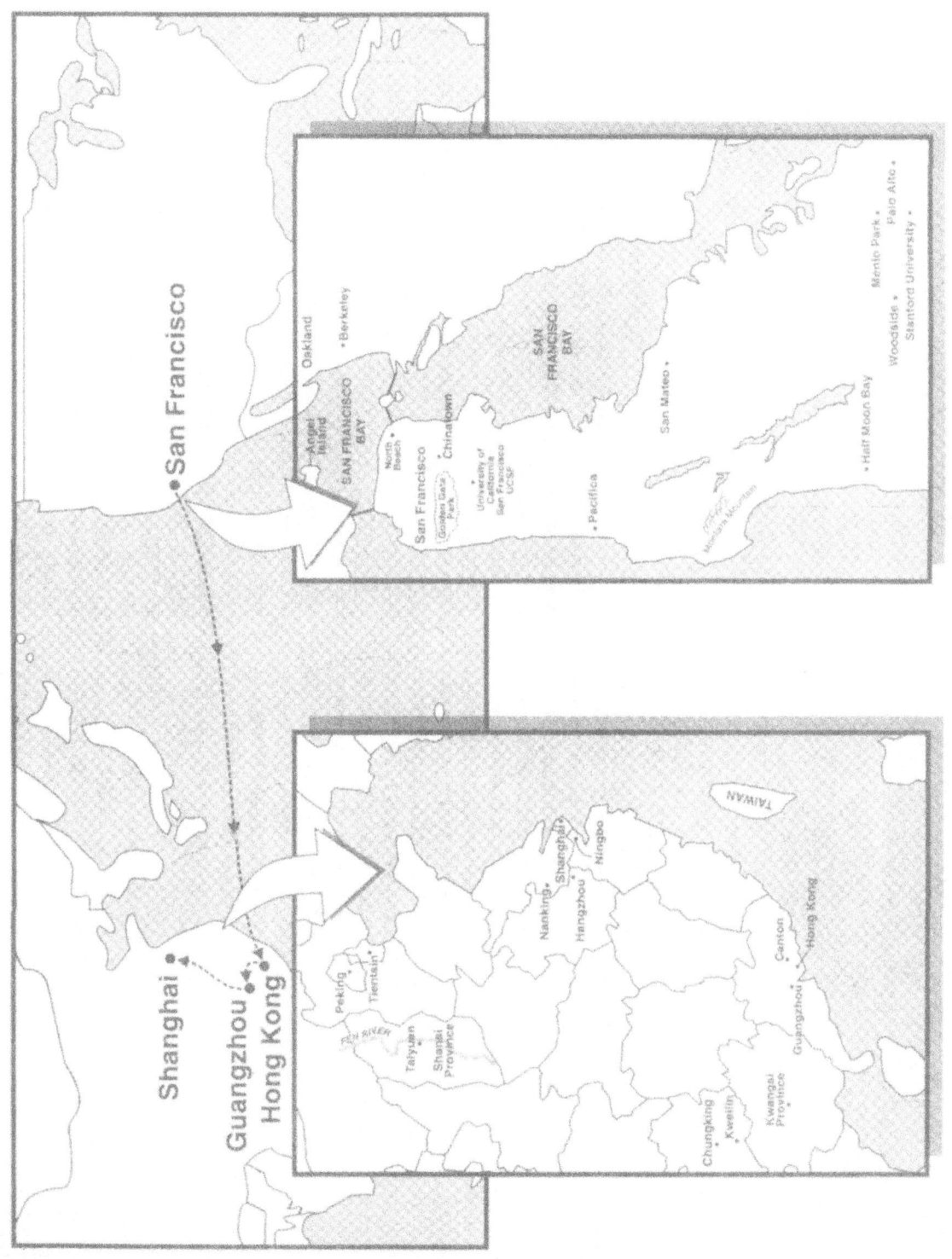

Julius Caesar
By William Shakespeare

Historical drama, ca. 1599

Geographical Summary

In the era preceding the founding of the Roman Empire, late republican Rome held a sizeable hegemony that spread north over Gaul and parts of Britannia, south to North Africa, and throughout Asia Minor. William Shakespeare's play covers three points of the Mediterranean world in the first century B.C. At the time of Julius Caesar's assassination, Rome, which was vast by ancient standards, plus Sardis and Philippi take on international even global importance. Through drama, the Elizabethan audience contemplated the influence of Pompey the Great, Julius Caesar, Mark Antony, and Marcus Brutus and a political imbalance that affected much of the known world. Playgoers from the English Renaissance immersed themselves in the failings and downfall of the most famous warrior statesman in early European history. They relived his funeral and immolation before mobs gathered in the forum of Rome and sampled scenes from the civil war that erupted in his absence.

For stage purposes, the playwright manipulates the political scene and shifts main characters rapidly from Rome southeast to Sardis and from there northwest to Philippi, where the conflict ends. This facile transportation of people to distant places erroneously implies that travel was simple for conquerors and armies of the period. For dramatic purpose, Shakespeare's settings and time spans are usually nonspecific. He sets up the triumvirate's meeting at Mark Antony's home and deploys legions to the camp at Sardis and the battlefield at Philippi, both of which seem close in time and space, even though they are on separate continents. Stylistically, for the playgoer, these places become little more than backdrops for an ongoing power struggle.

Obviously, Shakespeare intended dialogue to take precedence over scenery and costumes. Even though the fifth act closes in Philippi, it is significant that the play ends with the winning army's respect for Brutus, a noble Roman and worthy citizen. Thus the geographic sweep of the play returns to its patriotic roots at Rome and to the original question concerning how citizens should react toward threats to civic freedoms. Because Rome has lost significant noblemen during the rebellion, purge, and civil war, it is fitting that all people who fall under Rome's influence should wonder who will return to Rome, tame the revolt, and restore order and government to the region's most powerful state.

Detailed Itinerary

1. Streets of Rome

The play opens in late February 44 B.C., on the Feast of the Lupercal and with a ritual footrace held in the streets of Rome. On an unspecified street, possibly the Via Flaminia (now called the Via del Corso) or the main thoroughfare, Julius Caesar processes grandly into the city, which rises on the banks of the Tiber River in west central Italy. The cityscape offers a stunning vista of two basilicas or government complexes—the Aemilia and a new facility that Julius Caesar built to replace the Basilica Porcia, which burned. Rome was known for its engineers and road builders, who anchored massive lava blocks over fill dirt and gravel as a means of linking the city with outlying protectorates and client tributaries. After the recent civil war of 49–47 B.C., Caius Julius Caesar, the triumphant Roman *imperator* (commander-in-chief), made public works, traffic control, and road improvement the major features of his political and governmental agenda.

2. Tiber River

While commoners celebrate Caesar's victory over Gnaeus Pompey and his sons, two tribunes, Flavius and Marullus, scold the fickle plebeians for shifting loyalties from one conquering general to another. They refer to Caesar's victory over Pompey, his relative by Caesar's marriage to Pompeia, his second wife. Pompey was also Caesar's son-in-law for five years, from the time of his betrothal to Caesar's daughter Julia in 59 B.C. to her death from miscarriage five years later. To holiday seekers, Flavius and Marullus emphasize the sanctity of the Tiber River and its overhanging banks, where commoners once shouted their support of Pompey the Great.

3. Circus Flaminius

The stage scene focuses on Caesar and his entourage, who approach the Circus Flaminius, a horse- and chariot-racing amphitheater erected in 220 B.C. by Consul Gaius Flaminius Nepos on the southern end of the Campus Martius, the floodplain of the Tiber River. Caesar and his followers pass by a seer who warns him to beware the ides of March, a calendar term meaning the middle day of the month. The great general, arrogant and overconfident after acquiring the title of dictator for life, dismisses the man as a dreamer and proceeds to the festivities. Citizens fix their attention on the race, a source of interest to Caesar, who supervised public games as a political ploy after his election to the post of *curule aedile* (civic supervisor) of public games and entertainment in 66 B.C.

4. The street

Meanwhile, Brutus, a man of unquestioned morals, remains in the street outside the racecourse because he doesn't feel "gamesome." Cassius, a malcontent who envies Caesar, engages Brutus in a discussion of Caesar's dangerous rise from military leader to absolute dictator. Cassius characterizes him as a power-hungry mortal who considers himself god-like and pictures him strutting about like the Colossus of Rhodes, a 110-foot harbor statue and lighthouse on a promontory of the island of Rhodes off the southwestern coast of Turkey.

Cassius emphasizes Caesar's unfitness for great office with specific examples of human weakness. Cassius recalls a time that Caesar nearly drowned while swimming the swollen Tiber River, which flooded annually from an influx of melted snow from the Apennine

Mountains. Cassius also cites a period when Caesar quaked with a fever during his campaign in what is now Andalusia and Portugal in the province of *Hispania* (Spain), where he served as *quaestor* (public treasurer) in 68 B.C. The post was a significant step on Caesar's rise up the political ladder.

Brutus, who is Caesar's colleague and an old family friend, does not share Cassius's discontent, but he does worry that Romans will lose their democratic rights if the dictator grows too powerful. The dilemma between patriotism and friendship unsettles Brutus. Cassius manipulates the inner conflict by persuading Brutus to value Rome over a personal friendship and to remove the threat that Caesar poses. When Caesar and company depart the race, he confides to Mark Antony, his loyal follower, that Cassius looks untrustworthy. Nonetheless, Caesar claims to be unafraid.

5. Racecourse

When the retinue moves on, Casca joins Brutus and Cassius and reports the events that took place offstage at the footrace. Antony thrice offered Caesar a crown, which he rejected, each time a little less strenuously. The public spectacle concluded when Caesar collapsed from an epileptic seizure, causing the audience to pity him.

6. The Capitol

During a thunderstorm, Cicero encounters Casca, who has seen strange omens—wind-tossed oaks, fire from heaven, flame erupting harmlessly around a slave's hand, and a lion walking by the Capitol. Built on the Capitoline Hill southeast of the Tiber River, the Capitol, alternately known as the Temple of Jupiter, is a public building and the city's center of business. Cicero learns that Caesar has dispatched Antony with a message to meet Caesar there the next day. Leaving Casca, Cicero hurries out of bad weather.

7. Pompey's Porch

On his way to confer with fellow plotters, Cassius meets briefly with Casca. The conspirators await Cassius at Pompey's Porch, the colonnade adorning the *Theatrum Pompei* (Pompey's Theater), a semicircular building that Pompey erected in 55 B.C. northwest of the Capitolium on the Campus Martius. The building, Rome's first permanent theater, bore the allegorical statue of *Venus Victrix* (Conquering Venus) as well as likenesses of *Honor, Virtus* (Strength), and *Felicitas* (Happiness). Before joining them, Cassius forges letters urging Brutus to take pity on Rome, which Caesar dominates. Cassius instructs Cinna to leave the letters at Brutus's residence in the magistrate's chair. Cassius is determined to bind Casca, Decius Brutus, Caius Ligarius, Cinna, Metellus Cimber, and Trebonius in an assassination plot.

8. The orchard of Brutus and Portia's home, west of the Capitol

Before 3:00 A.M., Brutus walks in his orchard and orders his servant Lucius to light a taper in the study. Wealthy noblemen like Brutus could afford to erect grand townhouses containing marble reception halls and dining halls, colonnaded gardens, slave quarters, and large kitchens detached from the main house. Lucius strikes a light and finds the forged letters, which he hands to his master. Brutus ponders the political dilemma along with the history of the city, which his ancestors cleansed of Tarquinius Superbus, an evil king, in 509 B.C. The date is the traditional end of the Roman monarchy and the founding of the Roman Republic.

The conspirators, their faces obscured by hats and cloaks, converge at Brutus's gate. Lucius shows them into the study, where they discuss their cabal with Brutus, who is now a willing participant. To men lurking about the streets in the dark of night, he declares that they must strike at Caesar in the open. Brutus rejects Cassius's call for the assassination of Mark Antony as well. To Cassius's fear that Caesar will not venture out after so fearful a storm, Decius Brutus promises to flatter him into appearing in public at 8:00 A.M.

9. The home of Julius Caesar and Calpurnia

Because of the tempestuous night, Calpurnia, Caesar's third and last wife, suffers a terrifying dream in which clouds shaped like fiery warriors dripped blood on the Capitol. She awakens on March 15—the ides of March—and pleads with him to forego his appearance in the Senate. Augurers—state priests who determine the future by reading signs from nature and from the entrails of sacrificial animals—concur with her fears.

Initially, Caesar accedes to her wish that he stay home from the Senate session. Decius Brutus reinterprets Calpurnia's nightmare of Caesar's statue pouring blood as a positive omen, a sign of public nurturance. He convinces Caesar to attend to public duty lest Romans laugh at him for fearing a woman's dreams. Six more conspirators and Publius, a senator not involved in the plot, enter to accompany Caesar to the Capitol.

10. A Roman street leading to the Forum

On the road to the Forum, Artemidorus, a rhetorician or writing instructor, stands ready to warn Caesar of the conspiracy. At the city's heart, the Forum Romanum, which stretched between the Palatine and Capitoline hills, was the scene of major events in Roman history. It contained the *Via Sacra* (Sacred Way), the parade route for religious leaders and triumphant generals, as well as the ancient round Temple of Vesta, the rectangular temples of Saturn and the Dioscuri, and the *rostra* (speakers' platforms), where announcers delivered news to the people below. With moneys from his conquests, Julius Caesar erected a new Forum Julium, the site of a new *curia* (Senate house), *comitium* (assembly hall), enlarged *rostra*, vendors' stalls, and the Basilica Julia, a commercial and justice center completed by his nephew and successor Augustus Caesar, Rome's first emperor.

Fearing danger to her husband, Portia awaits Brutus at a narrow place in the street. She dispatches Lucius to bring news from the Senate and encounters the seer, who awaits Caesar with another warning. As Caesar, his colleagues, and hangers-on walk up the forum and approach the Capitol, the seer warns that the day is fraught with danger for Caesar. In vain, Artemidorus presses a letter on him and begs him to read it. A veiled comment from Popilius hints that the plot has leaked to others.

11. The Roman Senate

Upon entering the Senate, a gathering of elite male citizens, the conspirators crowd around Caesar to beg for the return of the exiled Publius, the brother of Metellus Cimber, Shakespeare's name for the historical figure Lucius Tillius Cimber. Trebonius draws Mark Antony aside as the conspirators ring Caesar and stab him many times. At the approach of the trusted Brutus, Caesar muffles his face in his cloak and at the feet of a statue of Pompey, collapses from the final blow.

Public turmoil disrupts the conspirators' plans. To ingratiate himself with the assassins, Mark Antony makes a show of supporting the killers' cause. He petitions Brutus for permission to speak at Caesar's funeral. Against Cassius's advice, Brutus grants the request. When the crowd departs, Antony speaks his anger in an emotional, vengeful soliloquy denouncing the murderers. To plunge Rome into bloody civil war, he intends to incense the mob at the funeral. A servant of Octavius states that his master is seven leagues outside the city. Antony replies with a message that Rome is too dangerous for Caesar's nephew, who was then a nineteen-year-old novice at politics. Antony and the servant carry the body away.

12. Public forum

In the public pulpit, Brutus carefully outlines the assassins' noble purpose in murdering Caesar to end his rise to power. After onlookers applaud Brutus and his explanation of the assassination, he yields the pulpit to Antony, who carries Caesar's body into public view. Antony plays on the crowd's emotions. By disclosing the blood-encrusted corpse and naming the assassins who stabbed his friend, he whips the crowd into an angry mob. Antony points out Caesar's mantle, the one he wore when he defeated the Nervii, a Celtic tribe that inhabited Artois in northern France adjacent to the English Channel.

Antony stays the people from rioting by reading Caesar's will, which leaves them his arbors and orchards to the north of the Tiber as public parks. By the end of Antony's funeral oration, the populace abandons sympathy with Brutus and the rest of the conspirators and howls for revenge. The wild crowd pours into the streets to kill the plotters and burn their houses. Brutus, Cassius, and the other members flee through the gates of Rome just as Octavius, Caesar's only heir, arrives.

13. Antony's house

Octavius allies with Antony and Lepidus to form the Second Triumvirate. The trio coordinates revenge on the assassins, whom they condemn along with the conspirators' families.

14. Outside Sardis

Brutus camps with his army at Sardis on the broad Hermus Valley plain in Asia Minor. Sardis, once the capital of Lydia and home of the fabled rich king Croesus, is now Izmir, Turkey. Cassius joins Brutus in the field. After ordering commanders out of earshot, the two withdraw to the privacy of Brutus's tent. Brutus accuses Cassius of defending the bribe-taker Lucius Pella and of withholding pay to his soldiers. Cassius demands respect as the more experienced leader and soldier. Their tempers cool.

After Titinius and Messala join them, the two leaders propose a purge of one hundred senators, including the venerable Cicero. Cassius prefers to wait for the armies of Antony and Octavius to attack, but Brutus opts to march to Philippi, a town in north central Macedonia ten miles north of the Aegean Sea. It was once fortified by Philip II, father of Alexander the Great. Cassius and Brutus depart friends. That night, Caesar's ghost appears to Brutus and promises to meet him again at Philippi.

15. Philippi

In the fall of 42 B.C., when the final two battles occur, the combatants meet for a parlay. To Antony's taunt that Brutus ripped a hole in Caesar's heart, Cassius retorts that Antony's words are sweeter than the bees of Hybla, a mountain in Sicily famous for honey production. On the field, Antony defeats Cassius; Brutus triumphs over Octavius. When Brutus sends Messala with dispatches, Cassius misinterprets the move and concludes that the opposing army has captured Brutus. Cassius falls on the sword that he used to stab Caesar. Brutus orders the body sent to Thasos, an island in the Aegean south of Macedonia, and arranges for a dignified Roman funeral. In the next clash, Antony's troops rout Brutus's men. With the aid of Strato, Brutus dies in a suicide similar to Cassius's death.

After Antony and Octavius locate Brutus's remains, Antony praises Brutus as the noblest and least blameworthy of the conspirators. All the other assassins envied Caesar, but Brutus acted out of love for Rome and its freedoms. Octavius orders that the army accord the body the respect and honor befitting a noble citizen.

Further Reading

Barter, James. *Julius Caesar and Ancient Rome in World History*. Springfield, N.J.: Enslow, 2001.

"Basilica Julia," http://kylemartin.ca/Forum/basilica_julia.html.

Bloom, Harold, ed. *Julius Caesar*. New York: Chelsea House, 1994.

Boyce, Charles. *Shakespeare A to Z*. New York: Facts on File, 1990.

"Campus Martius," http://www.skidmore.edu/~mmucha/campus.htm.

"Circus Flaminius," http://www.ukans.edu/history/index/europe/ancient_rome/E/Gazetteer/Places/Europe/Italy.

Claybourne, Anna, and Rebecca Treays. *The World of Shakespeare*. London: Usborne Publishing, 1996.

"The Colossus of Rhodes," http://ce.eng.usf.edu/pharos/wonders/colossus.html.

Connolly, Peter, and Hazel Dodge. *The Ancient City: Life in Classical Athens & Rome*. Oxford: Oxford University Press, 2000.

Derrick, Thomas J. *Understanding Shakespeare's Julius Caesar*. Westport, Conn.: Greenwood, 1998.

"The Flaminia Family," http://www.flumignano.com/FLAMINIA2.htm.

"Forum Julium," http://www.roman-empire.net/tours/rome/forum-julium.html.

Foster, Genevieve. *Augustus Caesar's World*. Sandwich, Mass.: Beautiful Feet Books, 1996.

McMurtry, Jo. *Julius Caesar*. Westport, Conn.: Greenwood Press, 1998.

_____. *Understanding Shakespeare's England*. Hamden, Conn.: Archon Books, 1989.

Nardo, Don, ed. *Readings on Julius Caesar*. Westport, Conn.: Greenwood Press, 1999.

"Theatrum Pompei," http://www.theaterofpompey.com/auditorium/theatrum.html

Thrasher, Thomas. *The Importance of William Shakespeare*. San Diego, Calif.: Lucent Books, 1999.

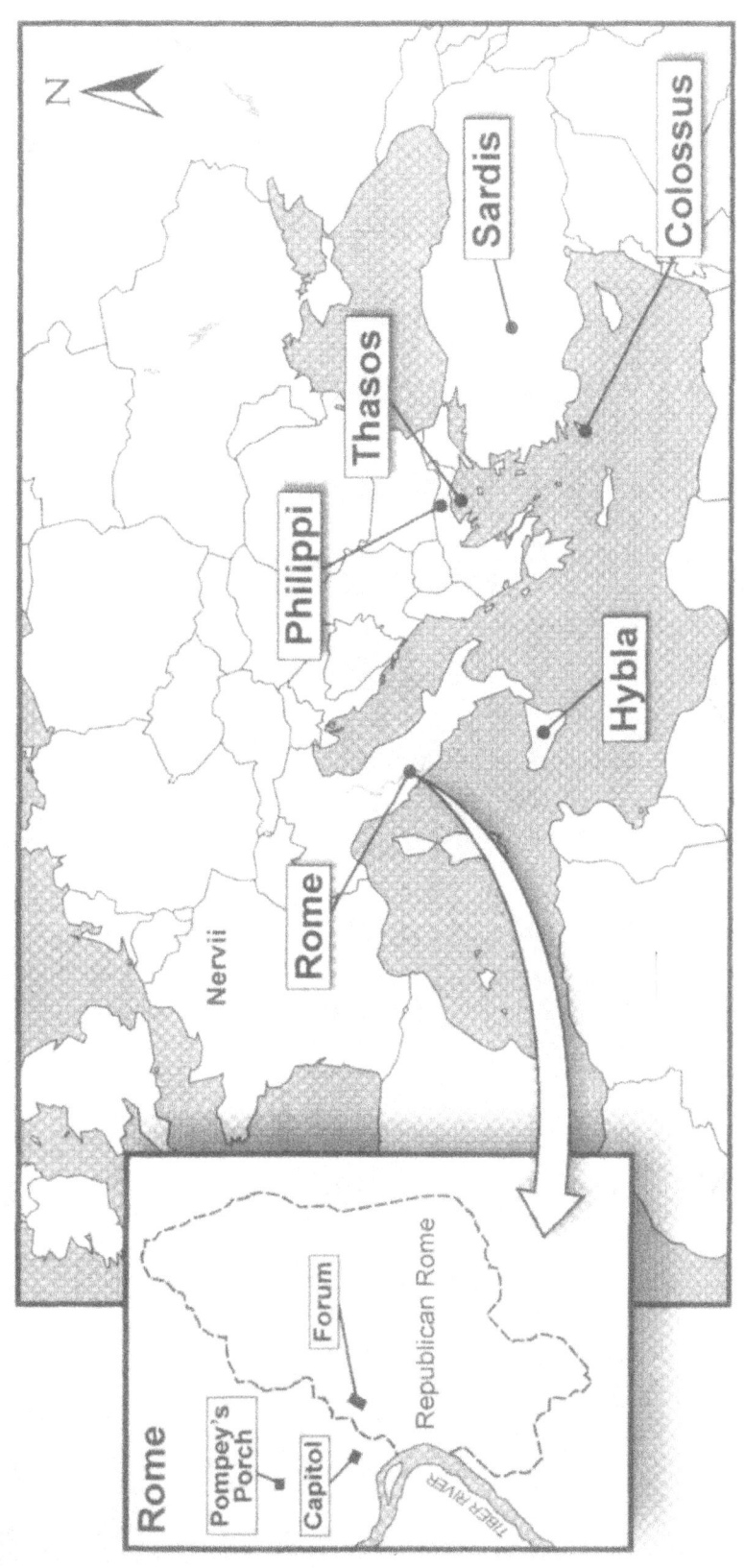

Kindred
By Octavia Butler

Classic science fiction, 1979

Geographical Summary

The time-trekking of Edana and Kevin Franklin, a biracial California couple, wrenches them back into slave times. The bizarre events begin June 6, 1976, a month before the U.S. bicentennial celebration. The couple is moving into a new home in Altadena on the outskirts of greater Los Angeles, where Dana attends classes at the University of Southern California. They cope with repeated and unpredictable time transportations back to slave days to assist Rufus Weylin, son of Tom Weylin, a savage plantation owner cultivating land near Easton, Maryland. During one episode, Kevin is parted from his wife. He travels through free states and considers buying land in Maine.

The location of the Weylin family estate—on the Delmarva Peninsula near Delaware to the northeast and across the Chesapeake Bay from Baltimore to the northwest—situates the unusual novel in a historic area torn by its reliance on slave labor to grow tobacco and on its pro-North leanings, which allied citizens with abolitionism. When the nightmarish back-and-forth from present to past ceases on July 4, 1976, Dana pays a heavy price for her loyalty by losing an arm in a freakish flight from a murder scene. In their own time, the Franklins return to Maryland to seek clues to the aftermath of Rufus's death. They study old newspapers and records of slave sales at the Maryland Historical Society in Baltimore to learn the result of Dana's knifing of Rufus, who grew into a brutal slavemaster like his father.

Detailed Itinerary

1. Altadena, California

On July 4, 1976, returning from time travel to an unknown location around 1808 or 1809, Dana Franklin, a black fiction writer, recalls her first journey on June 6. Unable to recognize time or place, she rescues a small boy from drowning in a river, probably the Tred Avon River, which flows through wooded land near Easton, Maryland. While his mother looks on, Dana resuscitates the boy.

Within minutes, Dana returns to 1976 and to her home in Altadena, a community directly north of Pasadena, California, on the northern fringe of greater Los Angeles and south of the San Gabriel Mountains. On entry to her house, she suffers an amputation after her arm is wrenched off. At her hospital room, Kevin, her husband, admits reporting to police that he discovered her pulling the detached arm from a hole in the wall of their new home.

2. Weylin plantation, Maryland

After a second dizzy spell, on June 7, 1976, Dana has no opportunity to recover before she returns to the year 1815 to help the same white boy, whose name is Rufus Weylin. She stops him in the act of burning draperies by pulling them down and throwing them out the window. Rufus admits burning the stable to spite his father, Tom Weylin, and discloses welts over old scars on his back that he received for stealing a dollar from his father's desk.

Dana finds herself a free, educated black among illiterate slaves of the Weylin plantation a few miles south of Easton, Maryland, which lies across the bay from Annapolis and southeast of Baltimore. The estate is part of historic Talbot County halfway up the western side of the Delmarva Peninsula. Rich farmland extends over the Chesapeake Bay on the Tred Avon Inlet and River, a business hub that steamboats served during the antebellum era.

Rufus confides his fondness for Alice Greenwood, a free-born black playmate. Connecting present with past, Dana recalls that her grandmother Hagar was the daughter of Alice Greenwood and Rufus Weylin. Dana concludes that the two episodes of time travel place her near Alice during the dangerous, uncertain slave era to guarantee her family's survival.

While searching the woods for Alice's mother, Dana encounters four white patrollers. They enter a log cabin and seize Alice's parents. They beat the child's father for failure to produce a pass, written proof that his master allows him to travel unaccompanied. The mother states that Tom Weylin persecutes her husband because her children are free born and not Weylin's slaves. One of the nightriders strikes Dana and attempts to rape her. She fights him off with a tree limb and returns to her own time.

3. Altadena, California

After two or three minutes of time travel, Dana reappears to Kevin. She chooses to sleep rather than seek medical treatment for the injuries she suffered in the scuffle. Before dawn the next day, she binds to her waist a canvas travel bag packed with a knife, shoes, and clothes. To assist her time treks, she finds a map of Maryland and studies black history books, which explain the handwritten passes used by free blacks to allow them to travel on errands for whites. With Kevin's help, she deduces that Rufus summons her when he is in fear of death.

4. Los Angeles, California

A flashback describes how Dana, a twenty-two-year-old freelance fiction writer and part-time worker in an auto-parts warehouse, meets Kevin Franklin, a published novelist who is white and twelve years older than Dana. She tells him she lives with relatives while taking extension courses at the University of California at Los Angeles. The school, which is located south of the city center, opened in 1919 at 405 Hilgard Avenue as a southern branch of the state education system.

5. Weylin plantation, Maryland

On June 9, 1976, when Dana experiences a third attack of dizziness, Kevin holds onto her and the canvas bag. The couple discovers Rufus downed by a broken leg after falling from a tree in 1819. Nigel, his black companion, fetches Tom, who returns the boy home by wagon. She confesses to Rufus that she and Kevin come from California in 1976. Kevin extends a bicentennial quarter as proof.

As was common practice in slave times, Kevin dines with the Weylins. Because she is black, Dana must eat at the cookhouse, where Sarah, the head cook, serves bowls of corn meal mush. Because California was not admitted to the Union until 1850, Dana fibs that she is from New York, a likely home for a free black of the period.

In private, Dana confesses to Kevin that she fears he will not return from time travel. He intends to work for the Weylins as Rufus's tutor. Dana wants to influence Rufus's character to keep him from growing into a brute like his father. She cleans the boy's room and sleeps in the attic during the six weeks that his leg heals. Because Margaret Weylin, the plantation mistress, flirts with Kevin, he wants to journey to Baltimore. Dana suggests Philadelphia, which is farther north in the free state of Pennsylvania. In the early nineteenth century, the city was an enclave of Quakers, a religious sect of pacifists and strong advocates of the abolition of slavery.

As Dana learns the role of slave, she worries about how quickly black people give in to mastery and lose the urge for freedom. Kevin tires of the plantation and considers going west. Because Nigel and Rufus read better than Tom, he accuses Dana of book theft and reading, which was a crime among slaves. He beats her into unconsciousness.

6. Las Vegas, Nevada

A flashback returns to the time when Kevin proposes to Dana four months after they met. Dana abandons an L.A. apartment on Crenshaw Boulevard, a major north-south thoroughfare west of the city that passes through an Africann American community. Kevin leaves his flat on Olympic, which crosses the city south of the fashion district. In 1972, they travel northeast to marry in Las Vegas, a common California getaway spot in southeastern Nevada.

7. Altadena, California

After her return from the third time trek, Dana enters the house alone, having left Kevin locked in the past. She soothes lash marks on her back; her blouse hangs in pieces. On June 10, 1976, she packs a denim bag with aspirin, soap, pen and paper, and a history of American slavery, which contains a map of Maryland. After more study of slave history, Dana packs sleeping pills for the next journey.

8. Baltimore, Maryland

On June 17, 1976, Dana arrives at the Weylin plantation in 1824—a year after Alice's mother died and Alice married Isaac. Alice reports that Kevin went "somewhere North." Tom's wife Margaret has moved to Baltimore, a wealthy Maryland harbor city that maintained ambivalence toward slavery during the antebellum era. Although the state didn't secede with the rebel Southern states, it suffered reprisals for its pro-slavery sentiments.

9. Weylin plantation, Maryland

Dana observes Rufus's fight with Isaac and accuses him of trying to rape Isaac's wife. Rufus, who is eighteen or nineteen years old, predicts that Isaac and Alice will suffer for striking a white man and threatens to conceal Kevin's whereabouts from Dana. When Dana reports Rufus's broken ribs to Tom, he states that Rufus has corresponded with Kevin, whose letters carry a Philadelphia address and disclose his plans to set out.

Rufus promises to intercede if Tom decides to sell Dana. She writes to Kevin and shows Rufus a book on black history. He reads about Frederick Douglass (ca. 1817–1895), who lived nearby in Talbot County, Maryland, and about abolitionist Harriet Ross Tubman (1820–1913), an agent of the Underground Railroad who lived a few miles south in

Dorchester County, Maryland. Farther south below Petersburg, Virginia, in Southampton County, which borders on North Carolina, Nat Turner (1800–1831) instigated a slave revolt. Rufus agrees to mail Dana's letter to Kevin.

After Alice is captured and enslaved, Rufus buys her from Judge Holman for an inflated price and returns her to the Weylin estate. He sleeps next to her while she recovers from dog bites. She recalls that captors cut off Isaac's ears and sold him to Mississippi. Along the Mississippi River Delta, white slavemasters flourished from a grueling cotton-based economy that rapidly wore down slaves.

Alice slowly recovers but is emotionally traumatized. With no choice but to comply with Rufus, she allows herself to become his concubine. A month after writing Kevin, Dana composes a second letter. Alice passes on Dana's original letters, which Rufus had hidden in his bed chest.

10. Delaware

At midnight, Dana sets out past Easton and Wye Mills, a former grist mill that ground flour for General George Washington's Continental Army at Valley Forge. Guided by the North Star or Polaris, the bright star in the handle of Ursa Minor (the Little Dipper), Dana intends to veer northeast up the Delmarva Peninsula toward Delaware, an Atlantic-coast state halfway between New York and Washington, D.C. Originally founded by tobacco growers, Delaware had supported slavery. Because of strong ties with Washington and federalism, landowners began abandoning the slave system after 1790. Consequently, the slave population dwindled.

11. Weylin plantation, Maryland

After Liza divulges that Dana has escaped, Tom and Rufus capture her. Tom kicks her into unconsciousness; Rufus orders her to be brave when Jake Edwards, the slave overseer, whips her with cowhide. Alice tends the lash marks. Dana contemplates suicide.

Kevin writes that he is on the way south to reunite with his wife. She learns that Tom wrote Kevin after discovering that Rufus lied about mailing her letters. After five years' absence, in 1821, Kevin, gray-bearded and dusty, arrives to fetch Dana. Rufus refuses to let her leave and holds them at rifle point.

12. Altadena, California

Kevin lands on Dana's lacerated back, forcing them both to return to California and 1976. Dana had been gone two months. Kevin relates that he almost bought a farm in Maine, the northernmost New England state. He confesses that he returned to Maryland to find her after a friend in Boston forwarded Dana's letter.

13. Weylin plantation, Maryland

Before Dana can prepare for time travel, she returns to the Weylin estate around July 1830 and finds Rufus lying face down and unconscious in a puddle. She treats him for malaria. Tom threatens to kill her if his son dies, but it is Tom who succumbs to a heart attack six days later. Because Dana failed at cardiopulmonary resuscitation, Rufus punishes her by having overseer Evan Fowler force her to cut corn stalks like a field hand. After Fowler beats her into unconsciousness, Rufus retrieves her from the fields and assigns her to tend Margaret.

Dana stays on edge because Rufus perceives her and Alice as two halves of the same woman, both of whom he desires. He terrifies her by selling off slaves according to his father's previous arrangements. While awaiting the birth of her grandmother Hagar, Dana keeps a journal in shorthand. When Alice gives birth to Hagar in February 1831, Dana feels less threatened. After Rufus strikes her for talking to Sam, while washing in the cookhouse, she slits her wrists.

14. Altadena, California

Awakening in her bed eight months later after being gone only three hours, Dana discovers that Kevin summoned Dr. Louis George to bandage her bleeding wrists. She recounts to Kevin the danger that Rufus will sell all the slaves to free his estate from debt. She fears that if she murders Rufus, she will be trapped in the past.

15. Weylin plantation, Maryland

On June 19, 1976, the fourth trip back into the time takes Dana to the Weylin home on the day that Alice hangs herself in the barn. Sarah explains that Rufus sold Alice's son and daughter because she ran away. Rufus admits that he faked the sale and that the children are safe in Baltimore with May, Margaret Weylin's sister. Dana insists that he free Alice's children and raise them as his own motherless offspring.

The next day at Easton, which had become the seat of Talbot County in 1788, Rufus drives to the courthouse and in Dana's presence, draws up certificates of freedom for his children. One morning in 1831, he travels to Baltimore by steamboat from Easton Point on the Tred Avon Inlet. On his return, he follows Dana to the attic and implies that he will take her as his next concubine. She locates her knife and fatally stabs him in the side. When Nigel bursts in, Rufus collapses with his arm draped across Dana's.

16. Altadena, California

On the way home to Altadena after spending eight months at the Weylin plantation, Dana loses her left arm, which becomes wedged in her living room wall as she emerges from the past. The event takes place on July 4, 1976, the nation's 200th birthday.

17. Historical Society, Baltimore, Maryland

Intent on learning the aftermath of Dana's escape from Rufus, Kevin and Dana travel Maryland in search of the Weylin estate and information on the owners and their slaves. Rufus reportedly burned to death when the house caught fire. Dana surmises that Nigel torched the attic to conceal her crime.

The Franklins proceed to the Maryland Historical Society, located at 201 West Monument Street in north central Baltimore. Established in 1844, it includes a library, museum, press, and educational programs that preserve and disseminate materials reflecting state heritage. Among old records, the couple pieces together a scenario that suggests that Nigel rescued Margaret Weylin from the fire. It appears that Nigel, Carrie, Joe, and Hagar were never sold and may have tended Margaret in Baltimore. Dana concludes that Rufus feared making a will freeing his children because he believed that Dana would murder him.

Further Reading

Allison, Dorothy, "The Future of Females: Octavia Butler's Mother Lode." In *Reading Black, Reading Feminist*. New York: Meridian, 1990.

Beal, Frances M., "Black Women and the Science Fiction Genre: Interview with Octavia Butler." *Black Scholar* (March–April 1986): 14–18.

Butler, Octavia, "A Few Rules for Predicting the Future." *Essence* (May 1, 2000).

Dubey, Madhu, "Folk and Urban Communities in African-American Women's Fiction." *Studies in American Fiction* (Spring 1999).

Fee, Elizabeth, et al, eds. *The Baltimore Book: New Views of Local History.* Philadelphia: Temple University Press, 1997.

Fry, Joan, "An Interview with Octavia Butler." *Poets and Writers* (March/April 1997): 58–69.

Gomez, Jewelle, "Black Women Heroes." *Black Scholar* (March–April 1986): 8–13.

Gregg, Sandra, "Writing Out of the Box." *Black Issues Book Review* (September 1, 2000).

Lambe, Dean R., "Review." *Science Fiction Review* (May 1984).

McHenry, Susan, "Otherworldly Vision: Octavia Butler." *Essence* (February 1, 1999).

McTyre, Robert E., "Octavia Butler: Black America's First Lady of Science Fiction." *Michigan Chronicle* (April 26, 1994).

Parisi, Luciana, "From Pleasure to Desire: Involution and Anticlimax in Octavia Butler's 'Dawn,' " http://www.ccru.demon.co.uk/archive/lilith.htm.

Rushdy, Ashraf H. A., "Families of Orphans: Relation and Disrelation in Octavia Butler's 'Kindred.' " *College English* (February 1993): 135–57.

Tilghman, Oswald. *History of Talbot County, Maryland, 1661–1861.* Baltimore: Clearfield Company, 1997.

A Lesson Before Dying

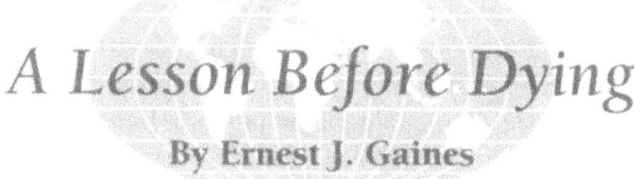

By Ernest J. Gaines

Multicultural contemporary fiction, 1993

Geographical Summary

Ernest Gaines writes knowledgeably, eloquently of his homeland, the rural agricultural South along the north shore of the Gulf of Mexico. Set at fictional Bayonne near Henri Pichot's plantation, Gaines's novel draws on memories of his childhood at Cherie Quarters on River Lake Plantation near New Roads, Pointe Coupée Parish, in eastern Louisiana. In the alluvial plain, the low country, a thriving agrarian center, lies between the Atchafalaya River and a loop of the Mississippi River near Mississippi's western border. Part of the story occurs in a village church, where Grant Wiggins teaches black children from late October to mid-April at a consecration table and pews. In the schoolyard, male students saw firewood into stove lengths that heat their classroom during cold weather. At noon, the children return to their homes in the black quarter to eat lunch with their families.

After Jefferson is arrested for murder and condemned to execution in the electric chair in fictional Bayonne, Grant grudgingly agrees to educate the boy. When landowner Henri Pichot needs to talk with Grant, his yardman hand delivers the written summons across the street to the school. To show his respect for whites, Grant remains in Pichot's kitchen until Pichot is ready to talk. The movements in the plot are small—Grant frequently drives ten miles under live oaks into the segregated town to drink at the bar of the Rainbow Club. On workdays, he gazes from his classroom at the cane fields where Jefferson worked at age six as waterboy for field laborers. After Étienne de Boré began the sugar industry in 1795, sugar cane became the area's money crop. It demands intense and dangerous hand labor of Bayonne blacks, who earn a pittance. In the mid-twentieth century, they live like their ancestors, the slaves who established Louisiana's plantation system.

Visits to the jail on the second story of the Bayonne courthouse are the most riveting of the novel's scenes. Down a corridor of locked cell doors, Grant and the deputy pass young male prisoners. Beyond an empty cell, the two men stop at the last door, where Grant finds Jefferson isolated behind bars. He lies stretched out on his bunk with his face to the wall. The only link with normality is a small window looking out on a sycamore tree and above, the blue sky.

Grant restores some sense of family and community to visitation by requesting that he and the boy's relatives and supporters meet in the jail's dayroom. The gatherings are pitiful scenarios in which Jefferson truculently receives his family, teacher, and preacher. Paul, a sympathetic deputy, leads Jefferson to a picnic table. In handcuffs and shackles, the boy is limited to a shuffling gait and haltingly attempts to feed himself. Multiple humiliations and inhumanity deepen Jefferson's hostility and widen the chasm that Grant must cross to ready him for execution.

Bayonne is unforgiving of black crime. In the Rainbow Club's darkened barroom and eating area, Grant feels obliged to fight two self-important mulatto bricklayers who denigrate Jefferson. At Morgan's department store, Grant purchases a radio from a supercilious clerk who keeps him waiting while she chats with a white customer. The expenditure is worth the effort for it connects Jefferson with music beamed from local stations and from Del Rio, Texas, and Nashville, Tennessee. Grant retreats to the school to await news of the execution. Jefferson's last written words reward the teacher. Returned to a scrap of his former humanity, the boy takes hope from a glimpse of the sky and finds beauty on his final day of life.

Detailed Itinerary

1. Courtroom in St. Raphael Parish, Louisiana

A Louisiana public school teacher in his late twenties, Grant Wiggins learns from his godmother, Emma Glenn, about the trial and condemnation of Jefferson, a young illiterate black who robbed and murdered Alcee Gropé, a white liquor store owner. The crime occurred in 1948 in fictional St. Raphael Parish, Louisiana, after Gropé shot Brother and Bear, two thieves who demanded credit until cane grinding ended. Jefferson, who was too stunned to flee, panicked and stole a bottle of liquor and cash from the till as two white men walked in. On a Friday in October, the judge rules that Jefferson is guilty of robbery and first-degree murder. The next Monday, Emma, Tante Lou, and Reverend Mose Ambrose hear the judge condemn the boy to electrocution.

2. Tante Lou's home in the Black Quarter, St. Raphael Parish

Before 4:00 P.M. Lou resolves that Grant will educate Jefferson before he dies. Lou intends to arrange jail visits through Henri Pichot, brother-in-law of Sheriff Sam Guidry. Both Emma and Lou have connections with the white Pichot family—Emma as cook and Lou as washwoman. Lou coerces her nephew to take on the task of preparing the prisoner for death.

3. Pichot's house, St. Raphael Parish

With the maid, Inez Lane, Emma, Lou, and Grant await an audience with Henri Pichot, who talks with another white man, Louis Rougon, in the library. Pichot disapproves of the idea of educating Jefferson, for whom he had been a character witness. Stubbornly, Pichot refuses to say when he will approach Sam to ask permission for Grant's jail visits.

4. Louisiana State University

Ten years earlier, Grant entered the state university, probably the Baton Rouge branch southeast of St. Raphael Parish, and returned home to teach. A land-grant and sea-grant facility evolved from l'Université de l'Etat de la Louisiane, the original Louisiana State University and Agricultural & Mechanical College, opened near Pineville north of Alexandria on January 2, 1860. Colonel William Tecumseh Sherman was superintendent in the year and a half the school remained in service before the outbreak of the Civil War. Four years after the war ended, the university reopened in 1869 at Baton Rouge.

5. Bayonne, St. Raphael Parish, Louisiana

Grant drives the two women home and proceeds along the St. Charles River ten miles to the Rainbow Club in Bayonne, the fictional parish seat of St. Raphael. He summons Vivian Baptiste, a native of fictional Free LaCove, whom he has dated for three years, and presses her to leave town with him. She insists on staying because of her teaching job and commitment to her children and estranged husband. She urges Grant to take the job of educating Jefferson.

6. Baton Rouge, Louisiana

Vivian and Grant make a date to visit friends in Baton Rouge on Friday, when they can share time alone. The state capital and the seat of East Baton Rouge parish, the city lies northwest of New Orleans on the east bank of the Mississippi River. A cosmopolitan center, Baton Rouge offers Grant and Vivian a respite from the racism and small-mindedness of backwoods St. Raphael Parish.

7. Pichot plantation, St. Raphael Parish, Louisiana

Under mid-twentieth-century racism, Grant lacks hope of elevating local children and takes out his frustrations on recalcitrant students who dawdle and count on their fingers. At 2:00 P.M., Farrell Jarreau, Pichot's groundskeeper, extends to Grant an invitation to come to the Pichot home at 5:00. Inez divulges to Grant that Henri and Louis Rougon bet that Grant will fail to educate Jefferson. At 7:15, Henri, Louis, Sam, and an unidentified fat man hear Grant's request to help Jefferson die with dignity. The sheriff agrees to allow Grant to visit the boy in a couple of weeks under the supervision of Chief Deputy Clark.

8. School, St. Raphael Parish, Louisiana

Meanwhile, Grant prepares his students for a visit from Dr. Joseph, the superintendent of schools. On Thursday before 2:00, Dr. Joseph quizzes Gloria Hebert and Louis Washington, examines teeth, and lectures on nutrition and hard work. Wearied of teaching from outdated and used materials from white schools, Grant requests up-to-date books and more supplies, but Dr. Joseph is more interested in hygiene and the pledge to the flag. The next week, Grant directs schoolboys to chop the school's winter firewood into stove lengths.

9. Poulaya, Louisiana

Grant thinks about fellow students during his university days and about his teacher, Matthew Antoine, whom he visited at fictional Poulaya. Antoine, who died early in 1943, warned him that he would fail at teaching ignorant students.

10. Courthouse Bayonne, Louisiana

At 1:30 P.M., Grant, Emma, and Lou carry clothing and a food basket for their visit to Jefferson at his solitary cell upstairs in the courthouse. Dispirited, he refuses food, but is curious about the date of the execution. Emma asks young Deputy Paul to distribute the contents of the basket to "the rest of them children."

In the next two visits, Grant gives inmates pocket change. On Friday, the fourth visit, Grant goes alone because there is no one else to send. Sulky and dirty, Jefferson kneels by the food bag and, in response to the defense attorney's insult, gobbles like a hog. Grant accuses him of letting the white man win.

11. Rainbow Club, Bayonne

Grant hears blacks exulting over the success of Jackie Robinson, the first African American athlete to play Major League baseball. Signed with the Brooklyn Dodgers in 1947, he helped them win the pennant. They voted him rookie of the year. Two years later at his peak, he led the league in batting and stolen bases. The league named him 1949's Most Valuable Player. Grant recalls 1938, when he listened by radio to the match between Joe Louis, the world heavyweight champion from 1937 to 1949, and Max Schmeling, a German boxer whom Louis knocked out in the first round.

12. Louisiana State University, Baton Rouge

At the university, Grant begins learning about heroes. Mr. Anderson lectures about Charles Stewart Parnell, an Irish freedom fighter and member of Parliament who raised money in 1879 to finance Ireland's battle against English overlords. He drew supporters with rabble-rousing speeches but lost public respect after the revelation of his adultery with a married woman. Anderson gives Grant a copy of James Joyce's "Ivy Day in the Committee Room," a short story anthologized in *Dubliners* (1914).

13. Bayonne, Louisiana

At Vivian's school, where she teaches sixth and seventh grades, Grant writes "*Je t'aime*" (I love you) in French three times on the blackboard. Because she fears that her ex-husband will take her children to live with him southwest from Bayonne in Houston, Texas, she refuses to go to Baton Rouge with Grant for the night. She replies on the board "*Je t'aimerais toujours*" (I will always love you.).

14. Black quarter, St. Raphael Parish, Louisiana

On Sunday, Vivian makes a surprise visit to Grant. They walk to the plantation cemetery and enter a cane field. They search for pecans and make love. She thinks they have conceived a child. After Grant introduces Vivian as his fiancée, Lou describes her as a "lady of quality."

Vivian is no longer married to the man she met at Xavier College. Located at 1 Drexel Drive in New Orleans, the college, which is sometimes confused with Xavier University, is a liberal arts institution founded in 1915 by Saint Katherine Drexel and the Sisters of the Blessed Sacrament. It is the only historically black Catholic college in the Western Hemisphere.

15. Courthouse, Bayonne, Louisiana

Because visits have been unpleasant, Grant urges Jefferson to respect his Great Aunt Emma. The sheriff complains that she requests that his wife, Edna Guidry, talk him into allowing supervised visits in the dayroom. Sam yields to Edna's plea, but he insists that Jefferson remain shackled. On the first visit, Jefferson refuses Emma's food. A few weeks before Christmas, Jefferson asks Grant about death by electrocution.

16. School, St. Raphael Parish, Louisiana

Grant dedicates to Jefferson the school children's Christmas program, consisting of the reenactment of Christ's birth, seasonal carols, and refreshments. Under the Christmas tree, the children place a wrapped package containing a sweater and socks for Jefferson.

17. Pichot's house, St. Raphael Parish, Louisiana

Late in February an hour before the end of school, Grant leaves his assistant, Irene Cole, in charge and visits Pichot's house across the street to confer with the sheriff and Henri. Sam announces the execution date as April 8, the second Friday after Easter, between noon and three. Grant departs to walk by the river and joins Vivian in comforting Emma.

18. Rainbow Club, Bayonne, Louisiana

Around 7:45, Grant meets Vivian at the Rainbow Club for a drink and talks about the strong women in his family—especially Lou, who raised him.

19. Courthouse, Bayonne, Louisiana

On Grant's next visit to the jail, Jefferson looks out the window at the sky and requests a gallon of ice cream for his last supper.

20. Morgan's department store, Bayonne, Louisiana

At Morgan's department store, Grant purchases a radio with donations from some old men and from Claiborne, the bartender at the Rainbow Club. The radio brings in two stations in Baton Rouge and one in New Orleans. At night, Grant anticipates that Jefferson can listen to music from Nashville, Tennessee, to the northeast and from Del Rio, Texas, to the west. With Paul's permission, Grant presents the radio to Jefferson. Angered that he wasn't consulted, the sheriff threatens to confiscate it.

Lou and Ambrose accuse Grant of tempting Jefferson with a "sin box." Grant reminds them that music has helped the boy abandon hate. On Wednesday, Jefferson enjoys listening to *Randy's Record Shop* and refuses to join visitors in the dayroom. Grant asks him to keep a notebook of his thoughts and rejoices that the boy is less hostile. After a successful session with Grant, Jefferson eats politely.

21. Rainbow Club, Bayonne, Louisiana

At 3:30, Grant is drinking with Vivian at the Rainbow Club when mulatto bricklayers complain that Jefferson should already have been "burned" for his crimes. Grant starts a brawl. Claiborne orders his wife Thelma to find Vivian and ends the fight by threatening the mulattos with a gun and knocking Grant unconscious. Vivian leads him from the bar. At her house while she prepares dinner, he quarrels and departs, then returns to bury his face in her lap.

22. Courthouse, Bayonne, Louisiana

Jefferson uses Paul's knife to sharpen a pencil and writes his first letter in a diary. When Grant's class visits the jail, the students kiss Jefferson. Bok, a retarded man, offers him a marble. The electric chair arrives at the courthouse by truck. Ambrose remains with Jefferson until midnight. The school children pray for him.

23. Port Allen, Louisiana

To escape the tension, at 10:30 P.M., Grant drives south to a bar in Port Allen in West Baton Rouge Parish. He refuses to discuss the execution with a man in the bar and returns home at midnight.

24. Courthouse, Bayonne, Louisiana

While school children kneel at noon until the execution is completed, the community grows quiet in anticipation. After Jefferson dies, Deputy Paul stops at the schoolyard and brings Grant the notebook. Realizing that he has succeeded in humanizing a condemned man, Grant weeps at Paul's praise of his influence on Jefferson.

Further Reading

"Biography of Ernest Gaines," http://www.uncfsu.edu/faculty/MCSHANE/ mozingo/GAINES.HTM.

Carmean, Karen. *Ernest J. Gaines*. Westport, Conn.: Greenwood, 1998.

"Communal Responsibility in Ernest J. Gaines's 'A Lesson Before Dying.' " *Mississippi Quarterly* (April 1, 1999).

Davis, Sandra D., "Review." *Detroit Free Press* (June 6, 1993): 7J.

"Ernest Gaines," *Melus* (March 22, 1995).

Ferris, Bill, "Meeting Ernest Gaines," http://www.neh.gov/html/magazine/98-07/gaines.html.

Gaudet, Marcia, and Carl Wooten. *Porch Talk with Ernest Gaines: Conversations on the Writer's Craft*. Lafayette: Louisiana State University, 1990.

" 'G'enet,' 'Lesson Before Dying' Take Top National Book Awards." *Chicago Tribune* (February 14, 1994).

Laney, Ruth, "Southern Sage Savors His Rise to Success." *Emerge* (May 1994):, 66–67.

"Lesson Grim but Well Done." *Charlotte Observer* (May 26, 1999).

"Louisiana State University," http://www.lsu.edu.

Magnier, Bernard, "Ernest J. Gaines." *UNESCO Courier* (April 1995): 5–7.

"Meet the Author: Ernest Gaines." *Literary Cavalcade* (November 1, 1998).

Peterson, V. R., "Interview." *Essence* (August 1993).

Rehder, John B. *Delta Sugar: Louisiana's Vanishing Plantation Landscape*. Baltimore: Johns Hopkins University Press, 1999.

"Remember When: Cherie Quarters Housed Family and Many Friends of Author Ernest Gaines," *Baton Rouge Advocate,* June 20, 1999.

"Seattle Readers Share in Author's Powerful Homecoming." *Seattle Times* (November 14, 1999).

Sheppard, R. Z., "An A-Plus in Humanity," *Time* (March 20, 1993).

Summer, Bob, "Interview." *Publishers Weekly* (May 24, 1993): 62–63.

"A Talk with Ernest Gaines." *Scholastic Scope* (May 3, 1999).

Williams, Wendy J., "Television: 'Lessons' from Life." *Boston Herald* (May 22, 1999).

"Xavier University of Louisiana," http://www.xula.edu.

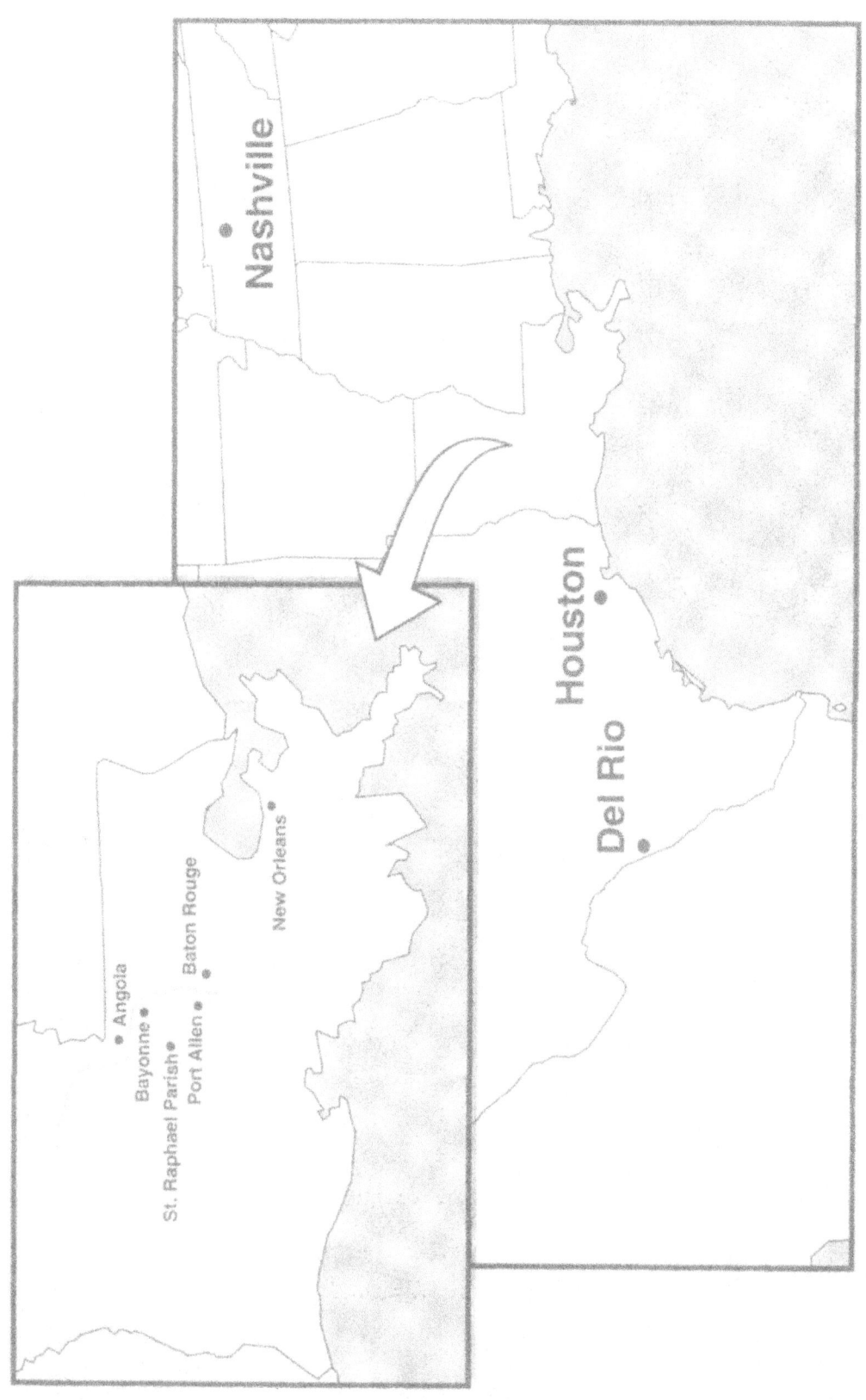

A Long Way from Chicago
By Richard Peck

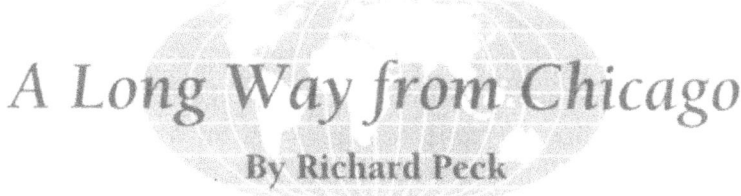

Historical fiction, 1998

Geographical Summary

Richard Wayne Peck, a native of Decatur, Illinois, and veteran of the military, relates the adventures of two city-wise Chicago children during seven consecutive summer visits with their eccentric Grandmother Dowdel, who lives alone in rural Piatt County. The children's mode of travel is the "Blue Bird," one route of the Wabash Railroad. The train line is a major Midwestern transporter comprising 2,500 miles of track stretching from Buffalo, New York, to Omaha, Nebraska. The novel's interlinking episodes refer to numerous significant events in Illinois—the Lincoln-Douglas debates, the Chicago crime wave of the 1920s, the St. Valentine's Day Massacre, the Great Depression, and the execution of bank robber John Dillinger—as well as the Mexican War, World War I, and World War II.

Although the episodic action takes place in central Illinois southwest of Chicago, mention of Lake Michigan, the Chicago Loop, Dearborn Station, Al Capone, and the Palmer House Hotel remind the reader of the big-city milieu that the children know best. Other references to Fort Sheridan, Decatur, Peoria, Palmyra, Springfield, Argenta, Farmer City, St. Louis, and Camp Leonard Wood express the importance of the Wabash Blue Bird in linking communities during an era when automobiles were few. The poignant closing scene suggests that city-smart Joey Dowdel carries with him into World War II the good sense and keen wit and humor of his country-smart grandmother.

Detailed Itinerary

1. Chicago, Illinois

Looking back over seven Augusts from 1929 to 1935, Joey Dowdel recalls how he and his sister Mary Alice spent part of their school vacation each year with Grandma Dowdel. In summer 1929, two months before the stock market crash that precipitated the Great Depression, the children's parents pack them off by train from Chicago, which was infested with gangsters and crime. The reign of the Chicago crime syndicate and gangster Al Capone began in the 1920s and fed on the prosperity of the corrupt prohibition era. After Capone eliminated his competition one by one, he finished the job on February 14, 1929, reputedly by hiring "Machine Gun" Jack McGurn to lure the goons of George "Bugsy" Moran for a daylight execution.

The crime was well planned. Dressed in police uniforms and driving a paddy wagon, Capone's men gunned down James Clark, Frank and Pete Gusenburg, John May, Adam Meyer, Dr. Reinhardt Schwimmer, and Al Weinshank at a Chicago garage on 2122 North Clark Street. The brazen deed became known as the St. Valentine's Day Massacre and boosted the notoriety of the Thompson submachine gun, nicknamed the "tommy gun." Joey assumes that Chicagoans never saw corpses because criminals weighted their feet with concrete and dropped them into Lake Michigan, which forms Chicago's eastern border.

2. Piatt County, Illinois

At age nine, Joey accompanies Mary Alice, two years younger, on the Wabash Railroad's Blue Bird, which leaves each morning out of Dearborn Station, a red brick and pink granite landmark graced by a twelve-story Romanesque clock tower. Erected on Dearborn Street in 1885 by architect Cyrus Lazelle Warner Eidlitz, the depot was the main departure point to southern California, the Grand Canyon, and the Southwest. The station accommodated the Erie Railroad; the Monon Route (later called the L. & N.), which served Cincinnati, Minneapolis, and Louisville; and the Santa Fe Railway, including its famous engines *Super Chief* and the *El Capitan,* the choice of celebrities who traveled regularly from Chicago to Hollywood, California.

On the way to St. Louis, Missouri, the Blue Bird travels southwest to the children's grandmother's house in Piatt County, established by James A. Piatt, Sr., in 1841 east of Champaign. The children's reserved, but eccentric grandmother rails against a reporter from Peoria. He seeks unsavory tidbits about "Shotgun" Cheatham, a local ne'er-do-well who had recently died.

3. Shiloh, Tennessee; Vicksburg, Mississippi

Grandma confides that Cheatham was a member of the Illinois Volunteers, who saw action at the Battle of Shiloh in southern Tennessee southwest of Nashville on April 6–7, 1862. The battle was a major Civil War victory for General Ulysses S. Grant and the Union Army. She claims that Cheatham was also with Grant's forces on July 4, 1863, at Vicksburg, Mississippi, a successful siege against the Confederacy's Mississippi River stronghold and one of the turning points of the Civil War.

4. Bull Run, Virginia

To the children's surprise, Grandma invites the reporter to sit by the casket that night in her living room and offers him homemade beer from the cellar. Mrs. Weidenbach joins the family and reports that Cheatham was wounded three times at the battle of Bull Run, an ambiguous reference to episodes of the Civil War fought in Virginia west of Washington, D.C. She could be referring to the first engagement on July 21, 1861, or the second on August 29–30, 1862. At midnight, Grandma's cat makes a disturbance at Cheatham's coffin. Grandma fires her double-barrel Winchester at the lid and terrifies the newsman, who leaps out the window.

5. Piatt County, Illinois

When the children return to Grandma's house in August 1930, nearly a year after the stock market crash of October 24, 1929, Joey brings along a jigsaw puzzle. The finished picture shows Colonel Charles A. Lindbergh, who flew a frail, stripped-down plane called the *Spirit of St. Louis* from Roosevelt Field in Long Island, New York, over Nova Scotia, Newfoundland, the Atlantic Ocean, and Ireland, to Le Bourget Airport in Paris, France, on May

20–21, 1927. Mary Alice skips rope to a jingle mentioning Calvin Coolidge, who was the U.S. president from 1923–1929. She also names Herbert Hoover, who followed him into office and faced much of the public's discontent and anger during the Great Depression. The children observe their grandma outsmart the Cowgills, a family of roughnecks, after the boys explode her mailbox. When she convinces their father that the boys put a mouse in her milk delivery, he beats them with a leather strop.

6. Chicago Loop

The next summer, Joey and Mary Alice depart the Chicago Loop, a thirty-five-block area of the downtown named for the track patterns of six elevated railroad lines that encircle the business district. In the city's financial and commercial core, which parallels the shore of Lake Michigan to the east, the loop encompasses State and La Salle streets, the Chicago Board of Trade, and the Home Insurance building, a metal-frame landmark demolished the following year.

7. Wabash Blue Bird from Detroit, Michigan, to St. Louis, Missouri

After boarding the Wabash Blue Bird when it stops at the Chicago depot on its way from Detroit, the children observe the worsening of the Great Depression from the windows of the train on its way southwest from Chicago to Piatt County. Destitute men walk the roads as they search for jobs.

8. Salt Creek in Piatt County, Illinois

After the Dowdel children arrive in Grandma's town, they spy a sign posted by Sheriff O. B. Dickerson warning out-of-work drifters to keep moving. At 5:00 A.M. Grandma and the children fish on Salt Creek southwest of town near posted land belonging to the Piatt County Rod & Gun Club. Grandma removes catfish from an illegal trap and rebaits it with foul-smelling homemade cheese. Ignoring Dickerson's complaint that she took his boat, she rows to the home of Aunt Puss Chapman, delivers a hamper of food, and cleans the kitchen.

9. Wabash Railroad Right-Of-Way

Late that evening, Grandma and the children carry fried fish, potatoes and onions, and beer to the Wabash Railroad bank and serve dinner to hungry hobos on the outer rim of the sheriff's jurisdiction. He and his deputies accuse Grandma of running an illegal soup kitchen that breaks health laws. She outfoxes them by hinting that she will take Mary Alice to a psychiatrist to work out the trauma of seeing the men of the gun club drunk while they sang and pranced in their underwear. After the hobos gobble up all the evidence, Earl Askew advises the sheriff to drop the issue.

10. Piatt County Fair, Illinois

By 1932, the Depression worsens as banks foreclose on local farms, leaving families homeless. Grandma practices making gooseberry pies, which she enters in the county fair held at the fairground near Monticello, the Piatt County seat. The county's founder, James A. Piatt, Sr., named the town after Thomas Jefferson's country estate, which the former U.S. president built two miles south of Charlottesville, Virginia. Grandma presents a blue ribbon to barnstormer Barnie Buchanan, who takes Joey for a ride in his biplane. Such planes had offered a military advantage to both sides during air battles over France and Germany during World War I.

11. The Great Fire, Chicago, Illinois

Grandma intrigues her grandchildren with the story of the Chicago Fire, which started in a barn at the city's center on October 8, 1871, and blazed out of control all the way to Fullerton Avenue two days later. The destruction killed 120 and covered 3.5 square miles, destroying 18,000 homes, the courthouse, Crosby's Opera House, the Palmer House Hotel, and the Field and Leiter store on State Street, the foundation of Marshall Field Department Store.

12. Wabash rail line from Decatur to Chicago, Illinois

Grandma tells the children of the Wabash Railroad brakeman. After volunteer firefighters boarded the train from Decatur, a town on Lake Decatur southwest of Piatt County, on the way to the Chicago Fire, a foggy night caused a mixup of tracks. The Decatur train ran head-on into the Wabash freight train a half mile from Grandma's house. According to local legend, the brakeman's ghost continues to search for the head he lost in the collision.

13. Piatt County, Illinois

The next day, Idella Eubanks drives up to Grandma's house to demand her daughter Vandalia, whom Mary Alice conceals upstairs. Grandma bars the pushy Idella from her home. Junior Stubbs, who sells insurance with his father, intends to elope with Vandalia. His parents, Merle and Lula Stubbs, arrive and complain that Vandalia is trying to steal their boy. Idella climbs a ladder to open the upstairs window and retrieve her daughter. Grandma removes the ladder; Idella falls into the snowball bushes.

14. Wabash Blue Bird, Detroit, Michigan, to St. Louis, Missouri

At 8:17 P.M. during the impasse, the Detroit-to-St.-Louis train arrives near Grandma's house. While the ghostly brakeman diverts onlookers' attention, Vandalia and Junior slip aboard the train and depart. Later, Grandma reveals that she knows that Mary Alice lied about hiding a fictitious puppy named Skipper in her upstairs room. Grandma is also aware that Joey had played the ghost by dressing in Grandpa's black overcoat and by swinging a lantern to flag the train.

15. Palmyra, Illinois

At the height of the Depression, when the children arrive in summer 1934, Grandma meets the train to accompany Effie Wilcox, an acquaintance who is leaving town. Like other victims of unemployment and hard times, she must depart because the bank foreclosed on her home. She travels to Palmyra, a small town southwest of Piatt County and north of St. Louis, Missouri.

16. Biograph Theatre, Chicago, Illinois

At noon, Joey and Mary Alice distract Grandma from her worry over Effie by telling her about John Dillinger, a notorious bank robber whom the FBI named Public Enemy Number One. After he escaped from prison in March 1934, an unnamed woman in red betrayed him to the FBI. Agents shot him to death on July 22 outside Chicago's Biograph Theatre on North Lincoln Avenue. The display of Dillinger's body was the source of gossip and legend during an era when criminals were Chicago celebrities.

17. Piatt County, Illinois

On the afternoon of the United Brethren Church rummage sale, Mrs. Weidenbach offers $15 dollars for a hat that Grandma donates from her attic. She claims that Effie discarded it from her house and displays on a quilt the initials M. T. L., suggesting the name Mary Todd Lincoln, the wife of the sixteenth president, Abraham Lincoln. The next day, Grandma nurtures a rumor that the items are Lincoln memorabilia and wonders whether the state might make the Wilcox house into a museum.

Another rumor connects the Wilcox parlor with the Lincoln-Douglas debates, a political challenge that caused Abraham Lincoln to lose the race for the Illinois Senate to Stephen A. Douglas. The actual face-off between the two politicians over slavery occurred at eight sessions between August 21 and October 15, 1858. The first debate took place in Ottawa, Illinois, on August 21. The venue passed to Freeport, August 27; Jonesboro, September 15; Charleston, September 18; Galesburg, October 7; Quincy, October 13; and Alton October 15. In a similar match between Grandma and Banker Weidenbach, she demands return of the title to the Wilcox house for Effie and two-dollar bills for Mary Alice and Joey. That evening, Ray Veech teaches Joey to drive. On the children's departure to Chicago, Effie arrives back from Palmyra aboard the Wabash Blue Bird.

18. Cerro Gordo, Mexico

When the children return in 1935 for one last summer visit at Grandma's house, she takes them to visit Aunt Mae and Uncle Grady Griswold, a veteran of the April 1847 battle of Cerro Gordo, Mexico, during the Mexican War. The fight between General Winfield Scott's soldiers and the forces of General Antonio López de Santa Anna developed sixty miles northwest of Veracruz on the Plan del Río in south central Mexico. The strategy of Captain Robert E. Lee enabled 8,500 Americans to rout 12,000 Mexicans, inflict heavy casualties, and collect more than 3,000 prisoners.

Piatt County's centennial celebration and parade draw people from as far away as Argenta southwest in adjacent Macon County and Farmer City to the north in adjacent DeWitt County. After Mary Alice dances in costume with Ray Veech at the centennial talent show, Grandma enrages Mrs. Weidenbach by parading Uncle Grady in his Mexican War uniform. When he proves that he is the oldest citizen of the county, a fight breaks out with Mrs. Weidenbach's father, who had claimed the title for himself.

19. Fort Sheridan

In 1942, twenty-two-year-old Joey Dowdel enters military service at the beginning of U.S. involvement in World War II, which was declared the day after the Japanese bombed Pearl Harbor, Hawaii, on December 7, 1941. On his way to basic training and flight school for the Army Air Corps, he departs from Fort Sheridan, a post on Lake Michigan twenty-five miles north of Chicago. The fort bears the name of Union cavalry officer Philip H. Sheridan, a hero of the Civil War. When the United States reinstituted the draft in 1940, Fort Sheridan became a recruit reception center and training post placing inexperienced men in combat simulations.

20. Dearborn Station, Chicago, to Camp Leonard Wood, Illinois

An hour late departing from Chicago's Dearborn Station, the troop train delays for another hour at Joliet, a few miles south of Chicago. The convoy passes through Piatt County on its way to Camp Leonard Wood in south central Missouri. It is named for the World War I major general who instituted reserve training at Fort Sheridan as a means of ensuring troop readiness. Looking into the night, Joey sees Grandma's house lit up in welcome. She faithfully waves from her door.

Further Reading

Drell, Adriene, ed. *20th Century Chicago: 100 Years—100 Voices*. Chicago: Chicago Sun Times, 1999.

"Featured Author: Richard Peck," http://www.carolhurst.com/authors/rpeck.html.

Freeman, Judy, "All You Need Is LOVE." *Instructor* (January 1, 2001).

Gallo, Donald R. *Presenting Richard Peck*. Boston: Twayne, 1989.

"Interview." *School Library Journal* (June 1990): 36–40.

Kovacs, Deborah. *Meet the Authors: 25 Writers of Upper Elementary and Middle School Books Talk about Their Work*. New York: Scholastic, 1995.

"The Loop—An Architectural Guide," http://www.yelodog.com/html/loop/loop.html.

"Making the Right Choices." *Reading Today* (December 1, 2000).

"Newbery Winners," http://www.carolhurst.com/subjects/newberycaldecott00.html.

Peck, Richard, "The Ezra Jack Keats Lecture," http://www.lib.usm.edu/~degrum/jm-2000/keatslecture.html.

"Richard Peck," http://tlc.ai.org/peck.htm.

"Richard Peck," http://www.carr.lib.md.us/mae/peck.htm.

"Richard Peck Papers," http://www.lib.usm.edu/~degrum/findaids/peck.htm.

"The St. Valentine's Day Massacre," http://members.home.net/fig1/mob/events/stvalmas.htm.

Szymanski, Lois, "Richard Peck," http://www.randomhouse.com/teachers/authors/peck.html.

"The Winners' Corner." *School Library Journal* (February 1, 2001).

Wolfe, Gerard R. *Chicago in and around the Loop: Walking Tours of Architecture and History*. New York: McGraw-Hill, 1996.

Macbeth
By William Shakespeare

Historical drama, ca. 1603–1606

Geographical Summary

The milieu of William Shakespeare's biographical drama about a medieval Scottish ruler moves from northwest of the Grampian Mountains to the south between Dundee and the port city of Perth, Scotland, encompassing much of the northern part of Britain, including numerous offshore islands. Historically, Macbeth (or Maelbetha), a mid-eleventh-century Scottish king, was the son of Finlegh of Moray, Thane of Ross, and husband of Gruoch, granddaughter of Kenneth II and widowed mother of Lulach, Macbeth's stepson. Macbeth probably ruled Ross-shire from Dingwall Castle in the west highlands northwest of the Moray Firth, a wide bay of the North Sea. The land is sparsely populated and contains less than 10 percent of Scotland's population.

The rugged coastal settings suit the rise and self-ruin of an ambitious Scottish warrior who goes from thane to king through a sequence of murderous conspiracies. In the play, at the end of successful combat against Sweno and his Norwegian invaders, King Duncan presents Macbeth a new title, the Thane of Cawdor. The motif reflects a battlefield promotion, a practice of the Middle Ages, when power was often a prize awarded on the spot to those who best served a monarch. The wartime elevation of Duncan's loyal general takes the form of a quid pro quo, with Macbeth assuming the title of the former thane, who is summarily dispatched for treason. Ironically, the traitor departs his life with the respect of his peers by facing death with honor. The postcombat execution foreshadows Macbeth's death in combat as a traitor and reprehensible king, the killer of Duncan, his benefactor, and the exterminator of women, children, and servants. The actual regicide occurred on August 14, 1040, at Bothganowan, Elgin, when Scotland's King Duncan was thirty-nine.

When the king and his entourage arrive at Macbeth's castle at Inverness, the scene shifts from rough wartime dealings to indoor relaxation and entertainment. Bearing the demeanor of a polite hostess and respectful subject, Lady Macbeth appears at the castle entrance to greet guests. The comforts of Macbeth's castle please King Duncan. Ironically, in the opening lines of Act I, Scene i, he notes, "This castle hath a pleasant seat. The air nimbly and sweetly recommends itself unto our gentle senses." Banquo adds that a martlet has built a nest at Macbeth's home. As the playwright emphasizes Lady Macbeth's mockery of welcome, these beneficent omens enhance the horror of the speakers' death at the hands of her ambitious husband.

Macbeth sinks deeper into rapacity, unleashing chaos with regicide, which Macduff characterizes as an atrocity committed against the Lord's anointed. From his castle at Forres, Macbeth does not hesitate to commission the slaughter of Lady Macduff and her children and domestic staff at their home in Fife southeast of Forres, where Macduff acceded in 1054. The deed earns the new king the suspicion and distrust of those nearest the throne. The guilt Lady Macbeth bears for Duncan's assassination so charges her conscience that she haunts the castle halls by night, laboring in vain to expunge invisible blood from her hands. When she dies, Macbeth is so deep into mayhem that he is unable to mourn or even show surprise.

The usurper Macbeth's comeuppance restores to Scotland the balance that his ill-gotten reign has violated. At Macbeth's castle at Dunsinane, troops take up leafy limbs from Birnam Wood to move up Dunsinane Hill against the king's stronghold, which he believes to be impregnable. After soldiers drop their screens and advance up Dunsinane plain, Macduff reveals his birth by cesarian section, another sign that Macbeth is soon to incur a bloody downfall. At his death, Malcolm, the Prince of Cumberland and rightful heir to Duncan's throne, summons friends from exile and prepares for the traditional crowning at Scone.

Detailed Itinerary

1. A heath near Forres

A storm and battle rage simultaneously on a desert heath north of Elgin near Forres in upper Scotland on the North Sea. Three witches gather in anticipation of meeting Macbeth, the Thane of Glamis, a stronghold northeast of the Firth of Forth and Edinburgh, the nation's most populous city.

2. A camp near Forres

A battle against Norwegian insurgents concludes near Forres, a coastal capital in Grampian in north Scotland southwest of Elgin on the Moray Firth. King Duncan I the Gracious of Scotland, who succeeded his grandfather Malcolm II of Alba in 1034, is victorious over the invading Norwegians, led by Sweno (or Sueno). His name survives in Sueno's Stone, located at the east end of Forres. A twenty-three-foot sculptured monolith, it may honor the Viking military leader Sweyn, who triumphed over the Scottish king Malcolm II in 1008.

3. St. Colme's Inch

The Thane of Ross demands payment of 10,000 dollars before Sweno's casualties can be buried at Saint Colme's Inch (also called Aemonia or Inchcolm), an island in the Firth of Forth northeast of Edinburgh on the North Sea. Built by King Alexander I in 1143 after he survived a storm at sea, the Abbey of Inchcolm was an Augustinian monastery and a monument marking the hazardous lives of sailors.

4. Royal Camp near Forres

A captain reports that royal troops have crushed a traitor, the Thane of Cawdor, a Scottish lord living near Inverness in the rugged northwest highlands on the Moray Firth. The camp is strategically located at the northern end of the Caledonian Canal, which slices through Scotland's high country from northeast to southwest, separating parallel mountain ranges. The original Thane of Cawdor defamed himself by siding with Sweno and his predatory Norsemen. The playwright transposes in time a foray led by Sweyn Alfivason, son of Canute II of England and Denmark and Aelfgiva of Northampton. Sweyn was king of Norway between 1030 and 1036 during the reign of the historical Duncan's grandfather. At the same time Duncan passes judgment on the traitor, he awards Macbeth the condemned man's title.

5. Heath near Forres

Still traversing the battlefield, Macbeth has not yet heard of the promotion. He crosses the heath with Banquo, his companion and fellow soldier, and encounters three hags, who state that Macbeth has been named Thane of Cawdor and will someday rule Scotland. They predict that Banquo will never rule, but his offspring will become a Scottish dynasty.

6. Royal Camp near Forres

In the royal camp, Macbeth invites Duncan to travel west to his home, Dingwall Castle, west of Inverness to the east of the mouth of Moray Firth in northwestern Scotland. There, Duncan intends to invest his eldest son as the Prince of Cumberland, the title traditionally borne by Scotland's heir to the throne. Macbeth precedes the royal cortege to prepare a fitting welcome. All the while, Macbeth thinks of Malcolm, the king's son and heir, as an impediment to his obtaining the Scottish crown.

7. Macbeth's castle, Inverness

From her husband's battlefield message, Lady Macbeth recognizes the possibilities initiated by her husband's promotion. With letter in hand, she summarizes his character flaws and deduces that he can never attain rule because he lacks the amorality and drive to seize it outright. As the king's train approaches Inverness, she plots his murder. Lacking her murderous impulse, Macbeth agrees to regicide, but he leaves Lady Macbeth in charge of arranging the details. When Duncan and his followers arrive, Lady Macbeth graciously welcomes them with music and torches and accepts a diamond from the king. For her husband, she plots the timing and method of Duncan's assassination. Her strength emboldens Macbeth to agree to the killing.

Lady Macbeth eases Macbeth's way to the king's chamber by indulging the royal chamberlains in wine and wassail. After Macbeth stabs Duncan, he overhears the royal princes at prayer. Their piety reminds Macbeth that his ambition has damned him. Shaking with guilt, Macbeth returns to his wife, who berates him for forgetting to leave the murder weapons with the attendants. She slips out to Duncan's quarters to smear the chamberlains with blood and leave the daggers with them to implicate them falsely in the king's murder. She then directs her husband to retire for the night.

8. Gate of Macbeth's castle

The porter, roused from a drunken sleep by knocking at the gate, believes he is in hell. He allows Lennox, the king's attendant, and Macduff, the semi-legendary Thane of Fife, to enter and join Macbeth. Fleeing mayhem in the king's chamber, Macduff raises the alarm that the king has been stabbed to death. After killing the chamberlains, Macbeth calls his wife and awakens the princes, Malcolm and Donalbain, who were only ages nine and seven at the time of the historical Duncan's death. Lady Macbeth pretends to faint. In private, the king's sons realize the danger of being blamed for the king's death and fear the killer's intent to assassinate them as well. The princes flee the castle, Malcolm south to England and Donalbain west to Ireland.

9. Colmekill on the isle of Iona

Outside the castle at Inverness, Ross and an old man discuss the chaos that follows regicide. Macduff reports that Macbeth has become king in place of the royal heirs, who have fallen under suspicion of killing their father. His body has been transported west of Scotland and south of the Isle of Skye to Colmekill or St. Columba's Cell, on Iona, one of the most sacred sites in all of the British Isles. In 563, St. Columba erected Iona Abbey, north Britain's most revered motherhouse.

10. Scone, Scotland

Macduff stays at his home at Fife south of Dunsinane on the Firth of Forth on the opposite shore from Edinburgh. Ross leaves to arrange Macbeth's crowning at Scone, a village near the River Tay north of Perth. Alexander I of Scotland transformed Scone, the traditional capital of the Picts, into an Augustinian abbey in 1120. Scone once housed the Stone of Scone (also called *Lia Fail* and the Stone of Destiny), a religious symbol imported from the Holy Land. Encased in a chair of state, it was the coronation site of Scotland's kings until Edward I of England removed the stone in 1296. It passed to Westminster Abbey in London, where Scotland's James VI fulfilled prophecy by succeeding the childless Queen Elizabeth I as James I of England. Uniting England and Scotland into Great Britain, he came to power as the first Stuart monarch in 1603, about the time that Shakespeare wrote *Macbeth*.

11. Macbeth's castle, Inverness

Banquo easily figures out that Macbeth killed Duncan. He tells Macbeth that he and his son Fleance will dine at the castle after a horseback ride, which will keep Banquo out an hour or two after dark. To prevent Banquo's line from succeeding to the throne as the witches foretold, Macbeth commissions two murderers to ambush him and Fleance. In private, Macbeth and his wife reassess their hold on power as the king gives in to jitters and bad thoughts.

12. A park near Macbeth's castle, Inverness

An unidentified third assassin joins the two killers. They murder Banquo but fail to kill Fleance, who escapes.

13. Macbeth's castle, Forres

At a state banquet, the lead assassin reports to Macbeth the success of only half their mission. Banquo's ghost sits in Macbeth's chair, causing the king to babble in terror. Lady Macbeth characterizes his hallucination as a chronic malady. The diners leave after a second incident of Macbeth's gibbering at the ghost. Lennox wishes the king better health. Macbeth resolves to locate the hags on the heath to learn more about his fate.

14. Heath near Forres

Hecate, the Roman goddess of the night and witchery, directs the other weird sisters to mix a potion for Macbeth. A powerful, complex deity originating in ancient Thrace, she was a Titan who conferred on humans power, wealth, military might, and wisdom, and also imparted good fortune to hunters and seamen. Connected with the queen of the underworld, Hecate came to symbolize the infernal regions, where she judged the souls of the dead. As queen of witches and high priestess of the occult, she ruled by night, when disembodied demons served her bidding in cemeteries, on roadways, and at blood-soaked sites of violent death.

15. Near Macbeth's castle at Forres

By 1050, Macbeth's reign had turned into blatant tyranny. In Shakespeare's version, Lennox and a royal attendant meet at Forres east of Macbeth's castle to discuss the sequence of events that have cost the lives of Duncan and Banquo. Malcolm has sought refuge in England, where the saintly Edward the Confessor was crowned king in 1042. Because Macduff has sided with the defector, Lennox foretells that the English will march on Macbeth to restore Scotland to Duncan's sons, the rightful heirs to the throne.

16. A cavern on the heath near Forres

Hecate and the hags add ingredients to their concoction. When Macbeth locates them to ask about his destiny, the three witches summon a procession of apparitions. Leading them is an armed head warning Macbeth to beware Macduff. A second vision displays a bloody infant, who states that no man born of woman can harm Macbeth. The last vision, a child wearing a crown and carrying a tree, guarantees that Macbeth shall remain undefeated until Birnam Wood comes to Dunsinane.

The predictions brighten Macbeth, who concludes that he will rule unchallenged. As an afterthought, he questions the hags about Fleance. A fourth vision displays Banquo preceding eight monarchs, the last carrying a glass. Shakespeare's fanciful depiction of the Stuart line transcends history, but bears a trace of fact from Raphael Holinshed's *Chronicles of England, Scotland and Ireland* (ca. 1587), the most reliable source available to Shakespeare at the time he wrote the play. Holinshed repeated history that Hector Boece recorded in *Scotorum Historiae* (History of the Scots; ca. 1530).

The three witches disappear. From Lennox, Macbeth discovers that Macduff has defected to Malcolm in England. To assure himself of no danger from Macduff, Macbeth plans to wipe out the man's entire family and all potential heirs to Fife.

17. Macduff's castle at Fife

At Fife, a stronghold far to the southeast, a messenger warns Lady Macduff of imminent danger. Before she can flee, the king's killers slay her, the children, and the family servants.

18. King's palace, England

At a meeting in England, Malcolm sounds out Macduff's loyalties, which are obviously pro-Scottish. Offstage, the English king, Edward the Confessor, touches victims of scrofula to confer healing. Ross divulges that Macbeth has slaughtered Macduff's whole family. Macduff shrieks in rage and demands vengeance on the "hell kite." He and Malcolm resolve to overthrow Macbeth with military force.

19. Macbeth's castle at Dunsinane

At Macbeth's castle at Dunsinane, northeast of Perth on the Firth of Tay, a doctor and female attendant observe Lady Macbeth's mental decline and her episodes of sleepwalking, ravings, and obsessive wiping of imaginary blood from her hands. From her frenzies, the onlookers deduce that she is aware of her husband's murderous tyranny. Outside the castle, Malcolm, Macduff, and Siward, an aged warrior, instruct their forces to cut branches from Birnam Wood as camouflage during the army's advance up Dunsinane Hill to Macbeth's castle. Historically, in 1057 at the battle of Lumphanan, five miles northeast of Aboyne and west of Aberdeen, Malcolm Canmore, Duncan's older son and the official Prince of Cumberland, led the rebellion to reclaim his father's throne.

Inside, Macbeth relies on the witches' prophecy as proof of his safety. In consultation with Lady Macbeth's physician, the king learns that there is no explanation of her derangement. As Malcolm's soldiers ready for attack, Seyton announces the queen's demise. Macbeth has expected the news.

20. Plain of Dunsinane outside Macbeth's castle

On the plain at Dunsinane after insurgent soldiers drop their leafy screens, Macbeth turns his attention to the English march on his stronghold. The realization of the hags' prediction wilts his bravado. He battles young Siward to the death before challenging Macduff. Old Siward hands over the castle to Macduff.

Macbeth courageously faces his nemesis and dies in the duel. Macduff displays the gory head of the usurper king to the soldiers and proclaims Malcolm the rightful Scottish king. Historically, after killing Macbeth's stepson Lulach and being crowned Malcolm III, the new king and his wife, St. Margaret of Scotland, remained in power until Malcolm's death in 1093 near Alnwick during an invasion of England.

Further Reading

Bell, Robert E. *Women of Classical Mythology: A Biographical Dictionary*. Santa Barbara, Calif.: ABC-Clio, 1991.

"Birnam Wood on the Net," http://www.geocities.com/Athens/Styx/5025/index.htm.

Bloom, Harold. *Macbeth*. New York: Chelsea House, 1991.

_____. *William Shakespeare's Macbeth*. New York: Chelsea House, 1987.

Boyce, Charles. *Shakespeare A to Z*. New York: Facts on File, 1990.

"The Chatelaine's Scottish Castles: Cawdor," http://www.castles.org/Chatelaine/CAWDOR.HTM.

Claybourne, Anna, and Rebecca Treays. *The World of Shakespeare*. London: Usborne, 1996.

Illsley, J. S., "The Ship of the Later Middle Ages," http://www.history.bangor. ac.uk/shipspecial/shlect88.htm.

"James VI of Scotland," http://www.cypass.com/greenwich2000/jamesI.htm.

"Macbeth," http://weber.u.washington.edu/~engl324a/macbeth.html.

"Macbeth," http://www.falconedlink.com/falcon/Macbeth.html.

"Macbeth: An Analysis," http://tqd.advanced.org/2888.

"Macbeth Notes," http://www.emporia.edu/s/www/english/courses/shakespr/macb_lec.htm.

"Macbeth Links," http://www.glen-net.ca/english/macbeth.html.

Maclean, Fitzroy, and Magnus Linklater. *Scotland: A Concise History*. London: Thames & Hudson, 2001.

McMurtry, Jo. *Understanding Shakespeare's England*. Hamden, Conn.: Archon Books, 1989.

Pugliatti, Paolo. *Shakespeare the Historian*. New York: St. Martin's Press, 1996.

"Raphael Holinshed's Chronicles," http://jefferson.village.virg inia.edu/courses/ ennc986/class/germ3/holin.html.

Schoenbaum, Sam, ed. *Macbeth: Critical Essays*. New York: Garland, 1991.

Sinfield, Alan, ed. *Macbeth*. New York: St. Martin's Press, 1992.

Thrasher, Thomas. *The Importance of William Shakespeare.* San Diego, Calif.: Lucent Books, 1999.

"William Shakespeare" (audio), http://town.hall.org/Archives/radio/MS/Harper.Audio/020994_harp_ITH.html.

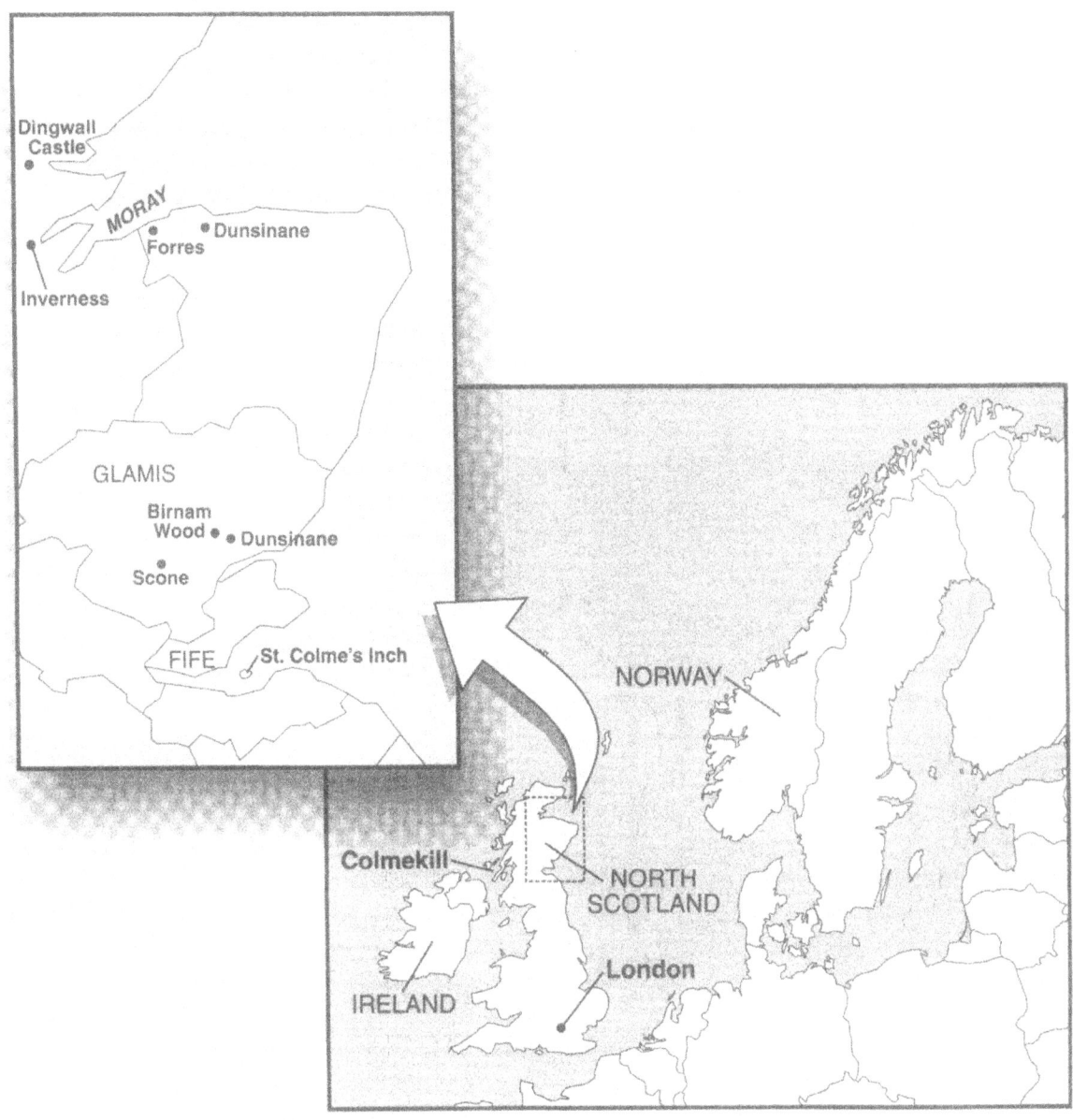

The Midwife's Apprentice
By Karen Cushman

Historical fiction, 1995

Geographical Summary

Young adult fiction writer Karen Cushman sets the story of Alyce, the midwife's apprentice, in an obscure medieval locale, probably in western England near Birkenhead and Chester in Cheshire. The time is most likely during the reign of Edward I, nicknamed Longshanks. A popular crusader king dubbed the "hammerer of the Scots," he ruled between 1272 and 1307. It is an era when young commoners lacked formal schooling and apprenticed with professionals as a means of mastering such skills as blacksmithing, baking, milling, carpentry, and midwifery.

Without a family to support or train her, Alyce, nicknamed Beetle, survives among strangers in an unnamed English village. Migrating from one warm perch to another, she manages a day at a time to earn food and a sheltered spot to sleep. From her point of view, medieval times seem difficult because of homeless wanderers living in dung heaps, infestations of fleas, venality of the clergy, and superstitions common to the uneducated. Daily tasks include washing clothes at a stream, herding livestock, grinding grain at a flour mill, harvesting hay, collecting apples, and journeying on foot to a fair to make minor purchases. From observation and the instruction of others, Alyce learns how to gather nuts and to stir up candles and soap as well as how to comfort laboring mothers and to deliver newborns, a skill she copies from her friend, farmboy Will Russet, and from Jane, her employer.

After abruptly departing midwifery, Alyce feels like a failure. She finds work at John Dark's inn, later named the Cat and Cheese, a roadside hostel with second-story kitchen, stable, and loft. Alyce serves travelers at large tables, under which they sleep for the night. At Christmas, she hangs holly and ivy from the beams, which are charred from the blaze of the fireplace that serves residents for heat and cooking. In the inn's commons room, she observes Magister Richard Reese, a scholar whose writings for an encyclopedic "Mirror of the Universe" introduce Alyce to basic education.

Passing field laborers returning with bales and implements, Alyce boldly sets out for a nearby manor to visit Edward, whose love and dependence satisfy her maternal longings. After inquiring for him among the staff, she calls at the barn and reunites with the charming six-year-old, whom she identifies as her brother. In the kitchen, the two share a supper of bread and bacon and sleep on soft straw in the corner. Edward describes how masons erect a tower out of mortar and brick. The next day at the river, Alyce renews herself with a bath, shampoo, and clean clothes before returning to the inn.

When a merchant and his ailing wife arrive from Salisbury, a great city in southern England, he identifies the woman's agony as a "stomach worm." Jennet recognizes the ailment as birth pangs and tries to help the sufferer, who lies on the inn table. To aid the laboring mother, Alyce draws on her experience in birthing chambers to attend and comfort her and deliver her son.

Her confidence restored, Alyce discovers that she can choose from several opportunities. She can return to Salisbury with the merchant and his family or travel to Oxford to aid Reese's widowed sister. She rejects the offers, gives up her job at the Cat and Cheese, and returns to the midwife's cottage to demand more training in midwifery.

Detailed Itinerary

1. Dung heap at a cottage in northwestern England

Without a home or family, Brat, a thirteen-year-old itinerant farm laborer, makes her bed in a pile of rotting garbage, straw, and dung. To her pleas for food, Jane, a sharp-tongued midwife, offers her room and board if she will assist at housework and birthings. She renames her servant Beetle. At a nearby pond, Beetle intervenes to rescue a cat that village boys try to drown in a sack. On Lady Day (March 25), the cat revives and, in exchange for a chunk of stale cheese, makes friends with Beetle and becomes her pet.

Beetle learns that the area's only midwife is Jane, the energetic mother of six children, all deceased in babyhood. Without a kind word of encouragement, she assigns Beetle to do the sweeping, roasting bacon, and dishwashing as well as the gathering of honey, medicinal herbs, leeches, and spider webs, which control bleeding. When Jane attends pregnant women, Beetle accompanies her and carries a basket of linen and herbs.

2. A Nearby Field

Before May Day (May 1), Jane's work takes her to the side of Kate, Robert Weaver's daughter and wife of Thomas the Stutterer, who suddenly goes into labor in a field. In the outdoors, Beetle observes the hard-handed delivery, which Jane accompanies with insults and harsh pushing. Intrigued, Beetle begins watching Jane's methods through windows to learn what the midwife does to bring babies into the world.

3. Near the Old North Road

That summer, Jane assigns chores to Beetle to keep her busy while Jane secretly romances the miller, a married man with thirteen children. On June 22, Beetle returns by the Old North Road from an errand at the manor dairy and angers Jane by witnessing her passionately hugging and kissing the baker. At noon, the miller's wife goes into labor. In the midwife's absence, Beetle assists the frightened woman until Jane arrives. She drags Beetle away and, for weeks, scolds her for assuming the role of midwife.

4. Fair at Gobnet-under-Green near Barry-on-the-Birkenhead

In midsummer, Jane fractures her ankle. In her place, Beetle goes to the Saint Swithin's Day Fair on July 15 at Gobnet-under-Green, a distant village that bears the name of Saint Gobnet or Gobnata of Ballyvourney, Ireland. The village lies near Barry-on-the-Birkenhead, a coastal town on the Irish Sea. In the mid-ninth century, Swithin of Winchester served Prince Ethelwulf as teacher and adviser. When the boy was crowned king, Swithin remained a court counselor and became bishop of Winchester. Farmers welcome his feast day, which supposedly brings rain to parched crops.

While running errands for Jane, Beetle recognizes goods from Cornwall and Lincoln. During the day, she enjoys puppets, singers, horse races, and fortunetellers. Late that afternoon, she returns to her shopping list and buys nutmeg, pepper, leather flasks, and the bath water of a murdered man, which the hangman sells. After a man mistakes her for Alyce, she takes the name in place of Beetle.

5. Jane's cottage in northwestern England

On Alyce's return to the cottage, Jane is unimpressed with the new name. The cat answers to Purr. Will Russet and other village ruffians try to kiss Alyce, who takes refuge in a willow at the riverbank. When the boys fail to retrieve Will from his tumble into the water, Alyce inches down a branch, which dips low enough for him to grab and slide along on his way back to safety. His admiration for her bravery extends to the whole village, even to Jane. In autumn, during a time when people fear witches and demons, Alyce takes vengeance on the people who mock and tease her. At the end of a series of strange events, Alyce tosses hoof-shaped wood blocks into the river.

6. The gravel pit on the way to the abbey gardens

In September, Alyce helps Jane make soap and brew cider and wine. Jane sends her apprentice to the nearby abbey gardens to gather apples. Before she arrives, she answers Will's call to a gravel pit and attends Tansy, his laboring cow, who had fallen in. Until late afternoon, Alyce croons wordlessly and massages Tansy's flanks to calm her. Meanwhile, Will delivers the cow's twin calves, which he names Baldred and Billfrith. The first name honors a pious saint from Glasgow, Scotland; the second names a Northumberland holy man and saint from Lindisferne who was patron of goldsmiths.

7. The bailiff's house

When Joan the bailiff's wife goes into labor, Alyce stands outside her residence in the rain until after daylight. At Jane's command, Alyce runs home to fetch pepper and herbs to make the woman sneeze out her babe. Alyce watches over Joan while Jane, intending to earn two fees, takes a call from Lady Agnes at the manor. Both babies arrive near midnight, Lady Agnes's son and Joan's daughter, whom Alyce delivers. In gratitude for a healthy babe, Joan names her child Alyce Little.

8. Manor

At Will Russet's cowshed in early November, Alyce rescues a six-year-old boy named Runt, who shivers in the cold. She feeds him parsnip tops and cheese and names him Edward after England's king, Edward I, known as Longshanks. To assure the boy a more comfortable life, she dispatches him to the manor to demand a job helping the threshers.

9. Village in northwestern England

Shortly afterward, when Emma Blunt, sister of Joan the bailiff's wife, goes into labor, Emma sends her son Matthew for Alyce. Competition from the apprentice angers Jane, who accuses Alyce of thievery and stealing patients. When the birth is still not complete at noon,

Alyce realizes that midwifery requires competence, not magic spells. On November 11, Martinmas afternoon, she sinks into despair that she is too stupid to learn how to deliver babies. Taking the road from the village, she abandons her job as midwife's apprentice.

10. Cat and Cheese Inn

The next morning, Alyce walks an hour toward the crossroads that leads west to the Irish Sea. She finds kitchen work with innkeeper John Dark and his wife Jennet, who urges Alyce to make the job permanent. Shortly before February, Magister Richard Reese sits for weeks at the inn table compiling an encyclopedia, *The Great Mirror of the Universe.* He dedicates the work to the bishop of Chester. To help her learn the alphabet, numbers, and words along with body humors, planting times, and geography, Reese pretends to teach the cat while Alyce listens. At the woodpile, she scribbles letters in the frost with a twig or writes in chimney soot. When he discards a piece of vellum ruined by an inkblot, she studies it at night to locate familiar words.

At winter's end while considering what he should accomplish next, Reese asks Alyce what she plans to do with her life. She wants a place in the world, yet degrades herself as too stupid to be the midwife's apprentice. He describes her as clever enough to read. Nonetheless, she continues doing menial chores.

In May, Reese decides to stay another season at the inn. That same month, Jane Sharp appears. Alyce watches as Jane serves Reese as an expert on midwifery and on the effectiveness of sage tea to prevent miscarriage. Reese writes in his encyclopedia her cures for excessive bleeding. Jane states that she knows her apprentice works at the inn and confides that Alyce gave up and ran away.

11. Manor

During a slow season at the inn, while Jennet buys goods at the market fair at Edenwick, Alyce visits the manor by a secret path off the road that leads to the village. Among harvesters, the smithy, maid, laundress, and carpenters, she searches for Edward, who the cook thinks is Alyce's kin. Alyce treats Edward like a son.

The next day, while workers dam the river and wash black-faced sheep, Edward assists by matching ewe with lamb. In the pleasant flow, Alyce helps until the workers depart at mid-afternoon. Upriver in clean water, she bathes and washes her hair and clothes before departing from Edward. She promises to return on Christmas, Easter, and his saint's day.

12. Cat and Cheese Inn

After riders bring a merchant's suffering wife to the inn on June 1, Alyce volunteers to aid the woman and delivers her son. The boy's father invites Alyce to live with them at Salisbury, a cathedral city in southern England on the Avon River. Suddenly, Alyce sees possibilities for her future. Reese offers her a job helping his widowed sister in Oxford, a university city northeast of Salisbury and a strategic crossroads on the western routes to London. Out of her choices, Alyce opts to continue learning midwifery. Although Jane first refuses to take her back, Alyce persists and returns to the midwife's cottage.

Further Reading

Barnhouse, Rebecca, "Review." *Voice of Youth Advocates* (August 1995): 156–57.

Butler, Alban. *Lives of the Saints*. New York: Barnes & Noble, 1997.

Cushman, Karen, "Newbery Medal Acceptance." *Horn Book* (July–August 1996): 413–19.

Flowers, Ann A., "Review." *Horn Book* (July–August 1994): 457–58.

Langton, Jane, "Review." *New York Times Book Review* (September 24, 1995): 29.

"Language," http://www.regia.org/languag.htm.

Loer, Stephanie, "An Interview with Karen Cushman," http://www/eduplace.com/recj/author/cushman/index.html.

Love, Amy Umland, "Flying Starts." *Publisher's Weekly* (July 4, 1994): 39–40.

"Medieval English Towns," http://www.trytel.com/~tristan/towns/towns.html.

"Medieval Homepage," http://www.rockyview.ab.ca/bpeak/edge/medieval.html.

"The Midwife's Apprentice," http://www.bookwire.com/pw/forecasts/childrens/midwife.html

"The Midwife's Apprentice," http://www.harpercollins.com/catalog/children/006440630x.htm.

Miller, Sara, "Review." *School Library Journal* (May 1995): 118.

Ruddy, Tom, and Laurie Ferrone, "Learning about Karen Cushman," http://www.scils.rutgers.edu/special/kay/cushman.html.

Shook, Bruce Anne, "Review." *School Library Journal* (June 1994): 147.

Snodgrass, Mary Ellen. *Who's Who in the Middle Ages*. Jefferson, N.C.: McFarland, 2000.

Stevenson, Deborah, "Review." *Bulletin of the Center for Children's Books* (June 1994): 316.

The Miracle Worker
By William Gibson

Biographical drama, 1957

Geographical Summary

Through contrasting settings, American playwright William Gibson enhances the historical encounter between Helen Adams Keller of Tuscumbia, Alabama, and a determined teacher, Johanna Mansfield "Annie" Sullivan of Feeding Hills, Massachusetts. The first glimpses of Helen place her at Ivy Green, an estate a mile northwest of Tuscumbia. The grounds consist of a driveway, gardens, a gracious porch, and an outdoor well and pump, a common kitchen yard image of the rural antebellum South.

The Kellers occupied a white clapboard house that Helen's grandfather, David Keller, built in 1820. Because of her impairment, she is at the time of the play a virtual prisoner in a dark and silent world. Her parents allow her to prey on her family like an untamed animal. Servants, parents, an older half-brother, and an aunt protect her from self-harm or menace to Mildred Keller, her infant sister.

As Helen increases in bratty, willful behavior, she meets her nemesis in Annie, an indigent state ward of Massachusetts. In her early twenties, Annie adapted to trachoma, a chronic bacterial eye infection she contracted at age five. After the death of her mother, Alice Cloesy Sullivan, Annie entered the poorhouse at Tewksbury northwest of Boston.

Annie's recollections of a squalid childhood flash back to a substandard orphanage that also housed the elderly and insane. Six months later, her brother Jimmie, two years her junior, died of a tubercular hip. In 1880, she entered the Perkins Institute for the Blind in Boston, which opened in 1832 as the nation's first educational facility for blind children.

In flight from permanent dependence, Annie borrows ticket money from school director Dr. Michael Anagnos, an educator from Epirus, Greece, who recommends her for a job teaching Helen Keller. Annie travels by train southwest to Tuscumbia, Alabama. Among the Kellers, the dining room becomes no man's land as Helen exploits the sympathy and indulgence of her family. As staff members serve a meal, Helen rages and disrupts normal conversation and polite sharing of platters. By sniffing, grasping, and gobbling, she forces her three normal senses—smell, touch, and taste—to compensate for sight and hearing. To combat the lack of discipline that destroys family harmony, Annie retreats to her room to plot a strategy that will open the world to Helen.

Annie travels a short distance to the Keller summerhouse, where Helen must learn manners and courtesy. Living apart from her family for two weeks, she experiences her milieu reduced to familiar toys and furniture. The only recognizable beings are Belle, the family setter, and Annie. Unpampered all of her waking hours, she suppresses physical and emotional urges while acquiring patience, appropriate demeanor, and a workable communication system. At the end of the trial, Annie deserves credit for a promising beginning but no lasting victory.

Returned to a chaotic mealtime scene amid adoring family, Annie rages at Helen's regression into childish self-indulgence. The family insists that Helen enjoy her favorite foods. Annie determines to end the family's collusion in keeping Helen dependent. By forcing Helen to the yard to pump water into a pitcher, Annie makes her recognize the link between abstract letters of the alphabet and the words they spell.

Detailed Itinerary

1. Helen Keller's room at Ivy Green near Tuscumbia, Alabama

In December 1881, Captain Arthur H. Keller, a bewhiskered Confederate veteran, local marshal, and newspaper publisher, hovers over his daughter's crib at Ivy Green at Tuscumbia, a small Alabama town. An elderly physician attends nineteen-month-old Helen as she fights scarlet fever. Alone with the baby, Keller's second wife, Kate Adams Keller, tests the child's reactions to a lighted lamp and snap of the fingers and screams that Helen is blind and deaf.

2. Pump in the yard at Ivy Green

Five years later, two black children, Martha and Percy are playmates for Helen, a disheveled child enjoying paper dolls. She is confused by conversations she can neither see nor hear. She gropes Percy's lips and tongue to study the purpose of their movement. He bites her fingers, which she puts to her own lips. Raging out of control, Helen knocks Martha to the ground and snatches up the scissors. Percy runs to the porch to summon Kate.

3. Living room at Ivy Green

Kate hurries to Helen to supervise her use of the scissors. Aunt Ev urges Keller to take Helen to Dr. Chisholm, an oculist in Baltimore. After previous consultations with doctors in Alabama and Tennessee, Keller has lost hope of a medical miracle and stifles his son James, who proposes that the family send Helen to an asylum for the mentally defective.

Helen feels the head and limbs of her doll and notes the absence of eyes. In search of material, she yanks two buttons from Aunt Ev's dress, then dumps Mildred out of the crib to create a place for her doll. Although Kate restores order, she realizes that Helen needs a controlled education. Finally Keller agrees to write to the doctor in Baltimore.

4. Tewksbury, Massachusetts

Because of her poverty and partial blindness from trachoma, Annie Mansfield Sullivan, a bright single woman born to a poor Irish family in Feeding Hills, Massachusetts, grew up at the state almshouse at Tewksbury. Legislators originally intended it as an infirmary for victims of tuberculosis and other infectious diseases. Opened on May 1, 1854, as a shelter for immigrant paupers, it exceeded its capacity of five hundred in seven days. Seven months later, 2,193 indigents overran its facilities.

Annie mourns the death of her brother, Jimmie Sullivan, who was separated from her in the men's ward. Later, she describes for Keller and his wife the building's abysmal conditions—rats, tubercular and epileptic patients, prostitutes, sexual opportunism against the young, unwed mothers, abandoned babies, alcoholics in the throes of withdrawal, and insanity. For entertainment, Annie and Jimmie played in the dead house until the staff could bury corpses.

5. Perkins Institution for the Blind, Boston, Massachusetts

In Boston at the Perkins Institution for the Blind in spring 1887, Dr. Anagnos confers with Dr. Alexander Graham Bell, an expert in deaf education, on methods of training Helen. Anagnos recommends twenty-year-old Annie, a recent graduate, as a worthy governess and teacher. In private, Anagnos urges her to be humble. He lends her train fare, which she will repay from a monthly salary of $25.

6. Ivy Green near Tuscumbia, Alabama

Dressed in a pinafore, Helen snoops through the upstairs guest room. Frustrated in a disorderly home, Keller rages that Annie's arrival delays dinner.

7. Depot, Tuscumbia, Alabama

Annie, who has been on the train from Boston for several days, arrives armed with a suitcase and copy of the Perkins report. James retrieves her trunk. She is eager for a first glimpse of her pupil. Kate is courteous but dubious about Annie's ability to manage Helen. Annie offers as credentials her own limited vision, her youth, and the mastery of the writings of Dr. Samuel Gridley Howe, founder of the Perkins Institute for the Blind.

8. Annie Sullivan's upstairs room

On the porch at Ivy Green, Helen gropes Annie with her fingertips, then examines her suitcase and helps carry it to her room upstairs on the corner. Kate informs her husband that Annie has had nine eye operations, which restored partial sight. Keller stereotypes Annie as an inexperienced Yankee.

Meanwhile, Annie gives Helen the suitcase key. Displaying love for the doll, Helen rocks it. Annie finger-spells "doll" into Helen's hand, employing a method invented by Spanish monks under a vow of silence. Laura Dewey Bridgman, a seven-year-old, blind–deaf mute from Hanover, New Hampshire, first demonstrated it as a means of communication for the handicapped in 1837.

Intrigued by a new hand game, Helen repeats the meaningless finger manipulation. Grabbing the doll, Helen strikes Annie in the jaw, locks the door to her room, and departs. Annie, minus a tooth, waits for the family to discover her predicament.

9. Almshouse in Tewksbury, Massachusetts

Annie flashes back to her childhood at the poorhouse and relives Jimmie's suffering and death.

10. Annie Sullivan's upstairs room

While servants gawk, Keller retrieves Annie through her bedroom window and carries her down a ladder. Below, Helen plucks the bedroom key from her mouth and drops it into the well. Kate is curious about finger spelling. Annie promises to teach her the alphabet the next morning.

11. Keller dining room

At breakfast the following day, while a battle of wills rages between teacher and student, James discusses the capitulation of Vicksburg, Mississippi, a strategic point on the cliffs of Mississippi River during the Civil War. General Ulysses S. Grant's capture of the city on July 4, 1863, was a major victory for the Union army and a boost to morale on the nation's eighty-seventh anniversary.

Annie dismisses the family to counter spoiling and the resultant mealtime tantrums. In a private face-off, Annie forces Helen to eat from a plate with a spoon and to fold her napkin. The morning's instructions in manners leaves the dining room a shambles and Annie sore and unkempt. Kate weeps at Annie's success in teaching Helen rudimentary table manners.

12. Annie Sullivan's upstairs room, Tuscumbia, Alabama

Annie returns upstairs to reminisce about Jimmie. Certain she will be fired from her first job, she repacks the suitcase. Kate intervenes with her disgruntled husband, who condemns Annie's methods and insists on discharging her.

13. Garden house, Tuscumbia, Alabama

At the garden house away from the Keller home, Kate worries that Helen may have to live out her years in an asylum, a fate that dismays Annie. Kate persuades Keller to let Annie lay siege to Helen's barbaric behaviors while maintaining complete control of her for two weeks. By using the garden house as an isolated classroom, Helen can concentrate on lessons without family interference. The Kellers will furnish the building and transport Helen's belongings and toy box from the house.

After a two-hour buggy ride, Helen arrives at an unfamiliar building. At first, Helen resists Annie's attempt to spell words into her palm. Annie arouses jealousy in Helen by teaching Percy finger spelling. In her garden retreat, Helen learns to crochet and eat with a spoon and masters eighteen nouns and three verbs. By 6:00 p.m. at the end of the fourteen-day trial, Helen is well behaved. Annie asks for an extension of the agreed time, but Keller refuses. Annie feels defeated. In gratitude for Helen's cleanliness and polite behavior, Keller pays her $25.

14. Keller dining room, Tuscumbia, Alabama

After Keller escorts Annie to the dining room, Helen disarms the family with her sedate demeanor. At dinner, she tests the adults. Because she tosses water from a pitcher, Annie insists that she refill it. At Aunt Ev's insistence, Keller tries to stop the confrontation, but James and Kate support Annie.

15. Pump outside the Keller house

After dragging Helen across the porch to the pump, Annie makes her refill the pitcher. Annie spells *water* into Helen's hand. Recalling "wah wah," Helen recognizes the alphabet as a means of communication. Gleefully, Helen rings the bell to summon the family and identifies members by words.

Historically, 1887 was a pivotal year for Helen Keller and Annie Sullivan. Helen mastered 625 words in her first six months of education; Annie improved her vision with additional surgery. At age nine, Helen's first journey from home took her to the Perkins Institute from 1889 to1893. Her second year in Boston, she learned to speak at the local Horace Mann School for the Deaf. In her last year at school, she visited the Columbia Exposition in Chicago with Dr. Alexander Graham Bell.

Helen continued her studies at the Wright-Humason Oral School in New York City in 1894, the year she published a biographical treatise, *Light in My Darkness*. Two years later, she entered the Cambridge School for Young Ladies in Cambridge, Massachusetts, to study history, English, German, Latin, and math. Two years after graduation, simultaneous with the publication of *The Story of My Life* (1902), she entered Radcliffe College in Cambridge to study economics, the Bible, philosophy, and Shakespeare. In her junior year, she published *Optimism* (1903) and graduated cum laude in 1904.

Supported by a stipend from Andrew Carnegie, Helen helped found the Massachusetts Commission for the Blind on July 13, 1906, and served as one of the first five members. She became a familiar spokeswoman for the handicapped, women, and peace. Still influenced by Annie Sullivan, who married Harvard educator and literary critic John Albert Macy in 1905, Helen lived with the Macys at a farmhouse in Wrentham, Massachusetts, and rallied support for women's suffrage and socialism. She continued writing, publishing *The World I Live In* (1908), *The Song of the Stone Wall* (1910), and *Out of the Dark* (1913).

Helen traveled the world as an advocate for the blind and deaf. In 1915, she appeared at the San Francisco Exposition and initiated Helen Keller International, a charity assisting the rehabilitation of Allied soldiers blinded in World War I. She championed new methods of educating the deaf and blind and published articles in *Atlantic Monthly*, *Home*, *Ladies Home Journal*, *McClures*, and *Youth's Companion*. She joined other suffragists in establishing the American Civil Liberties Union, headquartered in New York City in 1917. In 1921, she launched a fundraising lecture series for the American Foundation for the Blind, which she helped found.

For humanitarian aid to the American Foundation for the Blind, the American Foundation for Overseas Blind, and the Helen Keller Endowment Fund, Helen earned global thanks. One admirer, First Lady Eleanor Roosevelt, named Helen "America's Goodwill Ambassador." Helen received a Legion of Honor, an achievement award from Radcliffe, and ribbons and medals from numerous foreign states. Her childhood home, Ivy Green, became a national shrine and has been the venue of summer enactments of *The Miracle Worker* since its debut in 1962.

Further Reading

"Academy Awards for Writing, 1960s and 1970s," www.host.ballet.cit.gu.edu/ Movies/Oscars/1960writing.html, December 19, 1996.

"Annie Mansfield Sullivan Macy," http://www.afb.org/afb/fs_asm.html.

Dash, Joan. *The World at Her Fingertips: The Story of Helen Keller*. New York: Scholastic, 2001.

"Helen Keller International," http://www.hki.org.

"Helen Keller Papers," http://www.afb.org/archives/papers/papers.html.

Herrmann, Dorothy. *Helen Keller: A Life*. New York: Alfred A. Knopf, 1998.

Howell, Julie, "The Life of Helen Keller," http://www.rnib.org.uk/wesupplyfctsheet/keller.htm, 1998.

"Ivy Green," http://helenkellerbirthplace.org/Grounds/grounds.html.

Keller, Helen, "Speech, Lions International Convention," www.uark/ALADDIN/flions/hk.html, December 19, 1996.

Kudlinski, Kathleen V. *Helen Keller: A Light for the Blind.* New York: Viking Kestrel, 1989.

"Official Alabama Outdoor Drama: The Miracle Worker," www.asc.edu/archives/emblems/stodram.html, December 19, 1996.

Sabin, Francene. *The Courage of Helen Keller.* New York: Troll Associates, 1998.

Schuur, Diane, "The Miracle: Helen Keller." *Time* (June 14, 1999).

"Tewksbury Hospital," http://www.publichealthmuseum.org/tewk-grounds.html.

Walker, Pam. *Helen Keller.* New York: Children's Press, 2000.

"Writings by Helen Keller," http://www.afb.org/info_documents.asp?kitid=84&collectionid=1

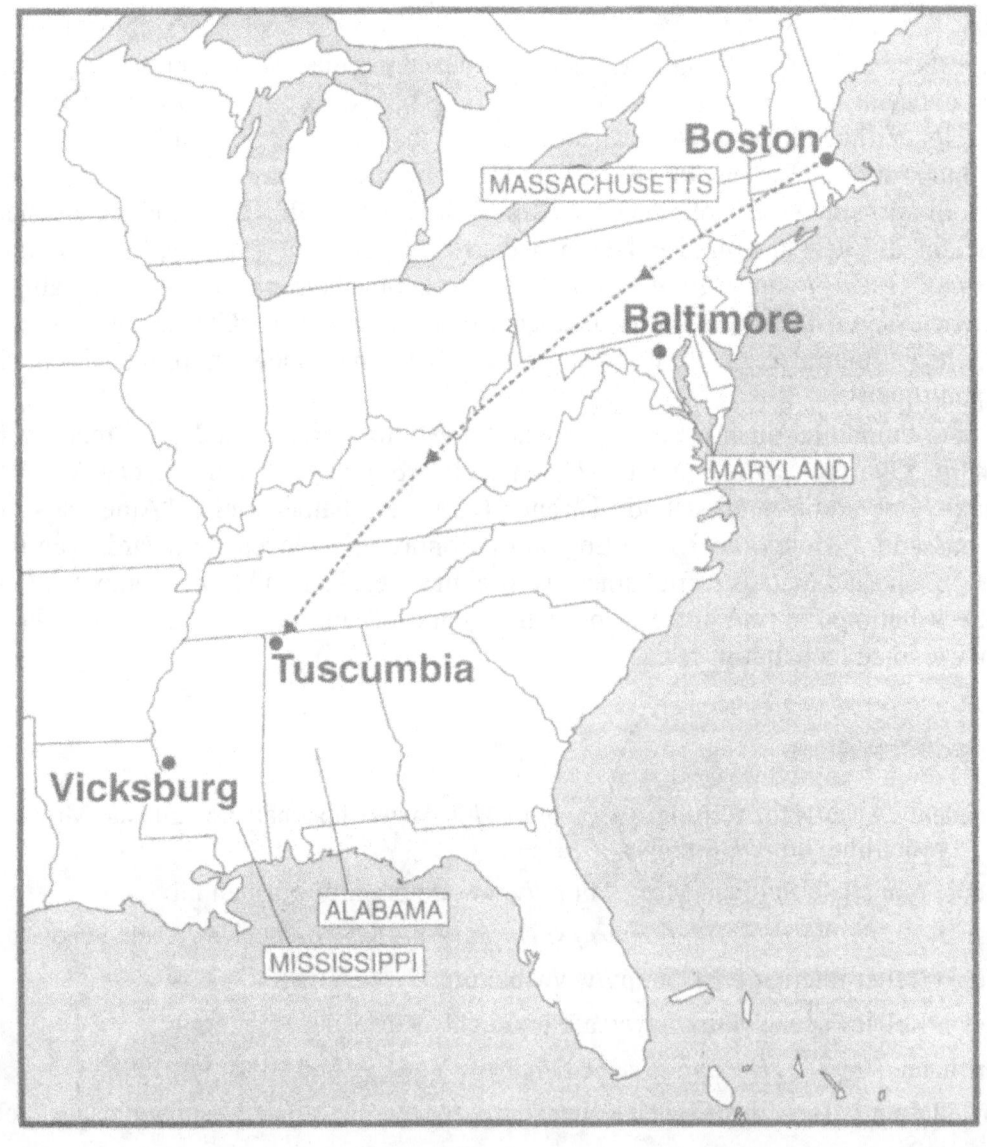

Moby Dick
By Herman Melville

Classic literary fiction, 1851

Geographical Summary

Setting out from New England, the whaling capital of North America since 1650, Herman Melville's fictional Ahab covers the global route of the nineteenth-century whaler. He progresses from the Western Hemisphere east across the Atlantic and Indian oceans toward the Pacific Ocean, where whalers first penetrated in 1790. The novel covers the epic voyage through a single eyewitness, Ishmael, the lone survivor of the last voyage of the *Pequod*. This New England whaling vessel was named for the Pequot (or Pequoit), a tribe of Algonquian-speaking Indians native to New London County, Connecticut.

Set in New Bedford, the opening chapters of *Moby Dick* summarize the uncertainty of a sailor's land existence in seacoast towns, bars, and inns among fellow seamen while the ship's mate hires more crew. Ishmael, the biblical wanderer, and tattooed harpooner Queequeg worship at a Whaleman's Chapel and observe Ramadan. After a few days of shore leave with local people during re-rigging and supplying, the *Pequod* sets sail on Christmas Day on a three-year voyage following whales migrating over the deep.

At sea, the setting focuses on the rhythm of work time, relaxation, and interaction among shipmates during the chasing and harpooning of sperm whales. The text follows the slicing of flesh and stripping of valuable oils, the source of income that sailors share. Because Captain Ahab's interest lies in vengeance rather than in the money his whale oil will bring, his faithful men must hold to the predetermined course, even during gales and a typhoon. Only the faithful mate Starbuck dares rebuke Ahab for his monomania. The natural setting dominates Ahab as he literally sniffs out Moby Dick southeast of Japan along the Equator.

Without pause, the *Pequod* plows the sperm whale hunting grounds in search of Moby Dick. No encounter with other ships and crews can dim Ahab's quest for vengeance. The lengthy course from New Bedford ends after a loop through Sumatra, Java, Formosa, and Japan. In the end, the vindictive whale ensnares and drowns Ahab and swims in circles to create a vortex that sinks the *Pequod*. The narrator Ishmael, clings to Queequeg's coffin, ironically adapted by the ship's carpenter into a lifeboat. After two days of bobbing on the sea, Ishmael gladly takes up residence on the *Rachel* after the *Pequod* vanishes.

Detailed Itinerary

1. New Bedford, Massachusetts

In December, Ishmael, a common sailor, departs "the insular city of the Manhattoes," a nation of Algonquian-speaking Indians on the north end of Manhattan. Ishmael continues northeast toward the great American whaling port, New Bedford, at the mouth of the Acushnet River. Ishmael misses the packet boat to Nantucket, an island twenty-eight miles south of Cape Cod, where the right whale regularly cruised close to land as it migrated north to the Gulf of St. Lawrence. Nantucket is the natural harbor from which North American whaling began. It and other New England ports, which Melville describes as "monopolizing the business of whaling," thrived when the demand for whale oil rose after the War of 1812. From thirty-eight whalers shipping out in 1816, the number increased to 722 when whaling peaked in 1846.

With two days to wait, Ishmael takes a room at Peter Coffin's Spouter Inn, a gabled building named for the geyser erupting from a whale's blowhole. Ishmael shares a bed with Queequeg, a cannibal, idol worshipper, and experienced harpooner from Rokovoko who sailed from home on a ship bound from Sag Harbor, New York.

While walking the town the next morning, Ishmael observes a multicultural community built on the wealth of the whaling industry. In the Whaleman's Chapel, a plaque names sailors killed or missing at sea. Father Mapple, the chaplain, mounts the chapel's rope ladder to a beaked pulpit to recount the story of Jonah and the whale.

2. Nantucket, Massachusetts

Back at the inn, Ishmael, a Presbyterian, finds Queequeg whittling on the pagan idol, named Yojo. At bedtime, they chat and smoke while Queequeg narrates his life. Aboard the *Moss*, they sail down the Acushnet River. After interviewing with captains Peleg and Bildad, Ishmael enlists on the *Pequod*, to which he brings Queequeg.

On board, the moody Captain Ahab departs from a young wife, whom he married when he was fifty. He continues his forty-year career at sea after recovering from the loss of a leg from the hip down to the bite of a whale. It bears the name Moby Dick, perhaps drawn from Jeremiah Reynolds's book *Mocha Dick, or the White Whale of the Pacific* (1839), an account of a Nantucket man who killed a seventy-foot whale that yielded one hundred barrels of clear oil. Melville appears to have drawn on two details—a seriously scarred body and some twenty harpoons piercing the whale's back. Other historical whaling memoirs tell of boat-eating whales and one animal that, in August 1819, sank the *Essex,* a Nantucket ship, one thousand miles from the Marquesas Islands.

Elijah tries to dissuade the two men from signing on with Ahab. After a night at the Try Pots, named for the boilers that extract oil from whale blubber, Ishmael and Queequeg board at 6:00 A.M. While Ahab remains out of sight, the crew assembles as Chief Mate Starbuck rises from his bunk.

3. Azores in the Atlantic Ocean

At noon on a cold Christmas Day, the *Pequod* sets out east from Nantucket toward the Azores, a Portuguese island cluster north of the Equator. Ishmael introduces Starbuck, an earnest Nantucket Quaker, along with second mate Stubb, from Cape Cod, and third mate Flask, a whaler from Tisbury who despises all whales.

4. Cape de Verdes off the Northwest Coast of Africa

Several days later, Ahab emerges from his cabin as the *Pequod* swings south. He paces ominously and steadies himself by slipping his peg leg into auger holes in the quarterdeck. He offers an ounce of Spanish gold for the sailor who sights the crook-jawed white whale with three holes in his right fluke. At his sea charts, Ahab plots the complex course of sperm whales. Ishmael learns that Moby Dick is known to attack whalers. The thought of pursuing him in a light boat is terrifying.

5. From the Azores and Cape de Verdes islands to the Rio de la Plata to the Carrol Ground and the Cape of Good Hope off the southern tip of Africa

The ship progresses over a standard route—from the Azores south toward the Cape de Verdes (Cape Verde Islands), a chain of volcanic islands in the Atlantic. The crew enjoys the easy weeks spent crisscrossing the southern Atlantic Ocean toward Africa from Rio de la Plata—called the "Plate"—an estuary of the Paraná and Uruguay rivers between Argentina and Uruguay. The *Pequod* sails east to Carrol Ground, southeast of St. Helena, a volcanic island in the South Pacific discovered by the Portuguese before becoming an English crown colony. It earned fame as the home of the exiled Napoleon Bonaparte from 1815 until his death on May 5, 1821. At midnight, the harpooner Fedallah makes the second sighting of a celestial plume of water outlined by moonlight. More mystical sightings of a solitary waterspout lead the crew to the Cape of Good Hope, which Ishmael calls "Cape Tormentoto," a major obstacle to whalers departing the Atlantic Ocean.

6. Crozetts in the Southern Indian Ocean

At the Crozetts, rugged French islands in the south Indian Ocean southeast from the Cape of Good Hope, the *Pequod* passes the *Albatross*. Ahab requests that the captain have his mail forwarded to the Pacific Ocean. Ahab determines to sail around the world in pursuit of Moby Dick. Intent on the prey, he avoids gamming, the practice of socializing with other whalers the *Pequod* passes along their route. Gamming was a natural instinct to men who had been at sea for months and could last several days while crews caught up on events, traded newspapers, and shared supplies, feasts, music, and dance. The approach required a skillful pilot at the wheel and a good judge of winds and current. On the second day in the southern Indian Ocean northeast from the Crozetts, the crew spots right whales named by whalers who considered it the "right" whale for its oil.

7. Java, Indonesia

The *Pequod* heads northeast toward Java, one of the line of Great Sunda Islands off the narrow Malaccan peninsula from Birmah (Burma) along with Bally, Sumatra, and Timor. Daggoo, an African whaler, spots the white whale. The next day, Ishmael points out a large sperm whale, a lucrative prey initially stalked in 1712, when a Nantucket whaler killed the first example and extracted spermaceti and a waxy oil that became more lucrative than the oil of the right whale. Pursuit of the free-ranging sperm whale led expeditions into warm Pacific climes, where blubber tended to rot. By 1760, whalers were stalking the sperm whale and rendering the fat from their flesh in try-works, brick ovens on board ship that ended the need to tow an unwieldy carcass to port.

Stubb kills the right whale with a lance thrust to the heart. On Sunday morning, the crew begins hoisting the carcass with block and tackle. They remove blubber with a hook by twirling the whale in water like an orange being peeled. Deckhands boil the skin to extract its oil while sharks and seabirds pick the carcass. As Ahab regards the gory head, a crewman sights the sail of the *Jeroboam* off the starboard bow. Captain Mayhew reports that Moby Dick killed Harry Macey, his mate. Gabriel, a deranged crewman, rows near and predicts that the whale will kill Ahab.

8. Cockatoo Point, Sumatra

The *Pequod* passes through the Strait of Sundra, which links the Indian Ocean with the Java Sea. The ship moves steadily northward by the Philippine Islands toward the west coast of Japan. Now in Moby Dick's home territory, the crew pursues a whale herd but captures only one whale. As the crew gives chase, they entangle Pip, the cabin boy, in the line. Stubb orders Tashtego to cut him loose, thus costing them a whale. The second time the boy snares himself in line, he bobs in the water while the men purse to more quarry. By the time they free Pip, he is insane.

9. To Japan and southeast toward the equator

Upon meeting the *Samuel Enderby* bound from London, Ahab converses with Captain Boomer, who lost an arm to Moby Dick because the harpoons in the whale's side slashed open the captain's flesh. Ahab claims the irons. Boomer saw the whale twice more but gave up chasing the cursed beast. Ahab quickly follows the *Samuel Enderby's* crew, who direct him southeast toward the Equator. Because the visit to the *Samuel Enderby* jeopardized Ahab's ivory peg leg, he has the ship's carpenter replace it with a substitute made of jaw ivory.

10. Formosa

The *Pequod* travels north to the Bashee (now Bashi or Bachi) Islands in the north Philippine chain, then continues toward Formosa. When the ship nears land, Ahab brandishes a musket at his first mate, who wants to stop for a week to repair leaky casks. Starbuck warns Ahab to beware his faults.

11. South Sea

The *Pequod* presses on northeast into the South Sea. Ahab determines to craft a suitable harpoon to kill Moby Dick.

12. Japan

Off Japan, the *Pequod* encounters a pleasant calm and summery weather. Toward the Japanese islands of Matsmai (Matsumae), Niphon (Nippon), and Sikoke (Shikoku), Melville describes the area as serene waters. On meeting the *Bachelor* from Nantucket, Ahab's sailors learn that the crew is rich in whale oil and heads back for New England. Ahab continues southeast toward the Equator after Moby Dick and captures four whales.

On the Japanese Sea, omens presage disaster. Ahab brandishes his harpoon and vows to hunt Moby Dick to the end of his strength. Starbuck considers shooting the captain with a musket, but is too honest to mutiny or murder the senior officer. The next morning, Ahab accuses the helmsman of lying about the ship's course. After striking him, the captain discovers that the typhoon disrupted the compass needle. He fashions a replacement from a steel lance point.

The next day, the crew of the *Rachel* reports spotting the white whale the previous day. The captain relates that the whale pulled his fastest boat under, drowning his son. When the captain requests the use of the *Pequod* for forty-eight hours, Ahab refuses to search for the boat and orders his crew to follow Moby Dick. For four days, they chase the whale.

On meeting the *Delight,* Ahab discovers that the whale attacked a longboat and killed five sailors. Starbuck begs him to return to Nantucket, but Ahab raves on. On the first night of the chase, he scents Moby Dick before the watchman locates him. The vengeful whaler pursues him for an hour; the whale bites the boat in two, forcing Ahab into the sea. When his men rescue him, he claims the doubloon but leaves it nailed to the mast until Moby Dick dies.

The next morning, the men have a second chance to spear Moby Dick, which again overturns Ahab's boat. On the third morning, Ahab spies the whale and leads the whalers in pursuit. After he plunges a steel harpoon into the white body, the whale sounds, then ascends, lifting into view the hapless Fedallah, enmeshed in harpoon ropes on Moby Dick's flank. In a final strike, Ahab tangles himself about the neck. The maddened whale circles the *Pequod,* creating a vortex that draws it under. Ishmael, the only survivor, floats aboard the coffin life buoy for a day until the *Rachel* picks up him.

Further Reading

Davis, Clark. *After the Whale: Melville in the Wake of Moby-Dick*. Tuscaloosa: University of Alabama, 1995.

Del Tredici, Robert. *Floodgates of the Wonderworld: A Moby-Dick Pictorial Celebrating the 150th Anniversary of Melville's Masterwork*. Kent, Ohio: University of Kent State Press, 2001.

Golding, William. *Herman Melville*. New York: Chelsea House, 1989.

"Herman Melville Online," http://www.melville.org/download.htm.

"The History of the Name Pequod," http://www.flash.net/~pthomp1/mason.htm.

Levine, Robert S., ed. *The Cambridge Companion to Herman Melville*. Cambridge: Cambridge University Press, 1998.

Mawer, Granville Allen. *Ahab's Trade: The Saga of South Sea Whaling*. New York: St. Martin Press, 2000.

"Moby Dick Literary Map," http://www.loc.gov/exhibits/treasures/images/1831s.jpg.

Norling, Lisa. *Captain Ahab Had a Wife: New England Women and the Whalefishery, 1720–1870*. Chapel Hill: University of North Carolina Press, 2000.

Paddock, Carl, and Lisa Paddock. *Herman Melville A to Z: The Essential Reference to His Life and Work*. New York: Facts on File, 2001.

Parker, Hershel. *Herman Melville: A Biography*. Baltimore: Johns Hopkins University Press, 1996.

Rollyson, Carl, and Lisa Paddock. *Herman Melville A to Z*. New York: Checkmark Books, 2001.

Selby, Nick, and Richard Beynon, eds. *Herman Melville: Moby-Dick*. New York: Columbia University Press, 1999.

Severin, Timothy. *In Search of Moby Dick: Quest for the White Whale*. New York: G. K. Hall, 2001.

Spencer, Duncan, "Wreck of the Whaleship That Spawned Moby-Dick," *Insight on the News*, September 20, 1999.

Stein, Suzanne. *The Pusher and the Sufferer: An Unsentimental Reading of "Moby Dick."* New York: Garland, 2000.

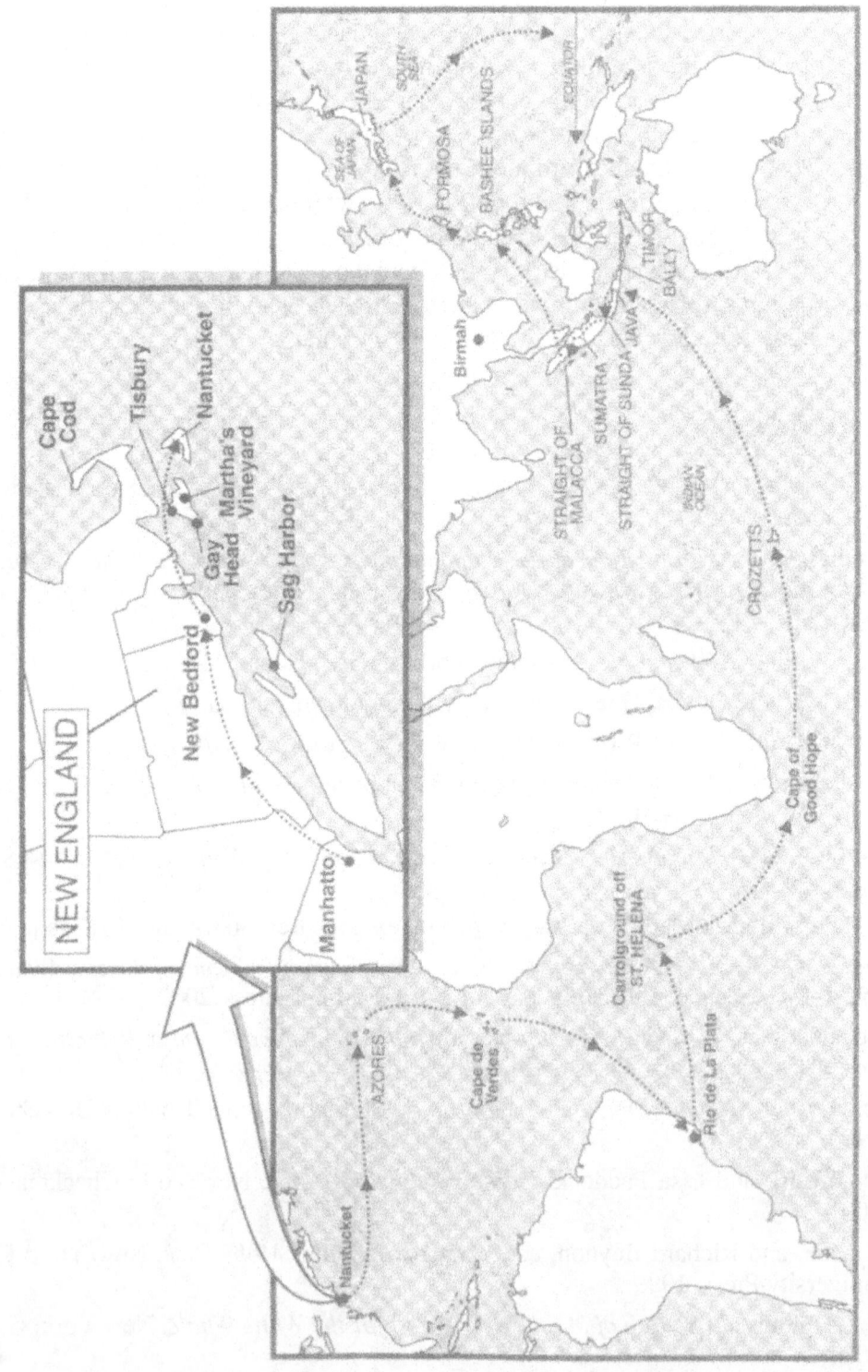

Monster

By Walter Dean Myers

Contemporary mainstream fiction, 1999

Geographical Summary

Walter Dean Myers's fictional protagonist, Steve Harmon, a contemplative sixteen-year-old student at New York City's Stuyvesant High School, composes an intimate confessional journal of his incarceration and trial for robbery and felony murder. He summarizes his experience in the style of a screenplay, complete with credits, voiceovers, and camera and sound direction. The focus of his jailing is the miserable cell of the Manhattan Detention Center at 125 White Street just north of Manhattan Criminal Court, where Steve is transported by prison van to await trial. Called the Tombs, the grim detention center comprises north and south towers connected by a bridge.

Before and after his arrest and trial, many of Steve's activities take place near home in the projects of Harlem, an area north of Manhattan that was beloved by author Walter Dean Myers. Although born in Martinsburg, West Virginia, after his mother's death in childbirth, Myers passed into the care of family friends living in Harlem. He acclimated well to the urban setting, where he attended church and school and played stoopball and Chinese handball with his pals. He recalled treasuring the George Bruce Branch of the public library, where he could read for free. For its meticulous background in law enforcement and verisimilitude of life in the Harlem projects, Dean's young adult novel *Monster* won the Michael L. Printz Award for Excellence in Young Adult Literature; the audio version from Listening Library received the 2000 Audio Earphones Award.

Detailed Itinerary

1. Cell Block D, Manhattan Detention Center, New York City

On July 6, sixteen-year-old Steve Harmon describes his life after his incarceration on suspicion of complicity in robbery and felony murder, for which prosecutor Sandra Petrocelli, assistant district attorney for the state of New York, seeks the death penalty. He dresses carefully for a court appearance, but he is too nervous to eat breakfast.

2. New York City Criminal Court Building

Taken by prison van from jail to the courthouse off Park Row and White Street in the Soho district of southern Manhattan, Steve enters the back door of the building. Guards lead him to the trial location. Handcuffed to the U-bolt on a bench, Steve watches the setup of guards and a stenographer and observes the bored judge, who has just returned from a Fourth of July break.

3. Stuyvesant High School

Steve flashes back to a film workshop led by club mentor George Sawicki at Stuyvesant High School, a high-profile public school at 345 East Chambers Street. The school opened on September 12, 1904, to provide college-prep and vocational courses. It earned a reputation for preparing gifted students for entry in the best universities and colleges. In September 1992, the school acquired a multimillion-dollar building in Battery Park City. The new setting provided computer labs and robotics shops to students of varying socioeconomic backgrounds. Located in the Stuyvesant Historic District, the school bears the name of Peter Stuyvesant, the last Dutch director-general of New York.

4. New York City Criminal Court Building

Sandra Petrocelli informs the jury that teen killers are monsters and describes the robbery and murder of Alguinaldo Nesbitt at his drugstore on Malcolm X Boulevard the previous year on December 22 at 4:00 P.M.. She charges Steve with being the lookout for the thieves, James King and Bobo Evans. Kathy O'Brien, Steve's attorney, charges that there is reasonable doubt Steve had any part in the crime.

5. Malcolm X Boulevard, Harlem

A major witness is José Delgado, an employee at Alguinaldo Nesbitt's drugstore. José testifies that on the day of the crime, he left the store around 4:35 P.M. for dinner and returned to find Nesbitt dead and five cartons of cigarettes stolen. A segment of Lenox Avenue as it passes the historic district of Harlem, Malcolm X Boulevard honors Malcolm Little, a native of Omaha, Nebraska, who established a ministry for the Nation of Islam.

6. Riker's Island

A second witness, Salvatore Zinzi, reports that he was incarcerated at Riker's Island, a penal colony in the East River due north of La Guardia Airport, Queens. He heard another prisoner, Wendell Bolden, claim to know who committed the crime. Zinzi called Detective Gluck and confided that Bolden got two cartons of the stolen cigarettes. On cross-examination, Zinzi admits being arrested for intending to deal dope and explains that he got cigarettes on December 24 from Bobo Evans, who helped James King rob the drugstore.

7. 141st Street, Harlem

A flashback has Steve Harmon talking with James King at a porch on 141st Street. With friends Peaches and Johnny, the two discuss committing a "getover" against an illegal alien.

8. Cell Block D, Manhattan Detention Center, New York City

The night of July 7, Steve hears a sexual attack on an inmate. The next day, Steve lets fellow inmate Sunset read his screenplay and receives a visit from a preacher in the afternoon.

9. Queens; New York University Law School
Steve worries that his lawyer, Kathy O'Brien, is losing hope of winning. He knows that she is from Queens, the borough east of Manhattan, and graduated from New York University Law School, a respected professional school in Greenwich Village. The lower Manhattan address is separated both geographically and culturally from Steve's mostly black milieu in Harlem.

10. Manhattan Detention Center, New York City
That afternoon, Mr. Harmon comforts his son in the visitation area but leaves sobbing.

11. St. Kitts
Steve recalls hearing women discuss Alguinaldo Nesbitt, a West Indian who immigrated to the United States from St. Kitts, an independent island in the east Caribbean Sea, a former British colony that severed its relationship with Britain in 1983. Most of the island's population are ancestors of slaves imported to the Western Hemisphere from West Africa.

12. 28th precinct
The previous December, Steve Harmon was watching the news at home with his brother Jerry when detectives Karyl and Williams took him for questioning at the 28th precinct headquarters in central Harlem. Steve's mother tried to follow but doesn't know where the police officers were escorting her son.

13. Manhattan Detention Center, New York City
Returned to jail, Steve mops the corridors with disinfectant and gags from the smell. More at home in a self-guided mental scenario than in the harsh jail atmosphere, he blames himself for wanting to be tough like James King and Bobo Evans, two career criminals.

14. New York City Criminal Court Building
City Clerk Allen Forbes testifies that since August 1989, Nesbitt had a permit for owning a gun. Detective Williams reports viewing the crime scene at 5:15 and receiving Evans's admission of guilt. Dr. James Moody, the medical examiner, describes how Nesbitt drowned in his own blood after a bullet passed through his upper chest.

15. Manhattan Detention Center, New York City
Mrs. Harmon arrives at the visitation area with a Bible in which she has marked an affirming passage. She assures her son that she knows he is innocent. Steve recalls how James King planned the robbery and asked him to be lookout. At 1:15 P.M. on Sunday, July 12, Steve sees Jerry and his parents in the street below. Steve anticipates testimony by the state's star witnesses on Monday.

16. New York City Criminal Court Building
On Monday, July 13, Lorelle Henry, a retired school librarian, testifies that she witnessed the crime. She picked out James King's picture from more than twenty police photos and identified him in a lineup.

17. Greenhaven
Asa Briggs, attorney for James King, complains to the judge that Bobo Evans arrives in court in a prison uniform from Greenhaven, a men's prison on Route 216 near Stormville.

Until September 1995, Greenhaven Prison was New York state's death house and the location of its electric chair.

18. New York City Criminal Court Building

On Tuesday, July 14, Dorothy Moore, James King's cousin, reports that he came to her house to give her a lamp at 3:30 P.M. the day of the robbery. George Nipping testifies that James King is left-handed, a weak retort to the fact that the bullet entered Nesbitt's left side, ostensibly by a right-handed shooter. Steve testifies that he wasn't a lookout for the crime and he spent the day taking mental notes for a school film project. George Sawicki states that he has known Steve for three years and that the boy is honest.

In Asa Briggs's opinion, no witness saw the murder. Kathy O'Brien adds that there is no proof that Steve served as lookout. The judge outlines to jurors the process of returning a verdict of guilty to felony murder. A guard confides to Steve that there is a pool of bets on the outcome of the trial. On Friday, July 17, the court awaits the arrival of the Nesbitt family. The jury finds James King guilty and exonerates Steve.

19. Harlem

Steve continues making films in Harlem. He worries that his father distances himself because he disapproves of Steve's friendships with criminals. Steve wonders about Kathy O'Brien's opinion of him.

Further Reading

Balshaw, Maria. *Looking for Harlem: Urban Aesthetics in African-American Literature*. New York: Pluto Press, 2000.

Bishop, Rudine Sims. *Walter Dean Myers*. Boston: Twayne, 1991.

"Book Award Winners Named." *Reading Today* (February 2001).

Cantor, George. *Historic Landmarks of Black America*. Detroit: Gale Research, 1991.

Corbett, Sue, " 'Monster' Writer Walter Dean Myers' Newest Work Is Destined to Be a Classic." *Tulsa World* (February 13, 2000): Books Section.

Favor, J. Martin. *Authentic Blackness: The Folk in the New Negro Renaissance*. Durham, N.C.: Duke University Press, 1999.

Hornberger, Eric, and Alice Hudson. *The Historical Atlas of New York City: A Visual Celebration of Nearly 400 Years of New York City's History*. New York: Henry Holt, 1998.

Jordan, Denise M. *Walter Dean Myers: Writer for Real Teens*. Berkeley Heights, N.J.: Enslow Publishers, 1999.

"Learning about Walter Dean Myers," http://mariner.rutgers.edu/special/kay/myers.html.

Margolis, Rick, "Business as Usual? No Way." *School Library Journal* (August 2000).

Moore, Claudia, "Monster." *School Library Journal* (December 1, 2000).

Myers, Walter Dean. *145th Street—Short Stories*. New York: Delacorte Press, 2000.

"Patrol Services Bureau: 28th Precinct," http://www.nyc.gov/html/nypd/html/pct/pct028.html.

"Publishing."*Selling to Kids* (January 24, 2001).

Shannon, Jerry Beth, "Tell It Like It Is!" *School Library Journal* (November 2000).

Shapiro, Stephanie, "Getting the Drift." *Chicago Sun* (January 29, 2000).

Short, Lynda N., "Monster." *School Library Journal* (September 1, 2000).

"2000 Horn Book Awards." *School Library Journal* (August 1, 2000).

"Walter Dean Myers," http://www.indiana.edu/~eric_rec/ieo/bibs/myers.html.

"Walter Dean Myers: African American Storyteller for Young Readers," http://www.familyhaven.com/books/walterdeanmyers.html.

"Walter Dean Myers's Biography," http://teacher.scholastic.com/authorsandbooks/authors/myers/bio.htm.

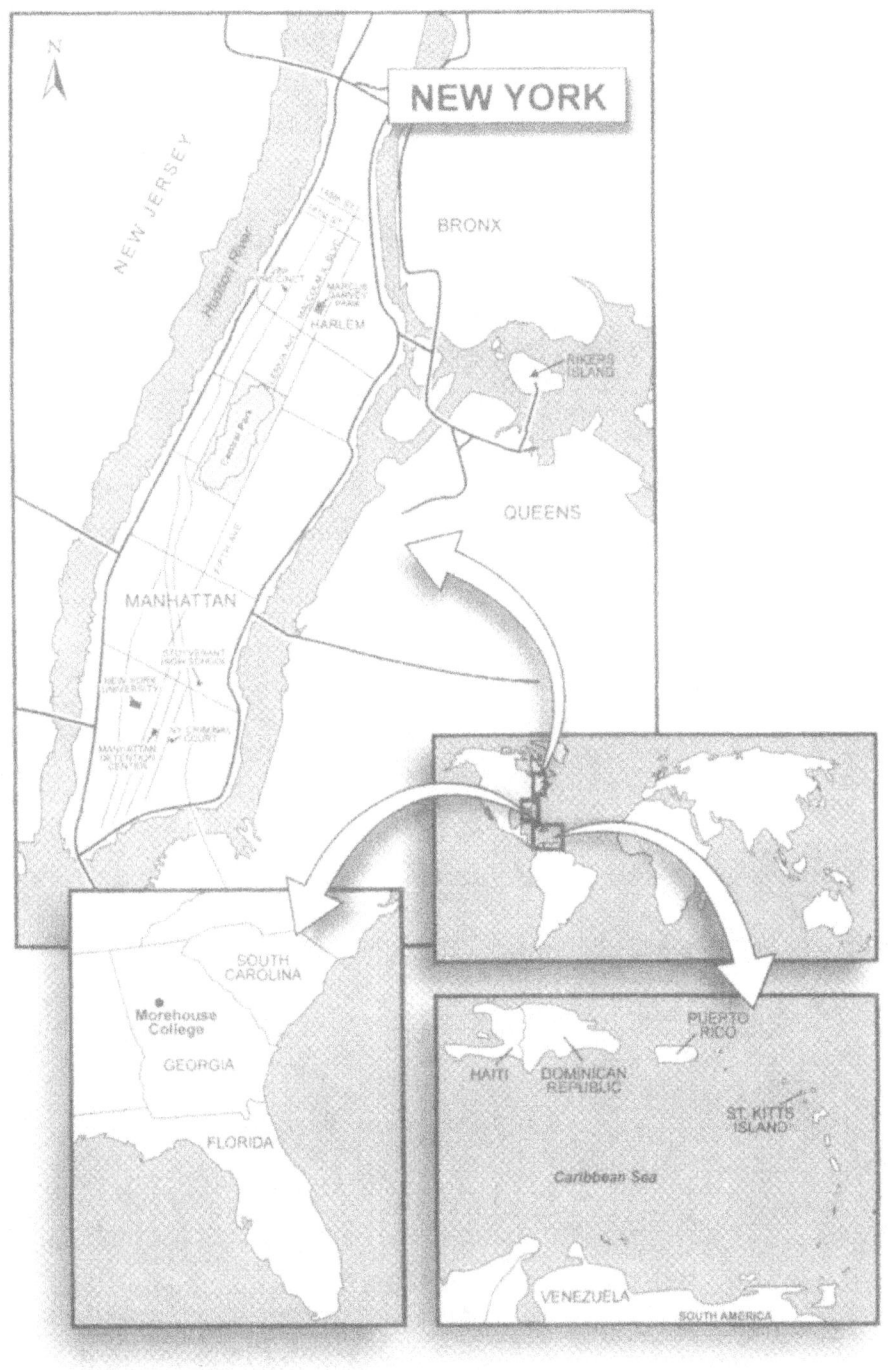

O Pioneers!
By Willa Cather

Classic historical fiction, 1913

Geographical Summary

Willa Cather's regional novel expresses a regard for the Midwest and its settlement by pioneers from many European regions. In 1884, the author's family moved to Red Cloud on wheat-growing land on the Republican River at the center of Nebraska's southern border with Kansas. Of her first view of the prairie, she recalled, "The land was open range and there was almost no fencing. As we drove further and further out into the country, I felt a good deal as if we had come to the end of everything—it was a kind of erasure of personality.. . . I had heard my father say you had to show grit in a new country" (Cather, "Basis in Early Experience").

Although the novel's fictional setting is never specified, the text orients the reader with numerous geographical landmarks, including Hastings, Omaha, the Platte and Missouri Rivers, the state prison in Lincoln, the Lindell Hotel, the Burlington Depot, and the University of Nebraska. The prairie's expansive flatland, the make-or-break element in characters' lives, "is like an iron country, and the spirit is oppressed by its rigor and melancholy." It mesmerizes Alexandra, who is willing to pledge her life to working the soil, even if she has to fight her brothers for possession of her inheritance.

On Alexandra' return from surveying riverfront property, the highlands infuse her with a will to apply nature's energies to enriching her family. She acknowledges that such a challenge dismays her weak-willed brothers, but a survey of lowlands along the river convinces her that she has made the right choice of staking a claim on the future. On her ride home to the farm, she becomes one of Cather's "dreamers on the frontier." After agreeing to marry the man she has always loved, she promises to follow him to the Yukon if he agrees to return with her to live on the Nebraska prairie.

Detailed Itinerary

1. Hanover and Omaha, Nebraska

In January around the middle of the nineteenth century, when the novel opens, the fictional town of Hanover in rural Nebraska lies in the state's tableland. Its landmarks include a squat red depot and grain elevator to the north and horse pond and lumberyard at the south.

Emil Bergson plays with a vivacious Bohemian child named Marie Tovesky, a newcomer from Omaha. Alexandra asks her friend Carl Linstrum to retrieve a kitten from the top of a pole. Around 4:00 P.M., she drives her wagon through a gale toward home with news that the doctor has diagnosed her father's illness as terminal.

2. From Sweden to the Bergson farm on the Nebraska prairie

At his log farmhouse on Norway Creek, John Bergson, a former shipyard worker in Sweden, regrets leaving the 640-acre prairie homestead, which lies in a ravine overgrown with brush, cottonwood, and dwarf ash trees. Earlier, his brother, Otto Bergson, had grown discouraged with agriculture. He had abandoned the farm to work in a bakery in Chicago, Illinois, an urban center east of Nebraska on Lake Michigan. For farm management, John depends on his business-minded daughter rather than on Lou and Oscar, her younger brothers. Mrs. Bergson, who misses Sweden, pickles food Scandinavian style.

3. Ivar's pond across the county line

In July, six months after John Bergson's death, Lou, Oscar, and Alexandra drive over the county line on a rough road to buy a twine hammock from Ivar, a Bible-crazed hermit and folk healer. He lives in a typical sod hut on a clay bank, works as a part-time farm laborer, and treats sick animals.

4. The Great Divide

West of Wyoming and Colorado along the eastern slope of the Great Divide, the rocky backbone that bisects North America, the Bergsons prosper in the three years after John's death. The stabilizer of the family is Alexandra, who understands and appreciates the land. During three years of drought and crop failure, the two older brothers grow restless and wish to join their Uncle Otto in Chicago.

5. Chicago, Illinois; St. Louis, Missouri

In September, during a period of widespread emigration from the Midwest, eighteen-year-old Carl Linstrum visits Alexandra. He reports that he and his father are leaving—his father to roll cigars in a factory in St. Louis, Missouri, to the south and Carl to learn engraving. From St. Louis, Carl plans to move on to Chicago to find work.

6. River Farms in the valley

Accompanied by her younger brother Emil, Alexandra journeys eastward down the valley from the Divide for a five-day survey of riverfront farmland near the fictional town of Brigham, Nebraska. She concludes that the Bergsons' high farmland will be more profitable than low-country acreage. Against the advice of the two older brothers, she decides to liquidate cattle and corn so she can buy the Linstrum, Struble, and Crow properties.

7. Bergson farm on the Nebraska prairie

Sixteen years after her father's death, Alexandra heads the motherless family and works a prosperous spread. Her initial hunch about the area was correct. The Divide is now thickly populated and thriving. In June, twenty-one-year-old Emil returns home from college. While he cuts grass in the Norwegian cemetery, he talks with a Czech farm wife, Marie Tovesky Shabata.

8. Hastings, Nebraska

Alexandra employs old Ivar, who lives in her barn. Because of his seizures, he fears that he will be sent to an asylum at Hastings in south central Nebraska.

9. Seattle, Washington; Alaska

On Sunday, after 16 years away from Nebraska, Carl Linstrum returns. He leaves his trunk in Hastings and arrives for a visit with the Bergsons before traveling to Seattle, Washington, and Alaska to work as an engraver. The gold strike in the Yukon Territory of western Canada on August 17, 1896, encourages a rush to the northwest after news reaches the United States in summer 1897.

10. Wall Street, New York City

To impress Carl, Lou blusters about the Wall Street scare of 1896.

11. Bergson farm on the Nebraska prairie

To Carl, Alexandra credits the land for enriching the farm, which she divided evenly after her brother's marriage. She brags that Emil will graduate in June from the University of Nebraska, founded in 1869 in Lincoln.

12. Shabata farm on the former Linstrum property

Marie lives adjacent to Bergson's original spread on the former Linstrum farm that Alexandra sold to the newlywed Shabatas. She exudes energy, and her love of life is common to immigrants from Bohemia, a Slavic kingdom added to Czechoslovakia in 1918. Alexandra tries to reason with Marie's melancholy husband Frank, who grouses that Mrs. Hiller's hogs wander into his wheat. Frank's mother reputedly owns a big farm in Bohemia's Elbe valley.

13. Union Station, St. Louis, Missouri

After Frank met sixteen-year-old Marie at a Bohemian picnic, her father feared Frank's good looks and fine clothes and dispatched her to St. Louis to the care of the Sisters of the Sacred Heart, a Roman Catholic congregation of women devoted to the education of girls. A year later, Marie met Frank at Union Station and eloped. Upon settling down with her, Frank acclimated to farm life but often drank with neighbor men and allowed himself a yearly fling in Hastings or Omaha.

14. Sainte-Agnes, Nebraska

While Frank carouses at Moses Marcel's saloon in fictional Sainte-Agnes, Emil mows his way toward the sound of Marie's cherries hitting the pail. In an intimate moment, they realize that their relationship has deepened with maturity. On Sunday, a month after Carl's arrival, he and Emil attend a Catholic fair. In the spirit of friendship, Amédée urges twenty-two-year-old Emil to get married. Emil makes Marie jealous by teasing Angélique, Amédée's fiancée.

15. Bergson farm on the Nebraska prairie

Lou and Oscar warn Alexandra that people gossip about her and Carl, whom they suspect of wanting to marry her for her money. The brothers contend that the Bergson family farmstead belongs to the Bergson men. At 7:30 P.M., Emil returns home and informs Alexandra that he wants to take a year from law school to go to the "City of Mexico." At dusk, Carl returns from a confrontation with Lou and Oscar and declares that Alexandra is always surrounded by little men. She counters that she has needed him for many years. He leaves for Alaska at once.

16. Gottland, Sweden

That winter, Alexandra sends Ivar to fetch Mrs. Lee for an annual visit. The elderly woman longs for the old times at a dairy farm in Gottland (now Gotland), an island off the southeast coast of Sweden. The largest island in the Baltic Sea, the former Viking stronghold of Gottland was a center for agriculture, herding, and Scandinavian trade with Russia and Germany.

17. Dawson, the Yukon

A week later, while having coffee with Marie, Alexandra reports that Carl sent her orange blossoms before leaving California. He arrived at Dawson, a frontier Canadian boomtown. Situated on the confluence of the Klondike and Yukon rivers, it drew speculators and prospectors after the discovery of placer gold on Bonanza Creek in August 1896. In a few months, it grew into a polyglot city of 30,000 and became capital of the Yukon Territory in 1898. Alexandra does not expect to hear again from Carl until the rivers thaw in spring.

18. Mexico City, Mexico

Alexandra shares Emil's letters with Marie. For her part, Marie weeps about the crankiness of her sour husband, who plays "California Jack" every evening with pals. Alexandra reads Emil's descriptions of happy times in the capital city, where President Porfirio Diaz rules with a strong hand. Emil enjoys an atmosphere energized by bullfighting, cock fighting, churches and fiestas, flower markets, fountains, street bands, and dancing. He mentions mingling with an international clientele at an Italian restaurant on San Francisco Street near city hall in the heart of the metropolis.

19. Sainte-Agnes, Nebraska

In June at a church supper, Alexandra shows off her handsome brother Emil, who is costumed as a Mexican. He tells of witnessing the death of a famous matador in the bullring. After dinner, Marie, the fortuneteller, receives Emil's gift of a handful of uncut turquoises. When the candle goes out, he embraces her.

20. Bergson farm on the Nebraska prairie

After a wedding, Emil follows Marie home. She insists that one of them must leave and confesses her love. Emil wanders the fields all night.

21. Omaha, Nebraska; Ann Arbor, Michigan

A week later, Emil prepares to go to Omaha to study law with a Swedish attorney. In October, Emil intends to enter law school at Ann Arbor, Michigan.

22. Sainte-Agnes, Nebraska

The next morning, Emil goes to the Chevalier house and finds his friend harvesting with a steam thresher. Amédée doggedly suffers a persistent pain in his side and keeps working. That evening, Doctor Paradis removes Amédée's appendix. The next morning, Alexandra tells Emil that Amédée died at 3:00 A.M.

23. Shabata farm

On Sunday at 3:00 P.M., Emil grows restless and hurries to the orchard to find Marie. That night, Frank finds Emil's horse in the stable and hears murmurs coming from the wheat field corner near the orchard hedge that stretches toward the Bergson pasture. Enraged at his unfaithful wife, he shoots Marie and Emil in the grass. Emil dies immediately; Marie struggles to touch him before collapsing and bleeding to death.

24. Train to Omaha, Nebraska

In terror of his rash act, Frank intends to catch the 1:00 train for Omaha. He realizes that his marriage is doomed and blames Marie for being careless. Halfway to Hanover, he suffers nausea. Meanwhile, Ivar reports the double murder.

25. State prison, Lincoln, Nebraska

Three months later, in mid-October, Alexandra longs for Carl's return. She intends to visit Frank, who is serving a ten-year sentence at the state prison in Lincoln. She arrives at the Burlington depot at 15th and P streets and stays the night at the Lindell Hotel. At 9:00 A.M. the next morning, she talks with Frank and encourages him by promising to petition the governor to pardon him. At the hotel, a telegram arrives from Carl, who has returned from Dawson and awaits her in Hanover.

26. Bergson farm on the Nebraska prairie

The next afternoon, Carl tells Alexandria that he did not receive her letter but read about the shooting in a month-old San Francisco paper. He proposes spending the winter with her and returning in the spring to gold fields along the Klondike River, a tributary of the Yukon River. She looks forward to wedding her old friend and agrees to go with him to Alaska but wants to return to her farm. With assurance that Alexandra is right, Carl murmurs, "You belong to the land . . . as you have always said. Now more than ever."

Further Reading

Acocella, Joan. *Willa Cather and the Politics of Criticism.* Lincoln: University of Nebraska Press, 1999.

Bloom, Harold. *Willa Cather.* New York: Chelsea House, 1999.

Cather, Willa, "Basis in Early Experience," *Historical Essay,* http://www.libfind.unl.edu/Cather/writings/novels/Antonia/Back/Historical.htm.

Downs, C. Catherine. *Becoming Modern: Willa Cather's Journalism.* Cranbury, N.J.: Susquehanna University Press, 1999.

Giannone, Richard. *Music in Willa Cather's Fiction.* Lincoln: University of Nebraska Press, 2001.

Kennicott, Philip, "In Cather Country, Works Live On." *Dallas Morning News* (June 29, 2000).

Kinnison, Dana C., "Cather's 'O Pioneers.' " *The Explicator* (Winter 2000): 97.

Macmillan, Kyle, "New Opera 'O Pioneers!' to Have Lincoln Premiere." *Omaha World-Herald,* (November 7, 1999).

March, John. *Reader's Companion to the Fiction of Willa Cather.* Westport, Conn.: Greenwood, 1993.

"My Antonia," *Reading Group Guides*, http://www.readinggroupguides.com/guides/my_antonia-author.html.

O'Connor, Margaret Anne, ed. *Willa Cather: The Contemporary Reviews*. Cambridge: Cambridge University Press, 2001.

Snodgrass, Mary Ellen. *Encyclopedia of Frontier Literature*. Santa Barbara, Calif.: ABC-Clio, 1997.

"University of Nebraska-Lincoln," http://www.unl.edu/unlpub/special/history/history.shtm.

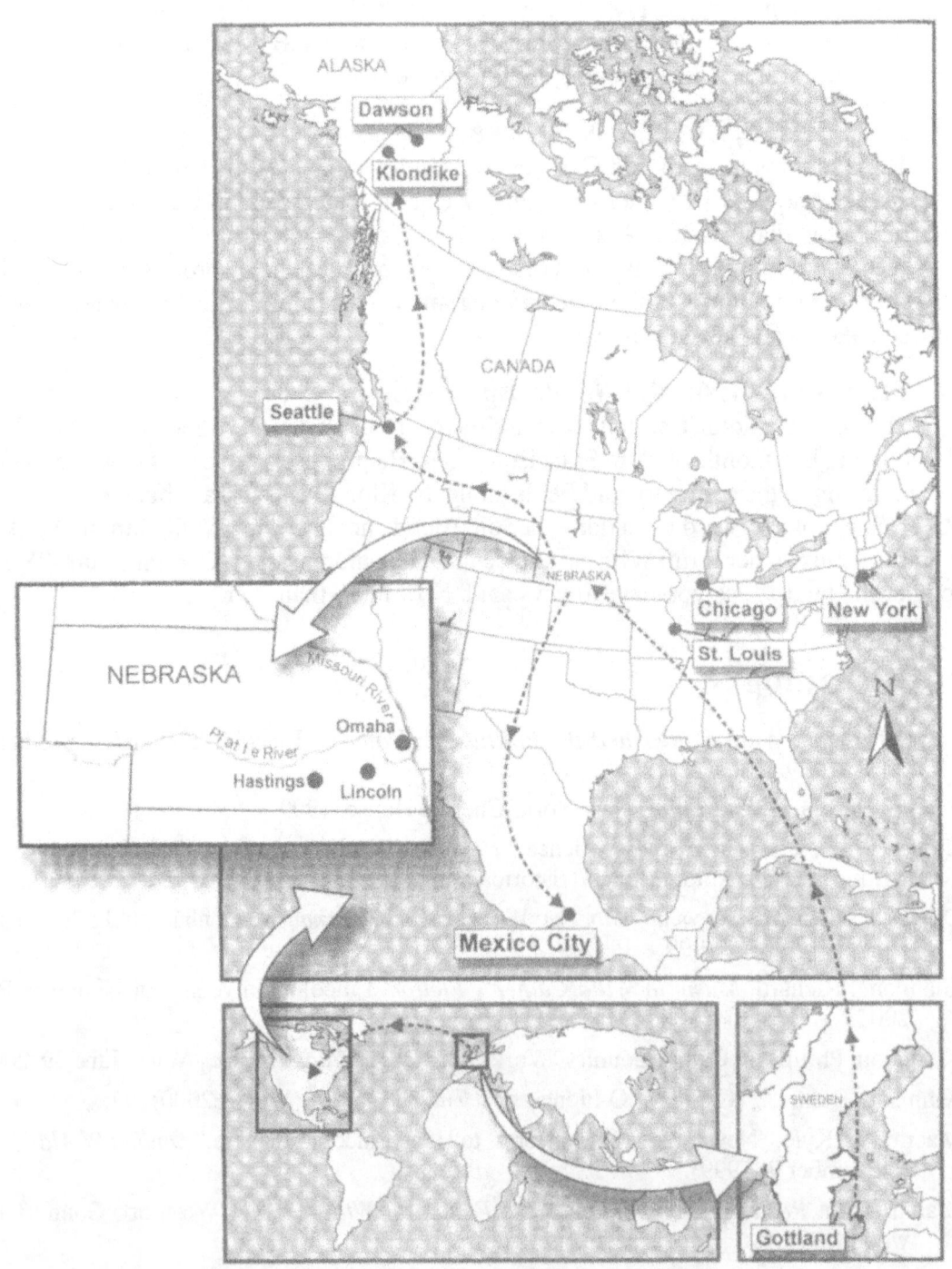

The Piano Lesson
By August Wilson

Multicultural drama, 1990

Geographical Summary

Opening in Pittsburgh in southwestern Pennsylvania, August Wilson's *The Piano Lesson* presents the drama of a historic southern heirloom and its meaning to a black family. A major coal, steel, and railroad center located on three navigable rivers, the Allegheny, Monongahela, and Ohio, the city offered jobs and opportunities to blacks migrating from racial oppression in the South. Settling among Irish, Scots, English, Germans, and Slovaks, blacks began arriving in the 1880s. In the 1920s, the African American influx produced the largest minority group, comprising 20 percent of the city's population.

The draw of Pittsburgh for Boy Willie Charles and his business partner Lymon corresponds with the lack of opportunity in the Yazoo Basin of northwestern Mississippi, a rural backwater where people earn about half the average U.S. per capita income. By 1987, when August Wilson produced his play for the National Playwrights Conference and opened at Yale in New Haven, Connecticut, counties along the Delta were losing population as blacks deserted agriculture and logging for industrial jobs in the urban North. The two fictional characters transport watermelons north by truck, which symbolizes their attempts to capitalize on Northern prosperity with the highly perishable farm products of the poverty-stricken South.

Detailed Itinerary

1. Stoner County, Mississippi, to West Virginia

Thirty-year-old Boy Willie Charles has been working in fictional Stoner County, Mississippi, cutting timber on land belonging to his partner Lymon's cousin. Boy Willie and Lymon travel northeast to sell a load of watermelons in Pittsburgh, Pennsylvania. Lymon sleeps in the truck to avoid Sheriff Stovall, who is looking for him. On the way, the two travelers have several truck breakdowns, two occurring in West Virginia southwest of Pennsylvania.

2. Pittsburgh, Pennsylvania

At 5:00 A.M. in Pittsburgh, Boy Willie awakens his Uncle Doaker, a railroad cook, and Boy Willie's thirty-five-year-old widowed sister Berniece, whose husband Crawley died three years earlier. Boy Willie reports that Cleotha died. Doaker heard the news from his older brother, Wining Boy, a footloose piano player who arrived a year ago for a two-week stay.

3. Stoner County, Mississippi

Wining Boy visited Mississippi two years before, when Boy Willie and Lymon were finishing three-year sentences at Parchman Farm, an isolated penal facility in a desolate stretch of Sunflower County in the Yazoo Basin south of Clarksdale. After Sutter's death, Boy Willie was eager to sell the family piano to buy the Sutter estate from the deceased's brother, who traveled south from Chicago to take charge of the land. He offers it to Boy Willie for $2,000 rather than sell it to Jim Stovall and gives Boy Willie two weeks to locate the money.

4. Pittsburgh, Pennsylvania

Doaker says that Berniece stopped playing the family piano after Mama Ola died seven years before. Berniece's daughter Maretha attends classes at Irene Kaufman's settlement house, a social outreach that gained popularity during the early 1900s as a means of teaching nutrition, hygiene, and other life skills to the needy. Berniece refuses to marry Avery Brown, the preacher who has been proposing to her for the past two years. Doaker knows that Berniece has already rejected a buyer's offer for the piano and is seeking a loan to start Avery's church. Berniece yells that Sutter's ghost stands at the top of the stairs. She turns on Boy Willie and orders him to leave for causing her husband's death.

5. Sunflower to Clarksdale, Mississippi

Doaker visits Mississippi once a month when the train passes through but avoids women since Coreen left him. He takes pride in having lined the track of the Yellow Dog from Sunflower to Clarksdale, a forty-mile stretch in northwestern Mississippi. The train takes its colorful name from the initials of the Yazoo Delta, a hot, dry section of the state's alluvial plain.

6. Kansas City, Kansas; New York

Three days later, Wining Boy arrives from Kansas City, Kansas, a trans-Mississippi railroad center on the Missouri River nearly five hundred miles southwest of Pittsburgh. He brings the news that his ex-wife, Cleotha Holman, whom he has known for thirty years, died on May 1. Doaker admits that he caused their break-up. He thought no more of Coreen after she left for New York City, a cultural and economic magnet for blacks escaping the Jim Crow South.

7. Pittsburgh, Pennsylvania

Boy Willie and Lymon have difficulty selling watermelons because their truck breaks down before they can get to white buyers at Squirrel Hill, a tony section of the city popular for ethnic restaurants, taverns, mansions and high rises, parks, boutiques, and theaters. The two men experience another breakdown and must sleep in the truck to protect the fruit from thieves.

8. Mississippi

Boy Willie says the Ghosts of the Yellow Dog got Sutter three weeks earlier. Wining Boy believes that evil spirits haunt the crossing of the Yellow Dog and Southern railroads in Moorhead, Mississippi. Boy Willie demands a drink and tells how he skimmed lumber from

Jim Miller. When white men retaliated, they killed Crawley and imprisoned Boy Willie and Lymon. Stovall paid the $100 fine and forced Lymon to carry water to laborers on the infamous Parchman farm.

Doaker tells about the situation three generations back when Sutter's grandfather, Robert Sutter, bought the piano for his wife Ophelia. Sutter paid for it by selling Nolander the pick of his slaves, Doaker's grandmother Berniece and her son, who was Doaker's father. Ophelia enjoyed the piano but missed Berniece, the domestic worker who kept her company. After Nolander and Sutter quarreled, Ophelia got sick. Sutter had Berniece's husband Willie Boy (the original Boy Willie) carve portraits of Berniece and her son on the piano. Willie Boy turned it into a collection of ancestral portraits by adding likenesses and scenes from the lives of his parents, Mama Esther and Boy Charles. Sutter disapproved, but the images pleased Ophelia.

Doaker's brother, Boy Charles, who died in 1911 at age thirty-one, wanted to repossess the piano from Sutter's house because he believed the family could never be free as long as its chief heirloom belonged to the white man who had enslaved and exploited them. On July 4 while the Sutter family attended a county picnic, Doaker and Wining Boy stole the piano and took it by wagon to Mama Ola's family. After someone torched Boy Charles's House, he fled on the 3:57 Yellow Dog. Whites stopped the train and burned the boxcar carrying him and four transients. Two months later, a suspect, Ed Saunders, drowned in his well. The incident precipitated the ghost story and the start of Berniece's enshrinement of the heirloom piano for which her father died.

9. Pittsburgh, Pennsylvania

Lymon contends that Boy Willie should stay in Pittsburgh, but Boy Willie longs for the familiar agrarian life in the South. He claims his share of the piano. When he and Lymon jostle it, the ghost sounds. The next morning, Doaker concludes that Berniece should sell the piano to end the family uproar. That evening, at Berniece's request, Avery promises to return the next day to exorcise the spirit. Late on Friday morning, Boy Willie anticipates a buyer who will pay $1,150 for the piano. The ghost sounds when the two men fail to move the piano. When Avery begins the exorcism, an unseen power twice tosses Boy Willie from the stairs. Berniece plays the piano and summons her grandparents and parents. Boy Willie prepares to take the train back to Mississippi.

Further Reading

August Wilson (video). San Francisco: California Newsreel, 1992.

"August Wilson," http://www.cee.umn.edu/ufv/catalog/data/659.html.

"August Wilson's Sacred Book," http://soundprint.brnadywine.American.edu/~soundprt/more_info/August_Wilson.html.

"Biography of August Wilson," http://www.dartmouth.edu/~awilson/bio.html.

Black Literature Criticism. Detroit: Gale Research, 1992.

Boan, Devon, "Call-and-Response: Parallel 'Slave Narrative' in August Wilson's 'The Piano Lesson.'" *African American Review* (Summer 1998).

Elkins, Marilyn, ed. *August Wilson: A Casebook*. New York: Garland, 1994.

Fitzgerald, Sharon, "August Wilson: The People's Playwright." *American Visions* (August 2000).

Lorant, Stefan, et al. *Pittsburgh, the Story of an American City*. Pittsburgh: Esselmont Books, 1999.

"The Mississippi Delta," http://www.glass-artist.co.uk/trip/trip16.html.

Nadel, Alan, and Henry Louis Gates. *May All Your Fences Have Gates*. Ames: University of Iowa Press, 1994.

Oshinsky, David M. *"Worse Than Slavery": Parchman Farm and the Ordeal of Jim Crow Justice*. New York: Free Press, 1997.

Pereira, Kim. *August Wilson and the African-American Odyssey*. Urbana: University of Illinois Press, 1995.

Shafer, Yvonne. *August Wilson: A Research and Production Sourcebook*. Westport, Conn.: Greenwood, 1998.

Shannon, Sandra G. *The Dramatic Vision of August Wilson*. Washington, D.C.: Howard University Press, 1996.

"Squirrel Hill," http://www.ece.cmu.edu/gradguide/neighborhoods/squirrel/.

"Sunflower County, Mississippi," http://www.rootsweb.com/~mssunflo/county.htm.

Taylor, William Banks. *Down on Parchman Farm: The Great Prison in the Mississippi Delta*. Columbus: Ohio State University Press, 1999.

"Where the Southern Cross the Dog," http://www.mrjumbo.com/contents/delta99/3delta/moorhead.html.

A Prayer for Owen Meany
By John Irving

Contemporary mainstream fiction, 1989

Geographical Summary

John Irving's New England and Canadian settings offer a microcosm of Canadian and American attitudes and actions during the years of protest against the Vietnam War. In the beginning, Paul Owen Meany Jr., the pale-skinned, undersized protagonist of Boston Irish background, seeks surrogate parents to replace his dysfunctional father and reclusive mother. He bonds with John Wheelwright's beautiful mother Tabby and aristocratic grandmother, Harriet Wheelwright. In 1950s, the boys grow up in Gravesend, a small fictional town patterned after Exeter, a colonial capital in southeastern New Hampshire on the Squamscott River nine miles northwest of Rye harbor and Hampton Beach on the Atlantic Ocean. By the 1960s, war threatens both the fictional characters and the nation.

Owen and John attend the fictional Gravesend Academy, a boy's prep school modeled on Phillips Exeter Academy at 20 Main Street, Exeter, New Hampshire. The two friends espouse personal and national causes through pranks and the campus newspaper. When they travel to Boston and Cambridge, the search for a doctor to treat Owen's unpleasant voice leads them to Graham McSwiney's studio. They inadvertently locate Jerrold's, the couturier shop where Tabby once bought a red dress. With a few clues and Owen's gift for logic, John begins to piece together his mother's double life as cabaret singer and unwed mother.

The escalation of the Vietnam War fills John's reflection on America's troubled era. Irving keeps Southeast Asia in the distance while focusing on John's quiet life as a Toronto schoolmaster. John grows disillusioned with the angry generation that transforms his cousin Hester into a war protester and Owen into a gung-ho, ROTC-trained second lieutenant. Scenes of the nation's anguish appear on Harriet Wheelwright's television, in summary of ethical and social decline. Ironically, her ambivalence toward the medium continues up to her death at Gravesend Retreat for the Elderly, where she dies painlessly at age ninety-nine while grasping the remote control.

The plot moves to Fort Huachuca, Arizona, a historic landmark of the Buffalo Soldier era. There, the Meany death business continues as Owen escorts soldiers' corpses home from Vietnam. In his busy task at California airports, he is remarkably unmoved by battlefield deaths. He calmly anticipates his own demise, which a dream implies will happen during a heroic action in Vietnam. Confused by the vision, he invites John to be with him in Arizona for his last days, which he details in a diary.

While grieving for Owen, John teaches Thomas Hardy's novels, which had been the focus of his master's thesis at the University of New Hampshire, to an English literature class of high school girls in Toronto, Canada. He limits his life to school and the Anglican Church. Dan Needham, John's sweet-natured adoptive father, urges him to abandon self-exile in Canada and to "forgive and forget" by returning home to Gravesend.

Detailed Itinerary

1. Gravesend, New Hampshire

In adulthood, John Wheelwright recalls Paul Owen Meany Jr., his working-class friend with the heavily graveled voice. John's mother, Tabitha "Tabby" Wheelwright, conceived John in the winter of 1941–1942 while traveling from her home at 80 Front Street, Gravesend, New Hampshire, southeast to Boston, Massachusetts, for weekly voice lessons. She hides the name of his father, whom she met while staying at a women's residential hotel.

When John is ten, Tabby meets her future husband on the Boston & Maine Railroad. A likely husband and father, Dan Needham is a Harvard graduate and a drama history teacher and theater coach at the fictional Gravesend Academy. After Dan adopts John, the family changes churches from Congregational to Episcopalian. At the Episcopalian Sunday school, John and his friend Mary Baird torment Owen.

At a Little League game in July 1953, Owen hits a baseball that strikes Tabby. To atone for her death, Owen delivers to John his most prized possession, a baseball card collection. Together, the boys sift clues in their search for John's unidentified father.

2. Gravesend Academy, Gravesend, New Hampshire

In fall 1958, Dan enrolls John at the academy to complete high school. Owen attends on scholarship. While John repeats ninth grade because of his learning disability, Owen likewise drops back one grade to coach his friend in reading comprehension.

3. Boston, Massachusetts

Grandmother Wheelwright takes Owen to Boston via the Boston & Maine Railroad to buy school clothes at Jordan Marsh and Filene's. The city, southeast of Gravesend, is significant in family history as the landing place of John's ancestor, John Wheelwright, who emigrated from Saleby, Lincolnshire, England, in 1636. After entry into the ministry, he became a Puritan and was banished from Massachusetts Bay Colony for holding unorthodox views that disrupted "the civil peace." The Reverend Wheelwright settled in Maine.

4. White Mountains, New Hampshire

In summer at the fictional Sawyer Depot near Loveless Lake and North Conway in the White Mountains of New Hampshire, John visits his cousins, Simon, Noah, and Hester. John loves the train ride aboard the Boston & Maine, which travels two hours north from Gravesend past Mount Chocorua and Ossipee Lake to his cousins' house. At Christmas during John's first year at the academy, the cousins do not invite him to their home because Hester is corresponding with a black boatman she met the previous year while vacation on

Tortola, the largest of the British Virgin Islands. Located in the Antilles chain stretching between the Caribbean Sea and the Atlantic Ocean east of Puerto Rico, the thirty-six islands were home to British planters who settled there in the sixteenth and seventeenth centuries and imported African slaves to work the land.

5. Gravesend Academy

The first Christmas after Tabby's death, John stays with Dan on campus at Waterhouse Hall. After playing the infant Jesus at the Christmas crèche reenactment, Owen takes the role of the ghost of Christmas future at Dan's Christmas Eve 1953 production of *A Christmas Carol*. On stage Owen has a vision of his own death. After driving him home, Dan discovers that the Meanys don't wait up for their son on Christmas Eve. At the academy, Owen is an outstanding student. In 1958, he begins dating Hester, who attends the University of New Hampshire, a liberal arts institution founded in 1866 in rural Durham.

6. Boston and Cambridge, Massachusetts

On a Saturday trip on the Boston & Maine Railroad southeast to Boston in November 1961, John and Owen cross the Charles River to visit Harvard Square in Cambridge. Around the corner from Newbury Street on Exeter Street, they recognize Jerrold's, the boutique where Tabby once bought a red dress. The owner, Giovanni Giordano, identifies her as "The Lady in Red," a popular singer at the Orange Grove, a supper club on Beacon Street. At Graham McSwiney's studio, Tabby's former singing instructor explains that he got Tabby the nightclub job singing Frank Sinatra songs, but he can't identify John's father.

7. Washington, D.C.

In Washington, D.C., in January 1961, American writer Robert Frost reads a poem, "The Gift Outright," at the outdoor inaugural ceremony of President John F. Kennedy. Owens watches the reading on television and regrets that a bitter wind blows the aged poet's hair.

8. Gravesend Academy

In spring 1962, within months of John and Owen's high school graduation, Headmaster White expels Owen for pranks. During psychological and spiritual counseling for multiple misbehaviors, Owen asks Reverend Merrill to pray for him. White protests the prayer, but Merrill refuses to shorten it. The standoff ends White's tenure as headmaster, which Merrill assumes.

9. University of New Hampshire

That summer, Owen lives with Hester at her apartment in Durham, New Hampshire. To be near John, he studies geology on an ROTC scholarship while John, with Owen's help, majors in English. They commute daily to campus from Gravesend.

10. Gravesend, New Hampshire

That summer, Owen works in his father's monument shop. After John Kennedy's assassination by rifle fire during a presidential motorcade through downtown Dallas, Texas, on November 22, 1963, Owen discusses with Reverend Merrill a recurrent dream in which Owen rescues Vietnamese children from an explosion. Hester punches Owen in the mouth and nose for wanting to fight in Vietnam.

11. Vietnam

On August 7, 1964, Congress passes the Tonkin Gulf Resolution supporting President Lyndon B. Johnson's troop buildup in Vietnam. On February 7, 1965, the Vietcong attack American ground troops. Four days later, formal bombing begins against North Vietnam. On March 8, U.S. Marines begin landing at Da Nang on the central coastline bordering the South China Sea, a western arm of the Pacific Ocean. In June, generals Nguyen Van Thieu and Nguyen Cao Ky seize South Vietnam. Owen predicts that the U.S. military will not escape intervention in the struggle.

12. Fort Huachuca, Arizona

After graduating with a bachelor of arts degree in spring 1966, John remains at the university for graduate study. Owen journeys to Lake Francis in northern New Hampshire with John and attends a going-away party at Grandmother Wheelwright's house. As a casualty assistance officer attached to the Adjutant General's Corps at Fort Huachuca in Cochise County, Arizona, he escorts the bodies of combat soldiers to their families. Located near the San Pedro River southeast of Tucson between Nogales and Sierra Vista, the fort is an army intelligence center that surveys the U.S.–Mexican border.

13. Gravesend, New Hampshire

After John is called up by the draft board in May 1967, Owen instructs him to avoid the physical examination. At the end of summer, Owen hurries home on leave and lovingly lops off John's trigger finger at the monument shop with a new diamond wheel to make John ineligible for military service. On October 21, 1967, John joins 50,000 antiwar protesters in Washington, D.C., for the March on the Pentagon and participates in other demonstrations in Boston and New York.

14. Toronto, Canada

After earning a master's degree in English with a thesis on Thomas Hardy, John teaches ninth-grade composition part-time for two years at Gravesend Academy. He emigrates to Canada in 1968 and arrives in Ottawa at the midpoint of draft resisters' defection to Canada. Without success, he interviews at Upper Canada College, on forty-three acres at 200 Lonsdale Road in the center of Toronto.

At Russell Hill Road near Grace Church, John locates a place to live and avoids the American media. Near the college, he finds a job teaching English at the Bishop Trachan School for girls. He applies for Canadian citizenship and accepts Canon Campbell's invitation to become a member of the Anglican church.

15. Phoenix Sky Harbor Airport, Arizona

Owen realizes that his death is near. At midnight on July 4, 1968, he calls from Oakland, California, to invite John to visit him at Fort Huachuca. After booking John's flight and a motel room, he meets his old friend on July 8 at the Phoenix Sky Harbor terminal, an international airport located northeast of the city. While assisting two nuns from Catholic Relief Services in leading Vietnamese orphan boys to the men's room, Owen meets his fate after receiving from John a Chicom grenade hurled by Dick Jarvits, a deranged family member awaiting the funeral of a deceased soldier. Owen slam-dunks the grenade out the window but dies of blood loss after the explosion rips off his forearms. On the restroom floor, a nun cradles him and wraps him in her habit. As he wished, he receives a posthumous Soldier's Medal.

16. Gravesend, New Hampshire

In conference with Mr. Meany, John learns that Owen was a virgin birth and he carved his own gravestone with proper dates when he was last home on leave. John requests that Reverend Merrill pray for Owen. On an order from Owen's disembodied voice, John retrieves the missing baseball from the minister's desk drawer and identifies Merrill as his father. John worries that Merrill has lost his faith.

At 10:00 P.M. John hurls the fatal baseball through the Congregational church window and terrorizes the unstable minister with Tabby's ghostly dressmaking mannequin. Merrill begs forgiveness from the apparition, which he thinks is Tabby's spirit. John disposes of the ball, Mary Magdalene's arms, and the dummy in Rye harbor. Merrill conducts Owen's funeral at Hurd's Church.

17. Toronto, Canada

In January 1987, John walks his dog at the St. Clair Reservoir east of Detroit, Michigan, in Toronto. His students admire him for knowing Hester the Molester, a randy, foul-mouthed hard-rock star. He denounces President Ronald Reagan for waging an illegal covert war against communism in Nicaragua via Anastasio Somoza's National Guard, organized and supplied by the U.S. Central Intelligence Agency.

18. Georgian Bay, Lake Huron, Canada

In summer 1987, John relaxes at the Reverend Katherine Keeling's island home on Georgian Bay, a picturesque getaway in the northeastern quadrant of Lake Huron. Located near Burnt Island, Peesay Point, and Hearts Content Island, the island had been in her family since 1933. Canon Mackie counsels him on expressing anti-Americanism. Dan urges John to end his grudge against the country that caused Owen's death. He invites John to return to New Hampshire to teach at Gravesend Academy.

Further Reading

Bernstein, Richard, "John Irving: 19th-Century Novelist for These Times." *New York Times* (April 25, 1989).

"Boston & Maine Historical Society," http://members.verizon.net/~vze264n3/bmrrhs/.

Byfield, Ted, and Virginia Byfield, "That Much Maligned 'Religious Right' May Yet Prove to Be Society's Salvation." *Alberta Report* (October 2, 1995): 37–39.

Campbell, Josie P. *John Irving: A Critical Companion*. Westport, Conn.: Greenwood, 1998.

"Divided Loyalties." *Maclean's* (April 15, 1996): 61.

Evans, David, "Review." *Quill Quire* (April 1989): 22.

French, Sean, "Review." *New Statesman* (May 12, 1989): 35.

Gussow, Mel, "John Irving: A Novelist Builds Out from Fact to Reach the Truth," *New York Times* (April 28, 1998).

Harvey, Dennis, "Simon Birch." *Variety* (August 31, 1998).

"The Idaho: A John Irving Page," http://www.cs.hmc.edu/~pkeller/ neo/irving.html.

Kazin, Alfred, "God's Own Little Squirt." *New York Times Book Review* (March 12, 1989): 1, 30–31.

Mutch, David, "Review." *Christian Science Monitor* (April 19, 1989): 13.

Nathan, Paul, "Author in Charge." *Publishers Weekly* (January 16, 1995): 315.

"Phillips Exeter Academy," http://www.exeter.edu/.

Prescott, Peter S., "Review." *Newsweek* (April 10, 1989): 64.

Pritchard, William, "Review." *New Republic* (May 22, 1989): 36.

Rechtshaffen, Michael, "Simon Birch." *Hollywood Reporter* (July 31, 1998).

Reilly, Edward C. *Understanding John Irving*. Columbia: University of South Carolina Press, 1991.

Renwick, Joyce, "John Irving: An Interview." *Fictional International* (1982): 5–18.

Sheppard, R. Z., "Review." *Time* (April 3, 1989): 80.

Shostak, Debra, "Plot as Repetition: John Irving's Narrative Experiments." *Critique* (Fall 1995): 51–71.

Smith, Joan, "A Man Who Takes His Lack of Talent Seriously." *Salon*, March 1997.

Steiner, Wendy, "Review." *Times Literary Supplement* (May 19, 1989): 535.

Towers, Robert, "Review." *New York Review of Books* (July 20, 1989): 30.

"University of New Hampshire," http://unhinfo.unh.edu.

"Vietnam Recollections," http://the-tech.mit.edu/V110/N22/thing.22a.html.

"World of Development According to Irving." *Variety* (January 10, 2000): 6.

Shabanu, Daughter of the Wind

By Suzanne Fisher Staples

Multicultural contemporary fiction, 1989

Geographical Summary

Through a coming-of-age study of a young Pakistani girl, Suzanne Fisher Staples depicts the attitudes, actions, and motivations of characters as elements of the Islamic culture of Pakistan, Afghanistan, and India and by implication, farther west in Iran and Saudi Arabia. Set on the border between India and Pakistan, the story draws on the weather patterns and privations of nomadic herders in the Cholistan Desert. The lifestyle of Shabanu and her people requires an annual trek from windswept wastes to more habitable lands and watering holes and to markets for trading livestock and purchasing supplies. Traveling west to the annual Sibi Fair by camel train with her father, Dalil Abassi, she searches the landscape for Fort Abbas, the Khanpur irrigation canal, Rahimyar Khan, the Punjabi Plains, Gudu Barrage, the Indus River, and tribal Baluchistan.

Implicit in Shabanu's behaviors is an awareness of the danger in shifting sand, drought, and harsh winds. A pelting sandstorm devastates even the experienced desert dweller and native animals, filling the eyes and noses with grit as it contours the terrain. A lethal storm takes the life of Shabanu's grandfather, Jindwadda Ali Abassi, a hero of the former nawab's camel corps. After allowing him to die peacefully, the family must rush to a burial site before the body decays in the intense heat. Later, in the month preceding the annual rains, Shabanu anticipates salt water, shriveled grass, dry camel udders, and weak babies. She awaits the monsoon, which rains sweet water for personal and livestock consumption in a land that is sparsely pocked with natural watercourses.

Along the tracks Shabanu's family follows, the emotional story of her betrothal, first to a sixteen-year-old family friend, then to Rahim, a mature man with three wives, impacts the long distances with dread and fleeting fantasies of married life in a house staffed with servants. The vicious strike of Nazir Mohammad, a greedy local landowner, disrupts Shabanu's future, leaving her sister without a fiancé and their two families in the throes of desert-style threats and negotiations. Shabanu's desperate flight into the dunes to escape an unpromising marriage proves fruitless and endangers Mithoo, her young camel. Held captive by gender more than place, she has no hope of living free of patriarchy.

Detailed Itinerary

1. Cholistan Desert, Pakistan

On the way back from the family's worm-infested cistern, twelve-year-old Shabanu battles the winter dust of the Cholistan Desert dunes while all eastern Pakistan suffers a two-year drought. At 16,000 square miles, the huge wasteland expanse is a dry, barren, wind-blasted stretch of ancient forts, worn tracks, and remote settlements southeast of the Punjab. In the courtyard of round thatched huts, she watches her mother and aunt, the proud wife of Dadi's brother, stitching a yellow silk wedding dress for Shabanu's sister Phulan, who has reached the marriageable age of thirteen. As the parent of two sons, Auntie needles Phulan and Shabanu's mother because the sonless family will never afford dowries and weddings for two girls.

2. Dingarh, Pakistan

Phulan and Shabanu's father, Dadi, worry about the lack of water for his camels in the *toba* (hill country). For the rest of the month until the Sibi fair, he decides to resituate the family northeast in Dingarh, site of an ancient baked-brick fort that once guarded the camel route. In addition to pondering over Phulan's betrothal to Hamir for a marriage after Ramadan, Shabanu recalls the journey the previous year to Mehrabpur, south of the Hakra River toward the Punjabi Plains, where her family pledged her to Murad, Hamir's younger brother. The marriages will place both girls in stable homes apart from the wandering life her family has known on the Cholistan Desert.

During rain the next day, Shabanu's family remains in their mud hut where Dadi brings the girls harness to mend. Grandfather Jindwadda Ali Abassi narrates memories of his military career with the Army Camel Corps of the Nawab of Bahawalpur, a former Sikh stronghold and state capital that became a cosmopolitan city and the headquarters of Islamia University. Auntie and her two young boys see little of Uncle, a government office worker. The following morning, Shabanu delights in watering Guluband, her prized dancing camel, as she gazes east over the dunes toward India. The rain allows the family to stay put until Hamir and Phulan's wedding.

Shabanu is knowledgeable about livestock and births a young camel. A month later, she names the baby Mithoo. She observes camels coupling and wonders if human experience is similar. Dadi helps her part their four-year-old stud Kalu from Tipu, a challenging male, and settles her with tiny Mithoo on Guluband for a quick escape.

3. Derawar Fort

In mid-February, before the departure for the livestock fair to the west, the girls adorn the seven male camels with henna swirls and bells. Dadi and Shabanu wear their best. To accommodate traditional modesty, Auntie gives Shabanu a *chadr,* a womanly garment that cloaks hair, neck, and part of the face. Mama insists that Shabanu wear the cumbrous scarf. Traveling west from sunup to nightfall, she and Dadi pass the ruins of Maujgarh Fort, built by moguls in the sixteenth and seventeenth centuries.

Dadi camps at Derawar Fort, built a century before with rounded palisades formed of sun-baked brick. A desert ranger, one of the men trained by the Pakistan Army to patrol the Pakistan–India border, offers to buy Guluband. He learns that Dadi and Shabanu will be traveling for ten days—southwest to the Khanpur irrigation canal and near the market city of Rahimyar Khan before turning west to cross the Indus River into Baluchistan, where other nomads will join them. In fear of losing her favorite camel, Shabanu runs toward the fort and encircles it, passing the ancient mosque where an Abassi prince once kept seventy wives in subterranean cells. The next day, Dadi and Shabanu pray at the mosque before continuing their journey.

4. Gudu Barrage over the Indus River

Dadi and Shabanu arrive near the Gudu Barrage, an irrigation dam over the Indus River just inside the Sind border. The river, the longest in southwestern Asia, travels 1,900 miles southwest from the Himalayan Mountains of Tibet to the Arabian Sea. Essential to irrigation, it produces an erratic flow that floods with the thaw of Himalayan snows, then decreases to a trickle during winter droughts.

Dadi and Shabanu encounter Bugti travelers pursuing a woman who has eloped with a Marri tribesman. The Bugti are Baluchti nomads who wander the desolate Sulaiman Range. The potential execution of the Bugti woman impresses Shabanu with the dangers faced by independent females in a male-dominated culture. With fellow livestock dealers, Dadi discusses prices paid by Afghan *mujahideen,* a band of Muslim wanderers. He declares that he does not sacrifice camels as food for the festival of Eid and refrains from selling to Arabs, who use camels for meat rather than transportation. Other herders admire his healthy stock.

5. Sibi fair

Beyond the Sulaiman Range in Baluchistan, a mountainous region sparsely forested with pine and juniper that extends from Karachi on the Arabian Sea north to Quetta, buyers bargain at the Sibi fairground. Because Shabanu may marry within the year and become a stay-at-home housewife, she knows that she will miss the annual trek to Sibi. Four armed Afghans from far to the north meet Dadi and Shabanu at camp. After Wardak, their chief, makes an offer for the camels, Dadi insists on double the price.

The third day of the fair, Dadi trades with a man from Zhob in northeastern Pakistan on the Afghanistan border. The buyer pays for all but one of the females and for Tipu, who brings a good price. Shabanu sells two wooden saddles and, with part of the proceeds, cooks chicken curry. After the rain, she serves Dadi's guests, who come to celebrate the sale. Dadi's profits are enough for his daughters' weddings and dowries. Some of the men consider driving their herds southwest through the Makran Range on the coast and into Iran, where Arabs eat camels.

6. Dingra to Rahimyar Khan

Late that night, Shabanu packs their goods for the remaining camel to carry on the return home. Before they depart for Jacobabad and northeast to Dingra, Dadi gives her a puppy, which he names Sher Dil. For two days, they worry about Dadi's money, the bulk of which he hides in his saddle frame as they cross the dangerous Bugti tribal area. On the eighth night of their travel over the northeast stretch beyond the Indus River toward home, Dadi and Shabanu visit Uncle at Rahimyar Khan and shop for Phulan's wedding.

7. Cholistan Desert, Pakistan

Four days later, Dadi and Shabanu rejoin Mama and Phulan and discover the birth of twenty-two baby camels during their month-long absence. At dusk, the family celebrates Dadi's lucrative trading and examines goods from the west. In March, with only a month left before the drought will force them out of the dunes, the family anticipates the May rains, a propitious time of weddings.

8. Channan Pir

On the night of the next full moon, the family makes a pilgrimage northwest over the dry Hakra River bed to the shrine at Channan Pir, a white marble tomb of a desert saint where women ask Allah for sons and good marriages for their daughters. Grandfather reminisces and relates events from ancient history. He misidentifies the battle in which he was a hero, when the army fought India over Kutch, a lowland area in southwestern India along the Arabian Sea that was the site of an ancient Indus Valley civilization.

At the shrine in February and March, where thousands gather annually, female worshippers kneel in the mud courtyard at the mosque near Channan's tomb and whip themselves into a frenzy. Their songs, wails, and chants honor the Muslim martyr and saint. Sharma sings a poetic song about Channan Pir. According to legend, after a vengeful raja abandoned him in the wilderness in infancy, he remained safe in a sandalwood cradle that dropped from heaven. He grew up among desert animals and became a sage respected by Hindus and Muslims. Sharma reminds Shabanu that she must honor her father, who has pledged his girls to worthy alliances.

9. Cholistan Desert, Pakistan

On their return through the desert, the family survives a catastrophic sandstorm that threatens to consume their camp and herd. Mama treats their lacerated eyes with mint, which stings and soothes. Late that afternoon, the quiet desert has an unfamiliar shape. As the family searches for Grandfather, Shabanu locates a dead baby camel. Before dawn, Dadi finds his elderly father. Nearing death, the old man requests a martyr's burial in Derawar. Mama tends his wounds while Auntie and Phulan pack for the journey west into the desert. They pass the place where, the previous day, they had prayed toward the holy city of Mecca, a sacred Arab site fifty miles from the Red Sea, where the prophet Muhammad was born in A.D. 570.

10. Derawar Fort

The family sets out with Grandfather nestled in a string cot on a camel. He wears his khaki fez and bronze star, symbol of the brave charge at Kutch. As required by their faith, they turn his head toward Mecca and pray for his soul. At sunset, they arrive at the century-old Derawar Fort and spy the minarets and marble dome of the nawab's mosque. The old man dies before sunrise.

The family chants prayers and hurries Grandfather's body, shrouded in his string cot, toward a grave before heat rots and distorts it. In the cemetery lie only the nawab's family and army heroes. In the desert, the family pounds clay into powder to mix with dung to pave a makeshift burial hole six feet deep. At sunset, they inter Grandfather and mark the spot with sticks and colored flags, where pilgrims can pray.

11. Mehrabpur

Because water is scarce and salty, the family departs Derawar and travels northeast toward Mehrabpur. After a two-day trip, they arrive at the irrigation ditch dug by Hamir's father. The two families erect a thatched cottage and fast in observance of Ramadan. Phulan is delighted with Hamir's thoughtfulness in building her a whitewashed cottage. While fetching pots of water, Phulan encounters quail hunters led by Nazir, who intends to present her to his guests as their entertainment for the duration of their visit. Hurling water jars at her pursuers, she runs.

Shabanu informs Dadi of Nazir's intent. As the family packs, Dadi goes to warn Hamir. Hastily, the women cut a hole in the hut and hurry out the back into the Cholistan Desert. On her flight to the southwest, Shabanu keeps the North Star or Polaris, the bright star in the handle of Ursa Minor (the Little Dipper), over her left shoulder and avoids the common track. When Shabanu and the other women meet Desert Rangers, their leader Spin Gul hurries back northeast toward Mehrabpur. Bloody but safe, Dadi and Murad reunite with the family and report Hamir's death. The rangers of Yazman guard Hamir's family while they negotiate a truce through Nazir's older brother Rahim, a politician.

12. Dingarh

The next morning, Auntie blames Shabanu for the family's predicament. After all-night negotiations by radio, Nazir accepts Hamir's death as an appeasement but threatens to seize Murad's property and cut off its water supply. Spin Gul and the rangers accompany the family to Dingarh, where Rahim will protect Murad's family. After a ten-hour ride, the family reaches Dingarh, the Wing Command headquarters of Colonel Haq.

When Shabanu rescues her young cousins after their ladder falls from a mango tree, a man Dadi's age steadies the ladder and jokes with Shabanu. She flashes her perfect teeth at the stranger. The negotiating continues into the night and the following morning. Bibi Lal reports that, in forty days, Phulan will wed Murad. Rahim, the stranger at whom Shabanu smiled, has formally requested her as his wife.

13. Mehrabpur

Five days after Hamir's murder, the family returns northeast to Mehrabpur. Rahim has erected a small village, given them a servant, and paid the bride price, which includes golden ornaments and other wedding gifts. Bibi Lal's family receives new houses. During the mourning period, pilgrims seek the grave of Hamir, which becomes a shrine.

14. Cholistan Desert, Pakistan

The family rides home in the rain. While everyone sleeps, Shabanu flees on Xhush Dil into the dunes. Mithoo, who straggles behind, breaks his leg in a foxhole. When Dadi arrives, he beats Shabanu with a stick, bloodying her shoulders, and then halts to hug her close.

Further Reading

Alter, Stephen. *Amritsar to Lahore: A Journey Across the India-Pakistan Border*. Philadelphia: University of Pennsylvania Press, 2000.

Caldwell, John C. *Pakistan*. New York: Chelsea House, 2000.

"Exploring Ancient World Cultures: Islam," http://eawc.evansville.edu/ispage.htm.

Fader, Ellen, "Review." *Horn Book* (January-February 1994).

Hasan, Shaikh Kurshid, "Talpurs and Their Tomb Architecture," http://royaltalpur.tripod.com/articles/arch1.htm.

"Islamic Weddings," http://www.jamiat.org.za/isl_wedding.html.

Kenoyer, Jonathan Mark, "Around the Indus in 90 Slides," http://www.harappa.com/indus/ubdys0.html.

"Kutch Peoples," http://budamusique.com/US/MONDE/ASIE/kutch.html.

McCray, Nancy, "Review." *Booklist* (August 1995).

McNulty, Faith, "Review." *New Yorker* (November 27, 1989).

Middleton, Susan, "Review." *School Library Journal* (August 1993).

Nilsen, Alleen Pace, and Ken Donelson, "Review." *English Journal* (December 1990).

Quick, Sheikh Abdullah Hakim, "Ramadan in History," http://www.al-muslim.org/ramadan/history.htm.

Raymond, Allen, "Suzanne Fisher Staples: Magical Storyteller." *Teaching PreK–8* (March 1994).

Richardson, Judy S., "A Read-Aloud for Cultural Diversity." *Journal of Adolescent & Adult Literacy* (October 1995).

Roback, Diane, "Review." *Publishers Weekly* (October 13, 1989).

Salzman, Philip Carl. *Black Tents of Baluchistan*. Washington, D.C.: Smithsonian Institution Press, 2000.

Sawyer, Walter E., and Jean C. Sawyer, "A Discussion with Suzanne Fisher Staples: The Author as Writer and Cultural Observer." *New Advocate* (Summer 1993).

"Shabanu," http://www.shorelin.wednet.edu/Shorewood/Classes/Honors10Rev/RevHTM/staplesS.html1.

Simon, Maurya, "Review." *New York Times Book Review* (November 12, 1989).

Snodgrass, Mary Ellen. *Encyclopedia of World Scripture*. Jefferson, N.C.: McFarland, 2001.

Staples, Suzanne Fisher, "Different Is Just Different." *ALAN Review* (Winter 1995).

"Sulaiman Range," http://www.nationalgeographic.com/wildworld/profiles/terrestrial/pa/pa1018.html.

"Suzanne Fisher Staples," http://www.indiana.edu/~eric_rec/ieo/bibs/staples.html.

"Suzanne Fisher Staples," http://www.ridgeret.org/event/Staples.htm#life.

Tuccillo, Diane P., "Review." *Wilson Library Bulletin* (May 1990).

Warwick, Ellen D., "Review." *School Library Journal* (November 1989).

Zeiger, Hanna B., "Review." *Horn Book* (January-February 1990).

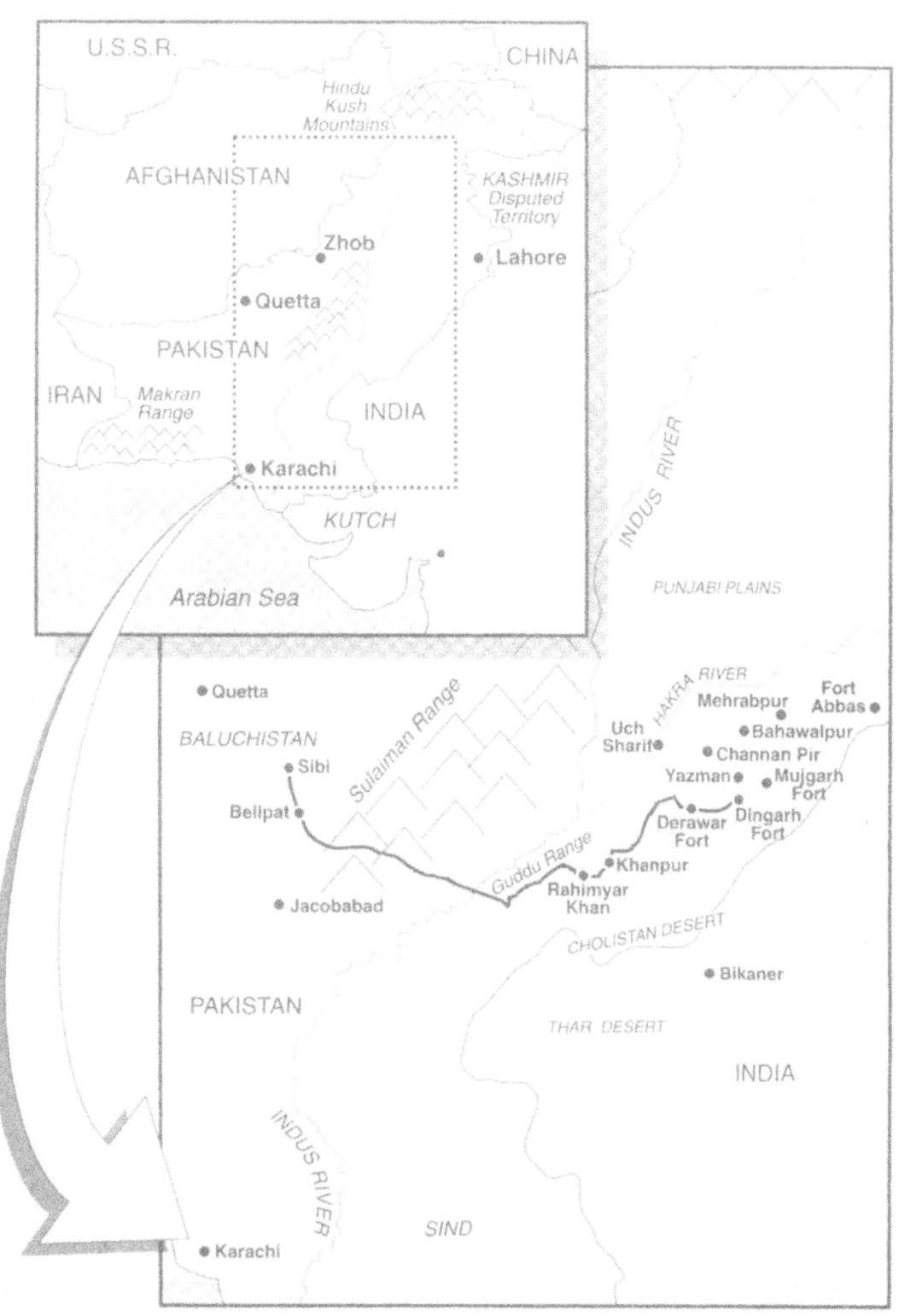

The Sign of the Beaver
By Elizabeth George Speare

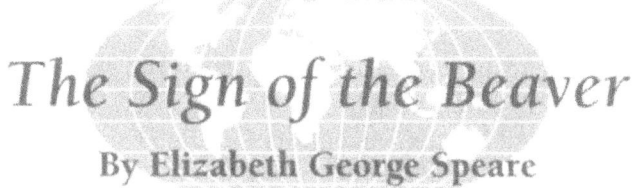

Historical fiction, 1983

Geographical Summary

Drawing on her familiarity with New England history, young adult writer Elizabeth George Speare sets her survival fiction in the coastal Maine wild along the Penobscot River. The story opens at a time when white families migrate inland from the original English colonies settlers had built near the Atlantic Coast. After the Hallowells buy land, Matt and his father erect a cabin and plant a garden on the Penobscot River in south central Maine.

Family business forces father and son to separate temporarily. Hallowell journeys southwest to Quincy, Massachusetts, to bring his wife and daughter to the new home. Alone, Matt manages against a thieving white hunter, wild animals, and bees. Unequal to forest dangers, he accepts the friendship of Penobscot Indians, an eastern Abenaki people who lived on forest game in winter and seafood in summer. They also traded furs, pottery, and birch bark crafts for corn, blankets, and ammunition.

Attean, a Penebscot boy, teaches Matt woodsmanship, how to make and shoot a bow and arrows, and how to snare birds and spear fish. By developing an intercultural understanding of forest natives, he comes to recognize the threat that whites pose to the Indians' ancestral homeland. By the time Matt reunites with his parents, he has grown into a mature, thoughtful man who has stored up ample food for winter. He learns of their sickness at the trading post and the long trek northeast by sled. At the novel's end, he sympathizes with the Penobscot, whom settlers have forced off their traditional hunting grounds.

Detailed Itinerary

1. Cabin on the Penobscot River, Maine

In 1768, Matthew Hallowell lives in the Maine wilderness at the mouth of the Penobscot River at his family's new cabin, the beginning of a new settlement. The area was the homeland of the Penobscot Indians, the largest Abenaki tribe, whose influence extended into central Maine. Northeast of the current citiy of Bangor, they settled at Old Town on Indian Island a few miles north of white settlements. Mr. Hallowell explains to Matt that most of the Indians have left for Canada to the north.

2. Massachusetts

The English had begun exploring Massachusetts 168 years before the story begins. Within seven years of their initial visit, in September 1620, the Pilgrims had boarded the *Mayflower* to cross the Atlantic Ocean and after exploring Cape Cod, landed at Plymouth on Massachusetts's southeastern shore on December 11, 1621. A decade later, John Winthrop led one hundred Puritan settlers, called the Massachusetts Bay Company, aboard the *Arbella* from England to chartered land between the Merrimack and Charles rivers. Chief Massasoit of the Wampanoag urged his people to seek peaceful alliance with the newcomers.

3. Quincy, Massachusetts

In summer, Matt's father travels southwest to fetch his family from their house in Quincy in the Massachusetts Bay Colony. The city, now a part of greater Boston on the southeastern edge of Boston Bay, was only a fort at the time of the story.

4. Cabin on the Penobscot River, Maine

Alone until August, Matt marks the passing days with seven notches per stick and counts four sticks per month. Ben, a heavyset white trapper, arrives as Matt skins a rabbit. Matt lies that his father will return momentarily. At a shared dinner of squirrel stew, corn cake, and molasses, Ben explains vaguely that he had to leave town to avoid hostile people. He states that most Indians have resettled farther west but that the Penobscot "stick like burrs" and return annually to harvest the steamer and quahog clams that live at the coast. After lighting a corncob pipe and narrating his capture by the Iroquois, he spends the night, then moves on toward the interior to trap beaver. The next morning, Matt is relieved that his guest has departed but realizes too late that Ben stole the rifle, leaving Matt to survive without a hunting weapon.

5. Loon Pond

In July, a week before his thirteenth birthday, Matt leaves the cabin door unbarred while he picks blueberries and fishes in the creek. A large mammal—probably a bear—ransacks the cabin and eats the family's supply of flour and molasses. Because the loss depletes Matt's stock of molasses, he robs a bee tree at the swampy end of Loon Pond and angers a swarm of bees. Losing a boot in the mud, he dashes toward the icy water, spraining his ankle on a fallen branch. Saknis, a kindly old Indian, rescues him.

6. Cabin on the Penobscot River, Maine

Later, Saknis doses Matt with bitter medicine that makes him sleep. Saknis returns later and introduces his grandson, Attean of the Beaver clan, who derides Matt for endangering himself in the bee tree. Saknis supplies Matt with stew and corn bread, a rough crutch, and moose hide moccasins with ties that wrap high up on his ankles. Matt rewards him with one of the two books on the Hallowells' shelf. He chooses a copy of *Robinson Crusoe* (1719), Daniel Defoe's fictionalized version of the marooning of Alexander Selkirk, whom privateers abandoned on the desolate Más a Tierra Island in the Juan Fernández cluster, four hundred miles west of Valparaíso, Chile. Attean concludes that the story of Crusoe's survival after shipwreck describes an inept protagonist who lacks the survival skills that Indians prize.

7. Woods on the Penobscot River, Maine

After a few days of reading lessons, Attean teaches Matt woodsmanship, beginning with shaping roots and saplings into snares for trapping small animals and birds.

8. A creek in the woods

Attean takes Matt spear fishing and discards a small catch, which he solemnly addresses before tossing it into the stream. Matt embarrasses himself by slipping into the water while trying to use a spear. A fish breaks his line and swims away with his only hook. Attean shows Matt how to carve twigs into hooks.

9. Beaver dam

In August, Attean and his dog Aremus lead Matt deep into the forest to a beaver dam. The animal is a tribal symbol, which clan members carve on trees as totemic markings of their hunting ground. Attean teaches Matt to identify stones, grass, and sticks with which Attean marked the trail and to gather spruce sap for chewing gum.

10. Turtle clan hunting ground

While stalking game in the forest, Attean denounces white hunters for causing a fox to suffer in an iron trap, a method only bad Indians imitate. Because the two boys are trespassing on the turtle clan's territory, he must leave the fox to chew off its foot. Matt is embarrassed by white cruelty.

11. Indian village

To Indian peers in his village, an hour's walk away, Attean relates the story of *Robinson Crusoe*. Matt tells Old Testament hero stories about David and Goliath, Samson, and Joseph and the coat of many colors. Attean matches them with the myths of the trickster Gluskabe and of the Great Spirit, a Penobscot deity. Matt is surprised Indians know a flood myth similar to Noah and the ark.

12. Beaver dam on the Penobscot River, Maine

On their way to the dam, Matt and Attean find a bear cub. Matt hurls a dead rabbit at the mother bear's nose while Attean shoots her between the eyes and below the shoulder. Both boys stab the dying bear. Attean atones for making the cub an orphan. He demonstrates that Indians waste nothing and never kill for sport. Squaws come from the village to collect the meat and hide. Attean strings bear claws on a cord to wear around his neck and paints his face for the victory feast.

13. Indian village on the Penobscot River

Matt travels upriver in Attean's canoe to the fortified stockade village to the celebration of Attean's courage. According to tradition, Attean, the hunter, must decline meat of the bear he killed. Matt enjoys the village festivities by sipping a maple sugar-flavored drink from a gourd, taking a draw on a long pipe, retelling the story of the kill, and watching a clown shaking a rattle. That night, Matt leaves the dancing to sleep in an empty wigwam on fur-covered mats.

The next morning when Matt arises, Indian women are at work weaving rush baskets and grinding grain in a mortar while the men stalk deer. Attean stays behind because he has no gun. Attean's grandmother thinks of Matt as one of the whites who shot and scalped Attean's mother while she was searching the woods for bark to make baskets. They also killed Attean's father, who attempted to avenge her death. Matt recalls that the Massachusetts governor offered bounty on native scalps. Saknis believes that peaceful coexistence is the only answer for Indians living near white settlers.

14. Turtle clan hunting ground

Matt goes back to the cabin. Late in September, the Hallowells have not returned. He roams the woods near the forbidden turtle trap and hears the whine of Attean's injured dog. Aremus's paw is broken. To get help, Matt runs along the trail to the Penobscot River and swims to the stockade at the Indian village.

15. Indian village

When Matt arrives, he encounters only women in residence after Attean joins the adult males in hunting. Attean's sister Marie paddles a canoe to the trail and hurries to free Attean's dog. Halfway back down the trail, they meet Attean.

Two days later, while touring the village, Matt observes women pounding corn kernels, drying berries on bark, and weaving birch bark baskets. He joins a game of discs, which costs him his only shirt. Before returning by canoe, he realizes that the clan now accepts him.

16. Woods on the Penobscot River, Maine

A week later, Attean begins a vision quest to find his *manitou*, an inner spirit that unifies him with nature. The ritual begins with fasting, purifying his body, and swallowing doses of a purgative. Alone in the woods, he sings and prays to ready himself for a dream that will identify him as an adult hunter. Matt discerns that the test is crucial to Attean's attainment of manhood.

17. North from the Penobscot River, Maine

In late October, Attean, now a village brave, sports a braided topknot and shaved scalp. After Saknis trades beaver skins for a gun, Attean is now armed like a man. The Beaver clan prepares to abandon summer camp and journey north into fresh territory that white hunters have not stripped of game. The villagers intend to separate from whites on a winter hunt. Saknis offers Matt a place in the clan as his foster grandson.

Matt surmises that Saknis fears the Hallowells are gone forever, but he keeps his faith in his father. Matt thanks Attean's grandfather, but remains at the family cabin. As the pair departs, Matt wonders if he would have abandoned white ways if the Indians had educated him in childhood. Four days later, the clan sets out for Indian lands in the west far from white settlers. Before departing, Attean comes to respect Matt for maintaining the family cabin as his father ordered.

18. Cabin on the Penobscot River, Maine

Matt survives the winter alone at the family residence and saves corn, dried pumpkin, nuts, and berries for food. When the skies threaten snow before Christmas, he readies the cabin for cold weather. He stacks extra fire logs and whittles a snow shovel. With his new snowshoes, he romps in the snow and delights in free movement. By night, he sits at the hearth to sip hemlock tea and reread *Robinson Crusoe*.

19. Trading Post, Quincy, Massachusetts Bay Colony
Three days later, the Hallowells return by sled after a bout of typhus, a noncontagious disease spread by lice infested with rickettsiae. The trio had delayed three weeks at the trading post while waiting for a guide.

20. Cabin on the Penobscot River, Maine
Mr. Hallowell unloads flour and molasses, a kettle, a whale oil lamp, pewter dishes, quilts, and a jacket, breeches, and new boots for Matt. His mother admires how healthy and manly her son has become and marvels at all the food he has stored. Mr. Hallowell expects three new families by spring and will share an oxen team with a family five miles away. Looking to the future, he envisions a mill, town, and school. Matt's parents are impressed with the survival skills he learned from Attean and the Beaver clan. Matt grieves that settlers drive Indians away from their ancestral New England homelands.

Further Reading

Ammon, B. D. *Handbook for the Newbery Medal and Honor Books, 1980–1989.* Hagerstown, Md.: Alleyside Press, 1991.

Apseloff, Marilyn Fain. *Elizabeth George Speare.* New York: Twayne, 1991.

Cantor, George. *North American Indian Landmarks.* Detroit: Gale Research, 1993.

Champagne, Duane, ed. *Chronology of Native North American History.* Detroit: Gale Research, 1994.

"The Doucette Index to K-12 Teaching Ideas for Literature," http://www.educ.ucalgary.ca/litindex.

"Elizabeth George Speare." *Biography Today* (September 1995): 102.

"Elizabeth George Speare," http://www.indiand.edu/~eric_recieo/bibs/speare.html.

"Elizabeth George Speare," http://www.mcdougallittell.com/lit/guest/speare/index.htm.

"Elizabeth George Speare," http://www.randomhouse.com/teachersbdd/spea.html.

Fritz, Jean, "Review." *New York Times Book Review* (May 8, 1983): 37.

Gray, Ruth. *Old Town, Maine.* Rockport, Maine: Picton Press, 1997.

Johansen, Bruce E., and Donald A Grinde, Jr. *The Encyclopedia of Native American Biography.* New York: Da Capo Press, 1998.

"Massachusetts Bay Colony Charter," http://www.sec.state.ri.us/rihist/richart.htm.

Moseley, Ann, "Signs in Speare's 'The Sign of the Bear.'" *ALAN Review* (Spring 1995).

"Newbery Award," http://www.sjpl.lib.ca.us/youth/x-newber.htm.

Patterson, Lotsee, and Mary Ellen Snodgrass. *Indian Terms of the Americas.* Englewood, Colo.: Libraries Unlimited, 1994.

"Penobscot: A People and Their River," http://www.clf.org/pubs/penob.htm.

"Penobscot Indian Nation Homepage," http://www.penobscotnation.org/.

"Penobscot Indians," http://www.knight.org/advent/cathen/11644a.htm.

Pritzker, Barry M. *A Native American Encyclopedia.* Oxford: Oxford University Press, 2000.

"Quincy Massachusetts History," http://www.key-biz.com/ssn/Quincy/history.html.

Schultz, Eric B., and Michael J. Tougias. *King Philip's Indian War: The History and Legacy of America's Forgotten Conflict*. Woodstock, Vt.: Countryman Press, 2000.

Speare, Elizabeth George, "Laura Ingalls Wilder Award Acceptance." *Horn Book* (July/August1989).

_____, "The Survival Story." *Horn Book* (March–April 1988): 163–72.

_____, "Report of a Journey: Newbery Award Acceptance." *Horn Book* (August 1962).

Sullivan, Emilie P., "Three Good Juvenile Books with Literacy Models." *Journal of Reading* (September 1994): 55.

Tighe, Mary Ann, and Charles Avinger, "Teaching Tomorrow's Classics." *ALAN Review* (Spring 1994): 9–13.

Waldman, Carl. *Who Was Who in Native American History*. New York: Facts on File, 1990.

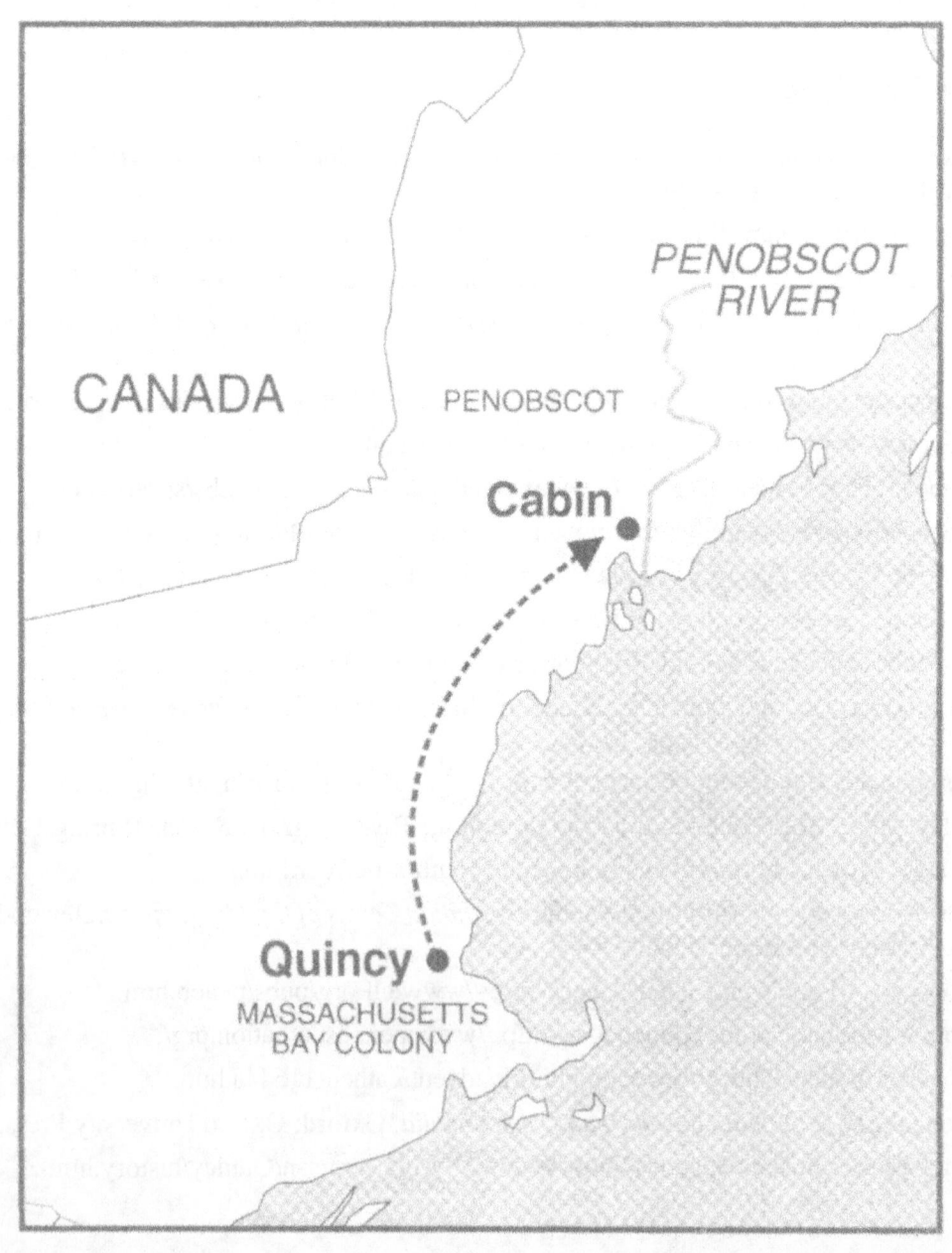

Snow Falling on Cedars
By David Guterson

Contemporary mainstream fiction, 1994

Geographical Summary

Immersed in memories of Puget Sound and the hard lives of stoop laborers, novelist David Guterson, a native of the Seattle area, sets *Snow Falling on Cedars* in the lush land of strawberry fields and sea teeming with fresh catch. The Japanese workers who arrived on fictional San Piedro Island in 1883 learned to adapt to the damp climate to wrest a living for their families. For schoolmates Kabuo Miyamoto and Carl Heine, Jr., advancement from agriculture to gill-netting salmon enhances the drama of a subsequent interracial dispute over truck farm acreage. Ironically, both men want to abandon sea fishing to return to the agrarian lives of their fathers. The accidental drowning of Carl Heine, Jr., in the wake of the freighter SS *West Corona* unsettles family harmony and threatens Kabuo with execution for an erroneous charge of murder.

In winter 1954, during Kabuo's trial at Amity Harbor courthouse, a fresh snow resurrects memories of World War II and forces local people to deal with the loss of electric power. The snow equalizes citizens facing immobilization of their island and causes the principal actors in the trial to seek justice by candlelight in cold rooms. Breaking the impasse is one kind deed—the unselfishness of Ishmael Chambers, who drives the Imadas home after they are stranded in the cold. After scouting new evidence, he determines to end his hatred of Kabuo's wife Hatsue, whose loss is the source of his postwar malaise.

Detailed Itinerary

1. Amity Harbor, San Piedro, Puget Sound, Washington

Awaiting the trial that accuses an innocent Japanese fisherman of clubbing to death a Caucasian gill-netter, at 8:50 on December 6, 1954, salmon fisherman Kabuo Miyamoto sits impassive before fellow islanders. He faces the insular community of Amity Harbor on San Piedro, a fictional part of the San Juan islands, a real cluster northwest of Seattle, Washington, off the east coast of Victoria, British Columbia. At Kabuo's trial, reporters from Anacortes, Bellingham, Seattle, and Victoria carry news of the event to mainland newspapers in Washington and British Columbia.

Sheltered from a snowstorm, the courthouse becomes a microcosm of the division between angry white residents and the Japanese supporters of Kabuo. He has languished in jail for ten weeks. Exacerbating the tension is Ishmael Chambers, the vindictive local reporter for the *San Piedro Review* who stokes hatred against the Japanese for catapulting the United States into World War II, the war that cost him an arm. The newspaper's founder—his father, Arthur Chambers—was a World War I veteran of the battles of Saint-Mihiel and Belleau Wood, France, in June 1918. He initiated the island press after he returned home.

2. White Sand Bay, San Piedro Island

According to testimony by Sheriff Art Moran, at 9:00 A.M. on September 16, Deputy Abel Martinson found the *Susan Marie*, Carl Heine's stern-picker, which trailed fishing nets from the rear. Erik Syvertsen, a Port Jensen fisherman, discovered the boat adrift in White Sand Bay on the northwest side of the island. Martinson helped Moran retrieve Carl's corpse, which was snared in his own net. Carl suffered a crushed skull above the left ear. The sheriff reported Carl's death to his wife, Susan Marie, at her home on Mill Run Road south of Amity Harbor.

Defense attorney Nels Gudmundsson discloses that the island was befogged on September 15. Muddling the investigation was the placement of a D-8 battery and an oversized D-6 wedged into the side flange of the battery well formerly occupied by Carl's dead spare.

3. Ship Channel Bank off San Piedro

According to Dale Middleton's testimony, the evening before Carl's death, he followed the *Susan Marie* to Ship Channel Bank at 6:30. An hour and a half later, Leonard George saw Heine at sea. Coroner Horace Whaley testifies that he found an empty knife sheath on Carl's corpse and a watch stopped at 1:47 A.M. Whaley determined that the victim entered the water alive but could not set a time for a cut extending from the victim's right palm to the wrist. He describes Carl's skull fracture in terms of the hard blow of a blunt instrument inflicted by Japanese kendo fighters. The coroner suggests the sheriff search for a bloody gun butt owned by a "right-handed Jap."

4. Manzanar, an internment camp in the Mojave Desert in southern California

The ancestors of local Japanese islanders prospered from labor at the Port Jefferson lumber mill and from agricultural work requiring intense stoop labor. On March 29, 1942, following the bombing of Pearl Harbor, Hawaii, on December 7, 1941, the U.S. government assigned local Japanese Americans to an internment camp at Manzanar for the rest of World War II. Hatsue's mother, Fujiko, struggled with the disappointment of marrying Hisao Imada, who had given the impression that he was rich. At her mother's insistence, Hatsue married Kabuo, who left for infantry training at Camp Shelby in Bolivar County, Mississippi.

5. Amity Harbor, San Piedro

Ishmael reminisces over his first love, fourteen-year-old Hatsue, who regularly met him in secret in the forest at a hollow cedar. Carl's mother Etta, an emigrant from Ingolstadt, Bavaria, testifies that, in 1934, her husband sold seven acres of farmland to Kabuo's father, Zenhichi Miyamoto, even though laws banned land purchase by immigrant Japanese. Carl Sr., disliked her anti-Asian racism and scolded her for insulting Zenhichi when he came to their home with the semi-annual payment of $250 on his debt. Carl had refused to take Zenhichi's savings and leave the family destitute.

After Carl, Sr., died of heart failure in October 1944, Etta refunded the sale price to the Miyamotos, who were still incarcerated in California, and earned $2,500 profit by selling all thirty acres to Ole Jurgensen, a local Scandinavian American. She refused to help Kabuo reclaim his family's farmland, which now belonged to Ole.

In court, Etta claims that Kabuo killed Carl, Jr., to retaliate for her racism and trickery. Ole testifies that he had no part in the land squabble. After suffering a stroke, Ole sold his property to Carl, Jr. Still eager to recover his family's farmland, Kabuo asked about the acreage after Ole and Carl, Jr., had reached their agreement.

6. Jail, Amity Harbor, San Piedro

Etta's testimony angers Kabuo, who loses control of his dignity. At noon recess, he returns to his cell and relives shooting a German soldier during the war. He thinks over his precipitate marriage at Manzanar, enlistment in the military, and life with a wife and children. He recalls that before the family departed for internment, his father had buried the family's treasures in the strawberry field. The family prized the courage of his great-grandfather, a former samurai who committed suicide in a failed rebellion in Kumamoto on the east central coast of Kyushu, Japan. The samurai revolt resulted from the collapse of knighthood that accompanied the abolition of Japanese feudalism during the Meiji Restoration in 1871.

7. Amity Harbor, San Piedro

Ishmael remembers four years of meeting with Hatsue and of seeing her crowned strawberry princess in 1941. As rumors implicated local Japanese Americans as agents of Japan, Arthur Chambers's editorial defended San Piedro's Asian settlers and called them neighbors rather than enemies. Local people retaliated against Arthur by canceling their subscriptions and refusing to advertise in his paper.

FBI agents questioned Hisao Imada and confiscated the twenty-four sticks of dynamite he used for clearing land. Agent Wilson arrested Hisao, handcuffed him, and jailed him in Seattle. He and eight other Japanese males were deported to a work camp farther east in Montana. On March 26, Arthur's editorial denounced the U.S. War Relocation Authority plan to remove and incarcerate islanders of Japanese descent. Two days later, Hatsue met Ishmael one last time. She resolved never to see him again.

8. Amity Harbor to Anacortes to Puyallup, Washington

At 7:00 the next morning, the Imadas traveled by army truck to the ferry at Amity Harbor. At 9:00 A.M., the *Kehloken* carried the sobbing family to the mainland. They traveled overland by train from Anacortes on the coast south to a transit camp at a horse stable at the Puyallup fairgrounds southeast of Tacoma, Washington. Three days later, another train transported them south across Oregon to California and deposited them at Manzanar, a hastily built tarpaper barracks encampment in the Mojave Desert.

After Hatsue's sister Sumiko intercepted a love letter from Ishmael, news of the secret love match immersed Fujiko in memories of herself as the picture bride of a Seattle pauper. She had lived in a Jackson Street boardinghouse and raised five daughters while her husband worked at the National Cannery Company. She rebuked Hatsue for deceiving her. Before Fujiko could mail a letter to the Chambers family, Hatsue declared that she cared nothing for Ishmael. After a few months, Fujiko encouraged the attentions of Kabuo, who came to the Imada quarters to build shelves and furnishings.

9. Parris Island, South Carolina, to Tarawa

Numb with grief, in late summer of 1942, Ishmael entered basic training at Parris Island in Beaufort County on South Carolina's southern tip, where some 14,500 marines trained before deployment in World War II. After completing radio school in North Island, New

Zealand, he traveled aboard the transport vessel *Heywood* from Nouméa, New Caledonia, to Betio, an island in the Tarawa cluster of the Gilbert Island chain in the western Pacific Ocean. During the landing on November 19, 1942, enemy fire depleted his company.

At 9:00 P.M., after three hundred of Ishmael's comrades topped the seawall, he was the only survivor. A sniper's bullet shattered his left arm. When the beach was secure, corpsmen relayed Ishmael to a ship, where a pharmacist's mate amputated the arm below the shoulder.

10. Amity Harbor, San Piedro

As the sheriff investigated the crime, Judge Fielding allowed limited search for a murder weapon on the strength of a tie line that suggested someone had boarded Carl's boat. The sheriff and his deputy checked Kabuo's boat, *Islander,* and located a gaff with blood on the handle. Fishermen cast doubt on Kabuo's relationship with Carl by testifying to quarrels at sea. Sergeant Victor Maples, who trained men at Camp Shelby, characterizes Kabuo as capable of murder with a kendo stick.

Susan Heine reflects on Kabuo's visit to their home on September 9. She knew that the war had grieved Carl, whose ship, the USS *Canton*, sank during the invasion of Okinawa in 1945. On return to San Piedro, Carl wanted to abandon salmon fishing and raise strawberries.

The elderly defense attorney Nels Gudmundsson begins cross-examination to determine Carl's state of mind at the time of death. When the storm cuts off power in Amity Harbor and darkens the courtroom, the state rests until noon. The jury withdraws to a cold, dark hotel.

Ishmael intends to carry groceries and supplies to his mother, who lives five miles away on the southeastern tip of San Piedro. On the way, he rescues the Imadas after their station wagon is disabled in a drainage ditch. Hatsue urges him to write something for the newspaper to ensure justice for Kabuo.

11. Point White Lighthouse, San Piedro

At the coast guard lighthouse at Point White on the San Piedro's northwestern peninsula, Ishmael combs records of the nights of September 15 and 16, 1954. Data recorded by Seaman Philip Milholland establishes that the SS *West Corona,* a Liberian freighter, entered the shipping lane. In its passage, it churned up a wall of water across Ship Channel Bank at 1:42 A.M. on September 16, five minutes before the victim's watch stopped. Because Philip transferred the next day west to Cape Flattery on Neah Bay at the far northwestern tip of Washington State, no one made the connection between the backwash and Carl's death.

12. Chambers home, San Piedro

On the opposite end of the island, Ishmael returns to his mother's house for soup. She worries that the war has made him dispassionate and emotionally distant and comments that his father was able to get beyond the animosity of World War I. As Ishmael ponders the evidence, she reminds him that Kabuo is a war veteran and a hardworking citizen and family man. Ishmael intends to write an upbeat editorial, but he resolves to hide the evidence he obtained at the lighthouse.

13. Amity Harbor, San Piedro

On December 8, the third day of the trial, Hatsue remembers seeing Kabuo dig up family memorabilia from the strawberry field in 1945 shortly before the birth of their first child. Four hours after the sheriff investigated the death scene, the Miyamotos learned of Carl's death, but they chose to conceal the land transaction that would pass the Heine farm to

Kabuo. He testifies that, near midnight, he loaned Carl a D-6 battery after discovering the *Susan Marie* disabled in the channel. In forcing the battery into the chamber, Carl cut his palm while hammering with Kabuo's gaff. According to their agreement, Kabuo would pay him $800 down on a debt of $8,400 in exchange for seven acres. Nels concludes that the case relies on local anti-Japanese prejudice resulting from the war.

After the jury begins deliberating at 3:00 P.M., Hatsue again urges Ishmael to establish justice for Kabuo. Three hours later, the jury has not reached a verdict. Ishmael's mother reminds him that the duty of a newspaper is to promote justice. At 10:30 P.M., Ishmael turns over his notes to the Imadas.

At 6:50 A.M., Hatsue comes to Mrs. Chambers's house to ask Ishmael to examine the *Susan Marie* for proof that Carl lashed his lantern to the mast when his battery failed. Ishmael persists over the sheriff's refusal and finds the lashings and traces of blood and three hairs from Carl's head. At 10:00 A.M., on the strength of Ishmael's evidence, the judge exonerates Kabuo of all charges.

Further Reading

Amend, Alison, "Snow Falling on Cedars," *Stanford Daily*, http://daily.stanford.org/intermission/BookIndex/S/SnowFalling.html, 1996.

"The Battle for Tarawa," http://www.uog.edu/faculty/ballendo/tarawa.htm.

Blades, John, "David Guterson: Stoic of the Pacific Northwest." *Publishers Weekly* (April 1999): 215.

"Collaboration on 'Snow Falling on Cedars' as Harmonious as a Haiku." *Fort Worth Star-Telegram* (December 19, 1999).

"David Guterson," http://www.forumdc.com/guterson.htm.

"David Guterson," http://www.randomhouse.com/vintage/read/snow/guterson.html.

"David Guterson," http://www.snowfallingoncedars.com/guterson.html.

"Executive Order 9066," http://www.ccnet.com/~suntzu75/eo9066/eo9066.htm.

"Ghostly Camps," http://thenation.com/issue/950918/bk_rev.htm.

Hai-Jew, Shalin, "Snow Falling on Cedars." *Northwest Asian Weekly* (February 1996): 16.

Holden, Stephen, "Prejudice Lingers in a Land of Mists." *New York Times* (December 22, 1999).

"Intelligent 'Snow' Falls Short of Oscar-Worthiness." *Chicago Tribune* (January 4, 2000).

"Interview." *The Bookseller* (April 14, 1995): 38.

"Japanese-American Internment," http://www.unc.edu/~jshields/ja/ iintgen.html.

"Japanese-American Internment Memorial," http://scuish.scu.edu/SCU/Programs/Diversity/memorial.html.

Kanner, Ellen, "Interview," http://www.bookpage.com/9601bp/fiction/snowfallingoncedars.html, 1996.

Mantell, Suzanne, "Interview." *Publishers Weekly* (December 18, 1995).

"Manzanar," http://www.sierra.cc.ca.us/us395/manzanar.htm.

"Manzanar Remembered." *Literary Cavalcade* (January 1, 1999): 27.

Marshall, John, "David Guterson and Chuck Palahniuk among NW Literary Notables on Stage." *Seattle Post-Intelligencer* (September 3, 1999).

Mathews, Linda, "Interview." *New York Times* (February 29, 1996).

Nordin, Kendra, "Beauty Can't Enliven This Story." *Christian Science Monitor* (May 6, 1999).

Pierce, J. Kingston, "Guterson on Guterson." *Seattle* (May 1, 1999): 12.

Sawicki, Walter, "Insight into a Dark Period," http://www.losangelesdowntown.com/Film_Art/Japanese_Museum.html.

Sherwin, Elisabeth, "New Writer Thanks Harper Lee for Leading the Way," http://test.dcn.davis.ca.us/go/gizmo/cedars.html, 1995.

"Snow Falling on Cedars," http://www.liglobal.com/readersbloc/reviews/snowfall.

"Snow Falling on Cedars," http://www.snowfallingoncedars.com/main.html.

Sullivan, Robert, "Bringing It All Back Home." *New York Times* (May 9, 1999).

Swanson, William, "When 'Snow' Turns to Gold." *Minneapolis-St. Paul Magazine* (April 1996): 30–33.

Whipp, Glenn, "More Than a Man on Trial in 'Snow Falling on Cedars.'" *Los Angeles Daily News* (December 22, 1999).

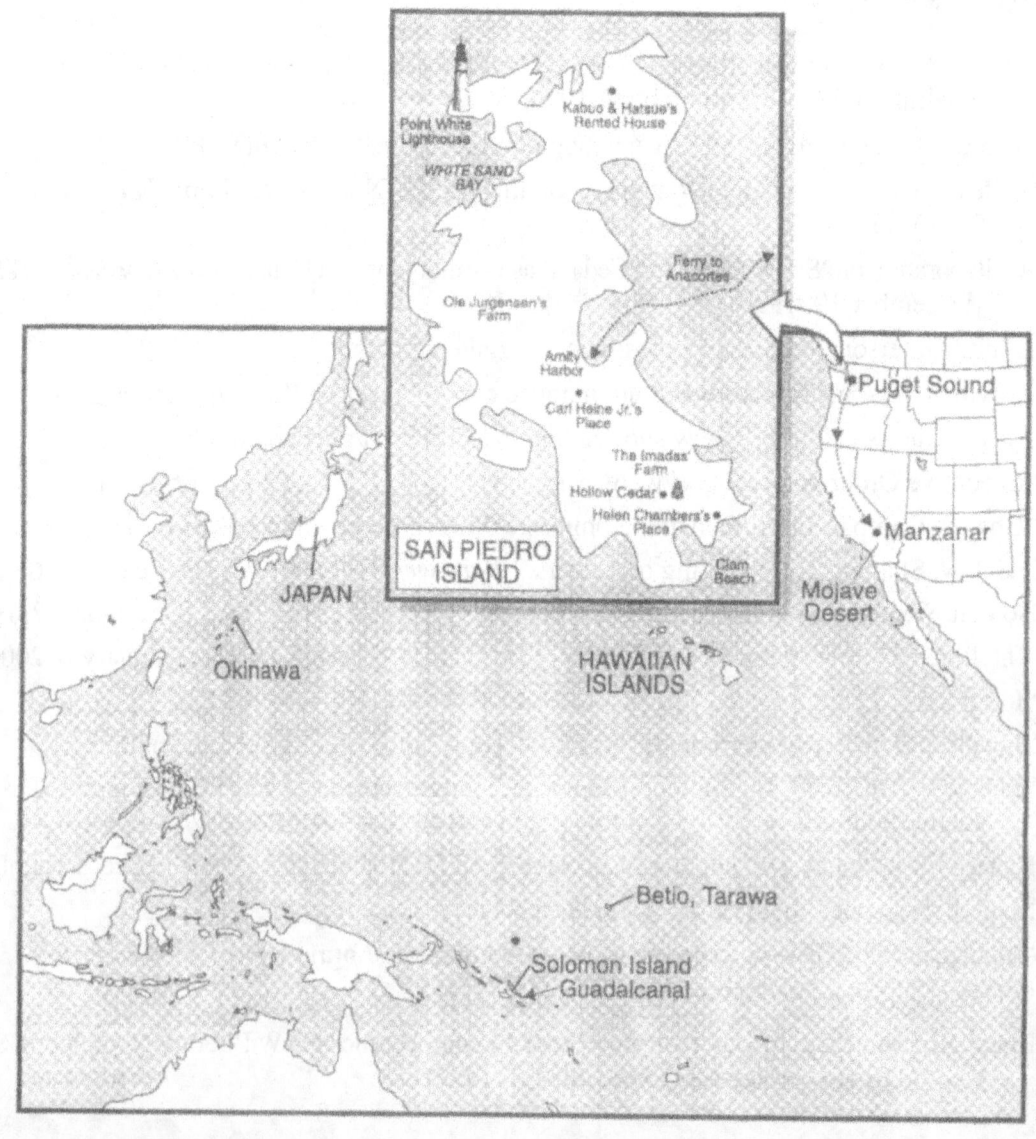

Song of Solomon
By Toni Morrison

Historical fiction, 1977

Geographical Summary

The contrasting settings of novelist Toni Morrison's *Song of Solomon* place the protagonist, Macon "Milkman" Dead, in the bucolic Virginia village of his forebears after his flight from Southside, a black community in upper Michigan on Lake Superior. His childhood odyssey begins with a friendship with Guitar, the streetwise teen who introduces him to working-class blacks at the barbershop, poolroom, and wine house of Aunt Pilate, a bootlegger who conducts an illicit but flourishing business.

After ridding himself of parental control and setting out for Danville, Pennsylvania, thrity-one-year-old Milkman travels by plane and bus to locate the cache of gold that Pilate supposedly left in Hunters Cave outside the town. He progresses toward Shalimar, a fictional black community that clings to legends of Solomon, the flying African. Milkman meets local men at a country store, hunts bobcat with them in Ryna's Gulch, gains information in Vernell's kitchen, and brings his Aunt Pilate to the region to bury his grandfather's remains.

Detailed Itinerary

1. Southside, Michigan, near Lake Superior

In the fictional town of Southside, Michigan, at 3:00 P.M. in 1931, Ruth Dead produces her firstborn, Macon, Jr., at Mercy Hospital on Not Doctor Street, named for Dr. Foster, Ruth's father, the black physician who settled in town in 1896. The boy's father, also called Macon Dead, moves into Dr. Foster's house when he marries Ruth and continues building a business renting houses and apartments to poor blacks. The boy's paternal grandfather, Jake, the first Macon Dead, was wrongly named in 1869 by a drunk Union clerk. He recorded the words "Macon" and "dead" in the wrong spaces on Jake's identification papers. The child's Aunt Pilate, who has been estranged from her brother since he was sixteen, returned to town in 1930 to run a wine house. She brings with her a daughter, Reba, and a granddaughter, Hagar.

2. Honoré, Michigan

On the weekly Sunday car ride, father Macon shows off his family and Packard while driving to Honoré, a fictional beach community on the lake where he intends to sell summer homes to middle-class blacks. The account of Honoré suggests the development of Idlewild, a black resort in Lake County in southwestern Michigan. Set up by white investors on the shore of Lake Michigan in 1912, the resort required the salesmanship of black agents to entice black buyers.

3. Montour County, Pennsylvania

To Milkman, his aunt explains how Grandfather Macon Dead was shot on his 150-acre farm north of the Susquehanna River, leaving Pilate and her brother to wander the woods of Montour County in the Appalachian mountains of east central Pennsylvania north of Danville. On a wagon moving north, the grandfather had met his future wife. After the family prospered, envious whites bilked his illiterate father out of his land.

4. Mississippi

Radio news relates the death of fourteen-year-old Emmett Till, a black Chicagoan visiting relatives in the small town of Money in LeFlore County in northwestern Mississippi. He was shot and stomped to death on August 28, 1955, after he fondled a white woman. His body, wrapped in barbed wire and weighted down with a cotton gin fan, was recovered from the Tallahatchie River three days later. Because of this atrocity, Guitar believes that blacks can never escape racism.

5. Culpeper, Virginia

Pilate narrates how she fled south to Virginia and lived with migrant workers, who ejected her after they discovered she was born without a navel. At each place she found work, she collected a rock as a memento. In October, she journeyed by wagon to Culpeper in north central Virginia, an historic spot in both the American Revolution and the Civil War, when both Northern and Confederate troops took up residence. There she learned about a colony of black farmers off the Virginia coast. She worked among the islanders for three months and conceived a daughter but rejected the father. For twenty years, she wandered, stopping only when her granddaughter Hagar was born. In 1930, Pilate contacted the Red Cross, Salvation Army, and Quakers to find her brother's address.

6. Southside, Michigan

Milkman learns that Guitar belongs to the Seven Days, a secret society of vigilantes who execute innocent white people to balance the loss of murdered blacks. The secret cabal started in 1920 to avenge two black soldiers maimed after they returned from service during World War I. Milkman compares Guitar to Malcolm X, the martyred Nation of Islam preacher who taught black brotherhood in Harlem, New York.

7. Danville, Pennsylvania

Father Macon and Pilate left home and lived with Circe, the midwife who delivered them. For two weeks, she concealed them in the upper story of her white employers' house. The children hid in a cave on the Susquehanna River, which flows from New York across Pennsylvania to the Chesapeake Bay in Maryland. Macon killed an elderly white man and discovered bags of gold nuggets. After he quarreled with Pilate, he fled the cave and returned three days later to find that both his sister and the gold had disappeared.

8. Sixteenth Street Baptist Church, Birmingham, Alabama

Guitar learns of the bombing deaths of Cynthia Wesley, Carol Robertson, Addie Mae Collins, and Denise McNair, a racist attack that also blinded Sarah Collins in one eye, injured twenty-one others, and damaged a church's foundation and five cars. The children were attending Sunday school on September 15, 1963, at 10:22 A.M. at the Sixteenth Street Baptist Church at 1530 Sixth Avenue North in Birmingham, Alabama.

9. Southside, Michigan

Believing they have located gold, Guitar and Milkman steal Pilate's green sack on September 19, 1963. The caper nets them a bag of bones. They go to jail overnight.

10. Pittsburgh to Danville, Pennsylvania

Milkman takes a plane southeast to Pittsburgh and a bus south to Danville, where he visits Circe. She relates that his grandmother Sing came from the fictional town of Charlemagne, Virginia. She identifies Hunters Cave as the site where killers dumped his grandfather's corpse. Milkman searches the cave but finds no gold.

11. Shalimar, Virginia.

At the fictional hamlet of Shalimar, his grandparents' hometown, Milkman receives a threatening message from Guitar. After a night hunt in Ryna's Gulch, Milkman is resting when Guitar approaches from behind and tries to strangle him with a wire. Milkman survives and learns from Vernell that his grandmother was Sing, an Indian girl reared by Heddy Byrd near Solomon's Leap. Intent on solving the family mystery, Milkman gathers information about his grandfather that connects him with legends of Solomon, a flying African. Milkman and Pilate return to Solomon's Leap to inter their grandfather's bones. Guitar shoots Pilate through the neck.

Further Reading

Allen, Robert, et al., "Black Writers in Praise of Toni Morrison." *New York Times Book Review* (January 24, 1988): 36.

Angelo, Bonnie, "The Pain of Being Black." *Time* (May 22, 1989): 120–21.

Bayles, Martha, "Special Effects, Special Pleading." *New Criterion* (January 1988): 34–40.

Bloom, Harold. *Toni Morrison's "Song of Solomon."* New York: Chelsea House, 1999.

Bouson, J. Brooks. *Quiet As It's Kept: Shame, Trauma, and Race in the Novels of Toni Morrison*. Albany: State University of New York Press, 2000.

Century, Douglas, and Nathan I. Higgins, eds. *Toni Morrison*. New York: Chelsea House, 1994.

Cohen, Diane, and A. Robert Jaeger, "Affirming Our Collective Stake in Safeguarding Sacred Places." *Historic Preservation News* (February–March 1995).

Darling, Marsha, "In the Realm of Responsibility: A Conversation with Toni Morrison." *Women's Review of Books* (March 1988): 5–6.

David, Ron. *Toni Morrison Explained: A Reader's Road Map to the Novels*. New York: Random House, 2000.

Donahue, Deirdre, "Morrison Taps Spirituality of Black People." *USA Today* (March 8, 1993): 1A–2A.

"Emmett Louis Till," http://www.findagrave.com/pictures/12300.html.

Furman, Jan. *Toni Morrison's Fiction*. Columbia: University of South Carolina, 1996.

Gates, David, "Keep Your Eyes on the Prize." *Newsweek* (October 18, 1993): 89.

Gillespie, Marcia Ann, "Toni Morrison." *Ms.* (January 1988): 60–61.

Harris, Trudier. *Fiction and Folklore: The Novels of Toni Morrison*. Knoxville: University of Tennessee Press, 1991.

Imbrie, Ann E., "What Shalimar Knew: Toni Morrison's 'Song of Solomon' as a Pastoral Novel." *College English* (September 1993): 473–90.

Kubitschek, Missy Dehn. *Toni Morrison*. Westport, Conn.: Greenwood, 1998.

Leonard, John, "To Ride the Air to Africa." *New York Times* (September 6, 1977).

Matus, Jill L. *Toni Morrison*. New York: Manchester University Press, 1998.

McKay, Nellie Y., ed. *Critical Essays on Toni Morrison*. Boston: G. K. Hall, 1988.

Page, Philip. *Dangerous Freedom: Fusion and Fragmentation in Toni Morrison's Novels*. Jackson: University Press of Mississippi, 1996.

Peach, Linda, ed. *Toni Morrison: Contemporary Critical Essays*. New York: St. Martin's Press, 1998.

Randolph, Laura B., "The Magic of Toni Morrison." *Ebony* (July 1988): 100–06.

Reyes-Cameron, Mark. *The Aesthetic Dimensions of Toni Morrison: Speaking the Unspeakable*. Jackson: University of Mississippi Press, 2000.

Rigney, Barbara. *The Voices of Toni Morrison*. Columbus: Ohio State University Press, 1992.

Samuels, Wilfred D., and Clenora Hudson. *Toni Morrison*. New York: Macmillan, 1990.

Smith, Valerie, ed. *New Essays on Song of Solomon*. New York: Cambridge University Press, 1995.

"Song of Solomon," http://members.tripod.com/SongSolomon/index.html.

Storhoff, Gary, "Anaconda Love: Parental Enmeshment in Toni Morrison's 'Song of Solomon,' " *Style* (Summer 1997): 290–310.

Subryan, Carmen, "Circles: Mother and Daughter Relationships in Toni Morrison's 'Song of Solomon.' " *Sage: A Scholarly Journal on Black Women* (Summer 1988): 34–36.

Taylor-Guthrie, Danille, ed. *Conversations with Toni Morrison*. Jackson: University of Mississippi Press, 1994.

Song of Solomon

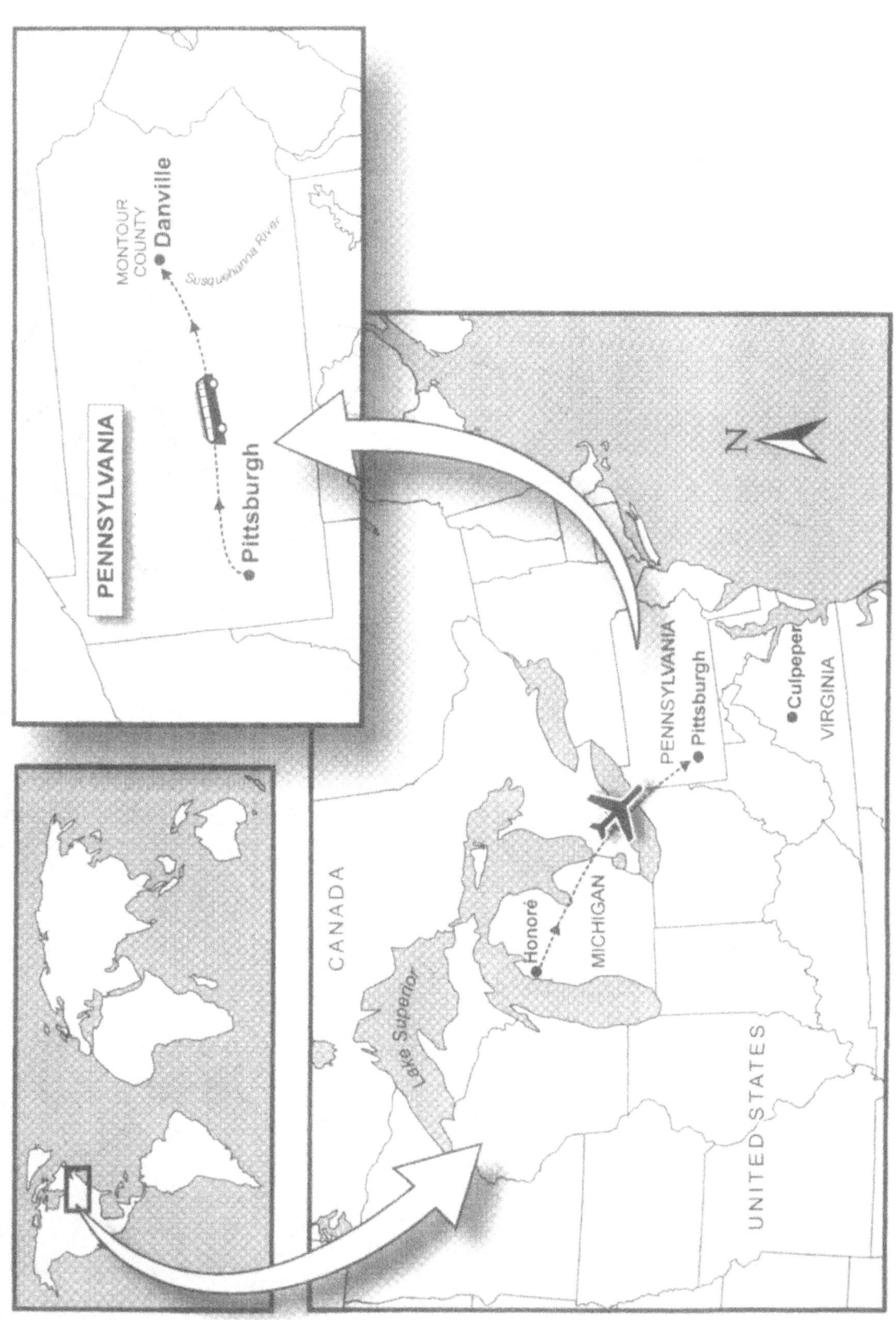

The Things They Carried
By Tim O'Brien

Historical fiction, 1990

Geographical Summary

The son of two World War II veterans—a sailor and a WAVE—Tim O'Brien grew up in Worthington, Minnesota, knowing his responsibility to his country. On April 21, 1999, he delivered the keynote address at Brown University's Writing Vietnam conference. He explained to the audience how in his youth he fled after receiving his draft notice to the Tip Top Lodge near International Falls, Minnesota, on the Canadian border. In sight of freedom from military service, he chose duty over higher ideals. Sickened by cowardice, O'Brien entered the army and soon found himself at an ambush site outside My Khe, Vietnam, where he lobbed the grenade that made his first kill.

O'Brien's war novel carries the reader around the environs of eastern Quang Ngai Province, including the capital, Quang Ngai City, Chu Lai, and the Batangan Peninsula, coastal areas along the South China Sea from which his unit, Alpha Company, goes on missions into the jungly highlands and Marble Mountains of central Vietnam. Most moving of his wartime experiences is the loss of his friend Kiowa, who died ignobly in a field outside Tra Bong, a village inundated by the Song Tra Bong River during the annual monsoon. The horror of seeing Kiowa hit by a mortar round and sucked into reeking mud torments O'Brien—the soldier and the writer—until he exorcises the memory in early middle age. Accompanied by his daughter Kathleen, he vacations in Vietnam and squires her about Saigon, the Cu Chi tunnels, and the countryside, then moves on to a spiritual cleansing. With Kathleen as commentator on his actions, he takes a jeep to the site of the fateful bivouac to deposit Kiowa's moccasins as a memorial to his death.

Detailed Itinerary

1. Than Khe near Chu Lai, Vietnam

First Lieutenant Jimmy Cross of Alpha Company escapes war in reveries of a one-sided love for Martha, an English major he met at fictional Mount Sebastian College in New Jersey. The school bears the name of Saint Sebastian, a Milanese soldier martyred at Rome around A.D. 288 during the persecution of Christians by the Roman emperor Diocletian. In art, St. Sebastian is depicted skewered by numerous arrows shot by a military execution squad.

Cross, whose name echoes the theme of Christian martyrdom, dreams of camping with Martha in New Hampshire's White Mountains. On April 16, his unit of seventeen men locates a tunnel complex at Than Khe south of Chu Lai, a coastal city of central Vietnam and south of the Demilitarized Zone in the bloodiest, most hotly contested area of the Vietnam War. After a lottery, Lee Strunk draws seventeen, the winning number, and enters the subterranean warren. Lee returns safely, but Ted Lavender dies of a bullet to the head. In retaliation, after a chopper carries Ted's corpse from a dry paddy to the rear, Alpha Company incinerates the village. Cross cultivates hatred of the enemy and leadership of his remaining fifteen men, who head west to greener country in Vietnam's interior.

2. Massachusetts

Years later, Cross visits a war buddy, Tim O'Brien, at his home in Massachusetts. O'Brien wants to write about Cross's experiences. The former lieutenant hesitantly gives his okay.

3. Batangan Peninsula

At age forty-three, O'Brien relives five days of following an old Vietnamese man through a minefield in Batangan Peninsula, a jut of land south of Danang bordering the South China Sea, a western arm of the Pacific Ocean. O'Brien's daughter Kathleen thinks her father is obsessed by war memories.

4. My Khe, Vietnam

O'Brien's worst memory is killing a young Vietnamese soldier with a hand grenade outside My Khe, a coastal city southeast of Danang on the South China Sea.

5. Worthington, Minnesota

On June 17, 1968, O'Brien, a Phi Beta Kappan and summa cum laude graduate only a month out of college, receives a draft notice. A pacifist liberal during a period of anti-war protests, he had modestly denounced the war. Rather than serve in the military, he intended to accept a scholarship for graduate work at Harvard, a prestigious university in Cambridge east of Boston, Massachusetts. Working as a declotter at a meatpacking plant in Worthington, an agricultural center in southwestern Minnesota near the Iowa border, he worries for a month. He muddles over the fate of the USS *Maddox* in the Gulf of Tonkin, a deep bay east of Hanoi, Vietnam's second largest city and the former capital of French Indochina. After North Vietnamese patrol boats fired on the destroyer, on August 2, 1964, President Lyndon B. Johnson initiated the Gulf of Tonkin Resolution, which escalated hostilities into full-blown war. In the midst of a grim political atmosphere, O'Brien yearns to flee to Winnipeg. The inviting refuge across the border has a long history, dating back to the 1860s, when men left the United States to keep from serving in the Civil War.

6. Rainy River, Minnesota

In October, O'Brien leaves a note for his family and drives north to Rainy River near International Falls, Minnesota, and lodges at the Tip Top Lodge on the border of Manitoba, Canada. For six days, the eighty-one-year-old innkeeper, Elroy Berdahl, respects the boy's privacy while O'Brien fights insomnia. On the sixth day, Elroy takes him fishing on Rainy River, a ploy that offers him a chance to dash to Canada. At age twenty-one, O'Brien can only weep and reject any form of flight from military responsibility. At noon the next day, he returns home to accept a role in the despised Vietnam conflict.

7. LZ Gator outside Chu Lai, Vietnam

In late July on patrol in a war zone called LZ Gator (Landing Zone G), Lee Strunk and Dave Jensen tussle over a missing jackknife. A month later, Jensen and Strunk sign a pact that each will end the other's life if it is compromised by severe injury. In October, Strunk loses his right leg at the knee from a mortar round. During the flight over Chu Lai, he dies of his injuries.

8. Inland from Chu Lai, Vietnam

After three days on a westward march into the jungle-covered Marble Mountains of central Vietnam, Curt Lemon dies after a detonator explodes while he and nineteen-year-old Bob "Rat" Kiley play catch with a smoke grenade. Kiley berates Lemon's sister, who does not reply to his letter relating details of her brother's death.

9. Quang Ngai, Vietnam

To illustrate the incredible experiences of war, O'Brien tells about Mitchell Sanders, who spends a week at a listening post on the wide, muddy Tra Khuc River north of the coastal town of Quang Ngai. He recalls hearing voices, music, choirs, and chanters. In the silence that falls at dawn, the listeners still hear the music. On return to base camp, they say nothing of their experience to the colonel. Sanders concludes, "Nobody listens." The next day, Sanders admits to O'Brien that he made up the extreme types of music they heard but that the basic facts are true.

10. The Rocket Pocket on the South China Sea opposite Chu Lai, Vietnam

Thinking over Lemon's life, O'Brien recalls how his comrade swaggered and played the part of the tough soldier. By February, the unit was patrolling the Rocket Pocket on the South China Sea opposite the airfield at Chu Lai.

11. Tra Bong west of Chu Lai, Vietnam

Kiley tells about a soldier's girlfriend who visited a medical detachment in Tra Bong village on the Song Tra Bong River in the mountains southwest of Chu Lai. From the helipad, personnel shipped casualties either northeast to Chu Lai or north to Danang. Without officers, the men lack military discipline and direction. They share the aid station with a macho Special Forces unit that arrived in the early 1960s. Eddie Diamond, who is the ranking aid station soldier, proposes sending for prostitutes from Saigon, the capital of Vietnam far to the south.

Mark Fossie invites his girl, Mary Anne Bell, a seventeen-year-old high school graduate from Cleveland Heights, a residential section in the northwest of Cleveland, Ohio. Six weeks later, she flies to Vietnam over a roundabout route that bypasses the war zone—from Los Angeles to Bangkok, west of Vietnam in Thailand, and east to Saigon. The two spend two weeks in a bunker on the camp's outer edge near a squad of six Green Berets, who keep to themselves. The second week, she visits the Tra Bong village, swims in the Song Tra Bong River, and helps the unit treat casualties.

Two months later, Kiley goes on R & R (rest and recuperation) in Bangkok. He encounters Diamond, who says that Mary Anne continued going on patrol barefoot and weaponless. She walked off into the mountains, perhaps to the Montagnards, highland tribes scattered throughout the rugged backbone of Cambodia, Laos, and Vietnam. She did not return. After a search by MPs (Military Police) and the CID (Central Intelligence Division), the government declared her missing. She became part of the war legend.

12. West of Batangan Peninsula

At an abandoned pagoda west of Batangan Peninsula, Alpha Company encounters two monks living in a tarpaper shack. During a week at the site, the two men assist with machine gun cleaning and offer four ripe watermelons from the younger man's garden. Dobbins considers entering the religious order so he can be "nice to people." Kiowa thinks that basing the unit in the pagoda is wrong. Dobbins rewards the monks with canned peaches and chocolate.

13. My Khe, Vietnam

O'Brien obsesses about the mutilated jaw of the young man he shot. He makes up a fantasy biography of a man born in 1956 on a farm at My Khe near the Quang Ngai Province coast. In 1964, he attended class at the university in south-central Saigon far to the south of Vietnam but died on his first day as a rifleman in the 48th Vietcong Battalion. Kiowa tries to draw O'Brien away from the corpse.

14. Massachusetts

Kathleen O'Brien asks if her father killed anyone. He lies and says he did not. To relieve his inner torment, he keeps writing stories and thinking of the man he killed with a grenade after seeing him go on dawn patrol.

15. Vietnam

At a burned hamlet, Alpha Company sees a fourteen-year-old girl dance on her toes with hands over her ears. After the unit marches away, Azar mocks her dance until Dobbins terrorizes him by threatening to drop him into a well.

16. Slater Park, Worthington, Minnesota

On Sunday, July 4, after the war, Norman Bowker drives his father's Chevy eight times around the lake, past Slater Park, across the causeway past Sunset Park, Chautauqua Park, and Centennial Beach. He carries seven medals for uncommon valor, but regrets he didn't earn the Silver Star. Bowker is haunted by memories of Alpha Company's bivouac in a malodorous swamp along the Song Tra Bong River, which flooded during the October monsoons. A Vietnamese woman warned them that the stinking field was the villagers' latrine. At midnight, the river overflowed its bank. As mortar fire pinned them down, Kiowa sank under the foul ooze. Bowker grabbed Kiowa's boot and nearly went under with his friend, whom he failed to rescue.

At 7:35 P.M., Bowker stops at A&W for a Mama Burger, fries, and root beer. Over the drive-in's intercom, he attempts to tell the order taker about the bad memories and then begins a tenth circuit in the Chevy. He tries to explain to his father about losing hold of Kiowa and about the Silver Star. On Bowker's twelfth turn around the park, he wades into the lake fully dressed to watch Fourth of July fireworks.

17. Massachusetts

In spring 1975, when Saigon finally collapses, O'Brien receives a disjointed letter from Bowker, who urges him to write a story about Kiowa's death. O'Brien first completes *Going after Cacciato* (1978), then begins writing about Kiowa's loss in a postwar chapter called "Speaking of Courage." O'Brien publishes it three weeks later and sends a copy to Bowker, who questions the absence of Kiowa's death in the text.

18. Worthington, Minnesota
Eight months later in August 1978, Bowker hangs himself in the locker room of the Worthington YMCA.

19. Swampy bivouac along the Song Tra Bong River
A decade later, O'Brien turns his first story into the true account of Kiowa's demise in the "shit field." Alpha company begins searching for Kiowa's remains. Lieutenant Cross, carrying a New Testament his father mailed him in January, blames himself for camping on boggy ground. Bowker and Sanders locate Kiowa's rucksack. Sanders blames the lieutenant for camping in so foul a place.

At age twenty-four, Cross regrets entering ROTC (Reserve Officers' Training Corps) at Mount Sebastian College. He castigates himself for encamping his unit on indefensible ground. Near noon, Bowker locates Kiowa's mangled body under two feet of water. He and Sanders drag the corpse to the surface, tape Kiowa's personal effects to his wrist, and call for a chopper pickup.

20. Massachusetts
At forty-three, Tim O'Brien feels that the death of the young Vietnamese soldier he shot is real but that events after the war are inventions. Because he was afraid to look at combat deaths, he continues writing stories to unearth the truth and "make things present." He has a choice to go on denying committing violent acts during the war or to confess to his daughter Kathleen that he did kill someone.

21. Quang Ngai City, Vietnam
After writing about Kiowa's death, O'Brien and ten-year-old Kathleen visit Vietnam in August. As a birthday present to her, they visit Hanoi far in the north and to the south, the Cu Chi tunnels, a tourist attraction on the outskirts of Saigon, now called Ho Chi Minh City. Hand-dug in the infamous "Iron Triangle" in the late 1940s to allow the peasant army to battle high-tech weapons, the 250 kilometers of shafts once were a death assignment to American insurgents called "tunnel rats." The subterranean network aided the Vietcong in surveillance of the outlying countryside until American bombers destroyed much of the tunneling late in the war.

At Quang Ngai City during the second week of August, Kathleen asks what her father wanted from the war. O'Brien replies, "To stay alive." On their two-hour jeep ride to the field where Kiowa died, O'Brien carries his friend's moccasins. O'Brien strips and wades into the Song Tra Bong where the mortar attack pinned the men in camp. He deposits Kiowa's moccasins in the soft river bottom and feels that he has finally worked his way out of bad memories and guilt.

22. Tri Binh, Vietnam
Around November 19, O'Brien is shot in the side at a pagoda in Tri Binh, where Kiley treats the wound. Returned to Alpha Company in mid-December after Kiley has been shipped to Japan for medical care, O'Brien takes a second hit, this time in the buttocks. An inexperienced medic, Bobby Jorgenson, bungles treatment. At the end of December, O'Brien leaves the 91st Evac Hospital to work at battalion supply headquarters. In relative safety, he misses the danger of combat.

23. My Khe, Vietnam

In March, Alpha Company takes a break from combat and reunites with O'Brien. He hears the story of Morty Phillips, who contracted paralytic polio from skinny-dipping in the river near My Khe down the coast from Danang.

24. Battalion Supply Headquarters

Three days later, O'Brien confesses to Sanders his grudge against Jorgenson. The next morning, Jorgenson apologizes to O'Brien for the poor treatment he gave O'Brien's wound. Teaming with Azar, O'Brien sets up a series of sounds to terrorize Jorgenson while he performs nighttime guard duty. O'Brien and Azar watch *Barbarella* (1967), a science fiction spoof starring American actress Jane Fonda, a radical antiwar spokesperson who angered patriotic Americans by challenging the legality and necessity of the war in Vietnam. Critics dubbed her "Hanoi Jane" after she visited North Vietnam in 1972. After departing the enlisted men's club, the duo rigs up flares, sandbags, ropes, and pulleys to simulate an enemy approach. An hour before dawn, O'Brien gives up the game. After Azar abandons O'Brien and their prank, Jorgenson cleans and bandages a gash on O'Brien's forehead.

25. Foothills west of Quang Ngai City

Sanders tells about Kiley's last days in the war, when the platoon moved at night for two weeks in central Vietnam west of Quang Ngai City. On March 16, 1968, the area was the site of the My Lai massacre of hundreds of Vietnamese civilians slaughtered by three companies of American infantry. Kiley shoots himself in the foot. As the evac chopper approaches, Cross promises to call the self-inflicted injury an accident.

26. A village along the South China Sea

Recalling his fourth day in the war, O'Brien asserts, "Stories can save us." In February 1969, after an air strike along the South China Sea, Jensen ridicules the corpse of an elderly Vietnamese man. Kiowa compliments O'Brien for not taking part in the mockery.

27. Main Street, Worthington, Minnesota

The corpse makes O'Brien think of nine-year-old Linda, whom he "dated" in spring 1956. O'Brien took Linda to see *The Man Who Never Was* (1955) at the State Theater on Main Street. A British thriller, it fictionalized the dropping of a corpse carrying phony papers behind enemy lines to confuse Germans during World War II.

In 1990, O'Brien recalls that he had wanted to save Linda from cancer. As a writer, he recognizes that war stories are soldiers' means of removing the terror of death and of keeping the dead alive. In 1990, O'Brien identifies his writing as "Tim trying to save Timmy's life with a story."

Further Reading

Blades, John, "Prisoners of War." *Chicago Tribune* (December 9, 1994).

Bonn, Maria S., "Can Stories Save Us? Tim O'Brien and the Efficacy of the Text." *Critique* (Fall 1994): 2–15.

Caldwell, Gail, "Staying True to Vietnam." *Boston Globe* (March 29, 1990).

Capuzzo, Mike, "A Novelist's Inner War." *Philadelphia Inquirer* (October 27, 1994).

Carlin, Margaret, "Vietnam Will Always Be One Thing Tim O'Brien Carries." *Rocky Mountain News* (November 20, 1994).

Chen, Tina, "Unraveling the Deeper Meaning." *Contemporary Literature* (Spring 1998): 77–98.

Coffey, Michael, "Tim O'Brien: Inventing a New Form Helps the Author Talk about War." *Publishers Weekly* (February 16, 1990): 60–61.

Cushman, Karen, "Newbery Medal Acceptance." *Horn Book* (July–August 1996): 413–19.

Galloway, Catherine, " 'How to Tell a True War Story': Metafiction in *The Things They Carried.*" *Critique* (Summer 1995): 249–57.

Getlin, Josh, "Vietnam and WWII: Myths and Memories." *Los Angeles Times* (April 9, 1995).

Harris, Robert R., "Review." *New York Times Book Review* (March 11, 1990): 8.

Herzog, T.C. *Tim O'Brien*. London: Prentice-Hall International, 1997.

Kaplan, Steven. *Understanding Tim O'Brien*. Columbia: University of South Carolina, 1995.

_____, "The Undying Uncertainty of the Narrator in Tim O'Brien's *The Things They Carried*." *Critique* (Fall 1993): 43–52.

Lannon, Linnea, "In War, Reality Becomes Surreal." *Detroit Free Press* (April 17, 1991).

Lee, Don, "About Tim O'Brien," *Ploughshares* (Winter 1995): 196–201.

Loose, Julian, "Review." *Times Literary Supplement* (June 29, 1990): 708.

McCaffery, Larry, "Interview," *Chicago Review*, 1982, 129–49.

Mort, John, "The Booklist Interview." *Booklist* (August 1994).

Naparsteck, Martin, "Interview." *Contemporary Literature* 32 (Spring 1991): 1–11.

"Rainy Lake-Rainy River," http://rainylake.org/.

Schroeder, Eric James, "The Past and the Possible: Tim O'Brien's Dialectic of Memory and the Imagination," in *Search and Clear*. Bowling Green, Ky.: Bowling Green State University Press, 1988.

_____, "Two Interviews: Talks with Tim O'Brien and Robert Stone," *Modern Fiction Studies* (Spring 1984): 135–64.

Steinberg, Sybil, "Review." *Publishers Weekly* (January 26, 1990): 404.

"Tim O'Brien's Home Page," http://www.scrtec.org/track/tracks/t06656.html.

Wetherell, W.D., "Dubious Martyrdom." *Chicago Tribune* (March 11, 1990).

"Writing Vietnam," http://www.stg.brown.edu/projects/WritingVietnam/obrien.html.

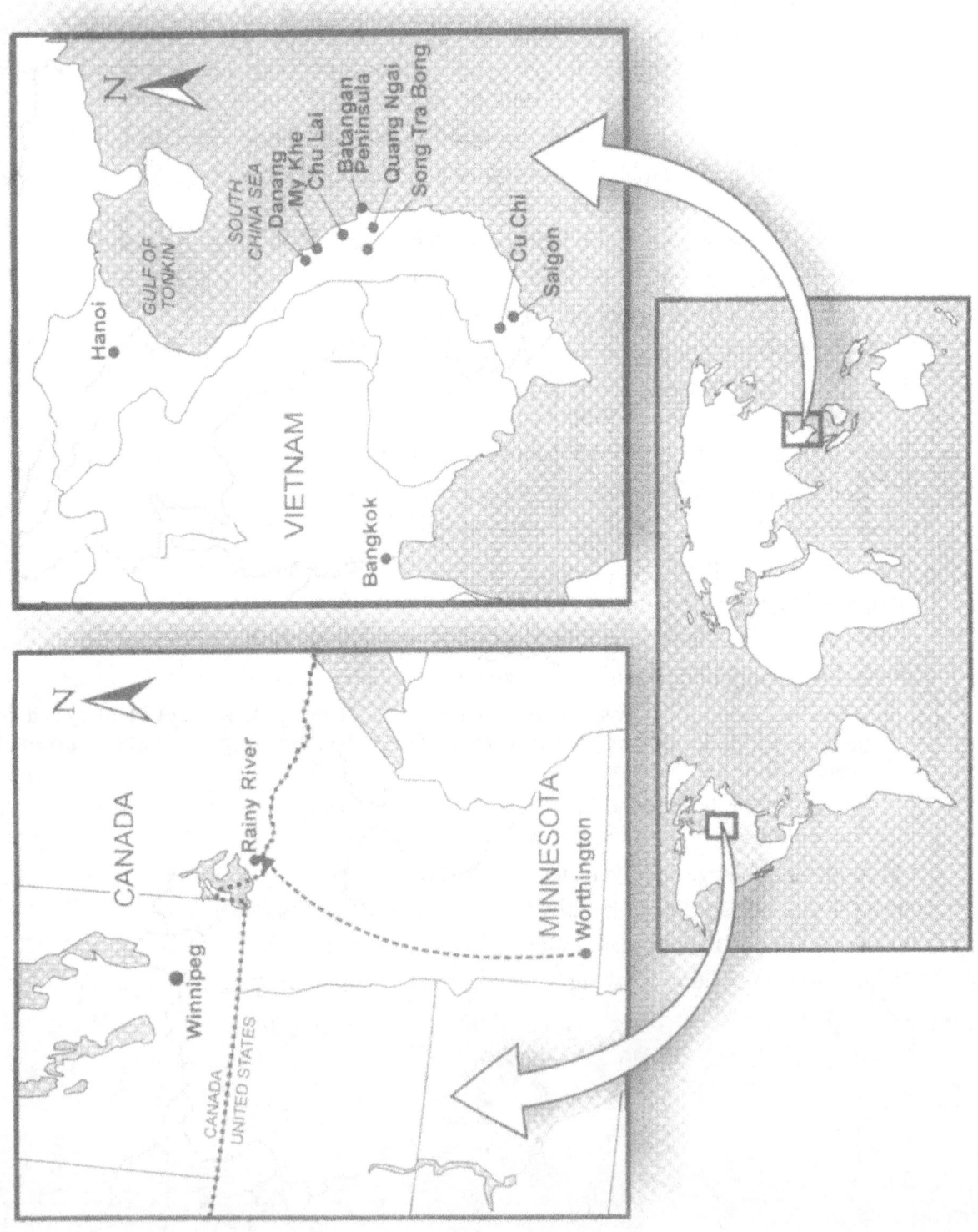

Who Killed My Daughter?
By Lois Duncan

True crime, 1992

Geographical Summary

The milieu of Lois Duncan's *Who Killed My Daughter? The True Story of a Mother's Search for Her Daughter's Murderer* shifts rapidly among numerous settings as the Arquette family pieces together the conspiracy and stalking preceding the assassination of eighteen-year-old Kaitlyn Clare Arquette, whom her mother used as a model for April in the young adult thriller *Don't Look Behind You* (1989). Beginning at the family residence in Albuquerque, New Mexico, the story follows the parents to the University of New Mexico Hospital, where Kait, on life support, fails to revive from a gunshot wound to the head. After the purchase of a plot at the Sunset Memorial Cemetery, Duncan reports on the funeral, retrieval of Kait's belongings from Alvarado Square Apartments, and subsequent meetings with Kait's boyfriend Dung, an initial suspect in the killing. Duncan encounters him at her home, at the hospital, where he is treated for a self-inflicted stomach wound at a dorm at Kirtland Air Force Base, and at the police station.

The rapid range of narration over places Kait visited and reasons for her movements supply the nonfiction inquiry with data about her apartment, Susan Smith's residence at Old Town, and Kait and Dung's flight from New Mexico to Orange County, California, on March 28, 1989, ostensibly to visit Disneyland. Instead, they rented a vehicle from Snappy Car Rental and took part in a traffic accident scam. In Albuquerque, Duncan and her daughter visit an Asian ghetto and cruise the Martineztown barrio to post flyers showing Kait's picture and asking for more information pertaining to her murder.

Duncan investigates psychic clues about the Desert Castle in the Sandia Mountains, a killer incarcerated in the grease pit of a garage, and the police concealment of the accident report and Kait's belongings. Duncan's precipitate departure from her deserted home after a suspicious car was parked outside suggests that even unconnected events heighten her fear. Kait's earthly presence begins to withdraw from her mother's consciousness and to move toward a new incarnation. More than a year after the shooting, Duncan is able to enjoy Christmas in Florida with her daughter Kerry and grandchildren. The story concludes with a summary of arrests in Southern California and information about a multistate drug ring that apparently ordered Kait's assassination.

Detailed Itinerary

1. Arquette residence, Albuquerque, New Mexico
On Sunday evening, July 16, 1989, hours before her murder, Kaitlyn "Kait" Arquette of Albuquerque, New Mexico, visits her parents, Donald Wayne and Lois Arquette, at their home south of Lomas Street, an east-west bisector of the city. Kait explains that she is dining with Susan Smith, a snow cone seller, at Susan's apartment in Old Town, a historic district south of Interstate 40 along the Rio Grande.

Kait's mother, who writes young adult fiction under the pseudonym Lois Duncan, suspects that Kait has fought with her boyfriend. She shares an apartment with an older man, Dung Nguyen, a Vietnamese refugee who joined the many children evacuated from South Vietnam by boat on April 30, 1957, after the country fell to Communist insurgents. Kait says that Dung refuses to move out of the apartment they share. She departs in her red Ford Tempo at 6:15 P.M.

2. University of New Mexico Hospital
Before midnight, someone from the staff of University of New Mexico Hospital east of Interstate 25 and south of Lomas Boulevard reports that Kait has been injured. As a result of a shot to the head, she is comatose from bullet wounds to the brain. The doctor warns that if Kait lives, she will never be the same.

3. Alvarado Square Apartments
To a detective from the APD Homicide Department, Duncan reports that Kait left home to dine with Susan Smith. Kait departed early from Smith's house in Old Town to study for a test at her own place at Alvarado Square Apartments, where she had lived since April of her senior year in high school. At 11:00 P.M., a half-hour after gunmen shot her in the head with an Uzi or small-caliber rifle, police found her still alive in her wrecked Ford Tempo on Lomas Street near Broadway Northeast west of a major interchange with Interstate 25.

4. University of New Mexico Hospital
After performing a CAT scan on Kait, the doctor offers little hope. Dung arrives and claims that the shooting was his fault. Friends and siblings gather along with the media, who imply that a cute blonde like Kait should not have driven her red Ford Tempo in a city filled with Mexicans. After blood fills the brain stem leaving Kait brain dead, Duncan insists that the staff keep her daughter on life-sustaining machines until Kait's sister Kerry arrives. Following Kerry's good-bye, on July 17 after 9:00 P.M., Kait dies when she is removed from life support.

5. Alvarado Square Apartments
Within minutes of Kait's death, An Le places two phone calls from her apartment to Bao Tran, who arranges bogus car accidents. Another call goes to Van Hong Phuc of Santa Ana southeast of greater Los Angeles, California. Duncan later learns from old friend Paul Becht that Tran works as a paralegal for Minh Nguyen Duy, an attorney in Garden Grove, south of greater Los Angeles, California.

6. Arquette residence, Albuquerque, New Mexico

Kerry discovers that Dung is involved in a Los Angeles vehicle-wreck scam. The family later confirms that he arranged the wreck of a car full of Vietnamese gang members with An Le's Plymouth Sundance on August 14, 1988, in Santa Ana. Don summons Detective Steve Gallegos and learns that Dung broke a door and window at Alvarado Square Apartments and threatened Kait with bodily harm. Dung and An Le, his best friend, attend the funeral. The *Albuquerque Journal* reports a search for a beige Volkswagen with a loud muffler and implies that the shooting was gang related.

7. Kirtland Air Force Base

That night, while visiting with An Le, Dung stabs himself in the abdomen with a four-inch folding knife at Khanh Pham's dorm at Kirtland Air Force Base, a 52,000-acre military installation southeast of Albuquerque. Police report that Dung attempted suicide because he believes that they and the Duncans suspected him of murdering Kait. On July 22, Kerry goes to a psychic, Betty Muench, who clarifies Dung's emotions about the killing. She describes Kait's feelings of betrayal.

At Dung's request, Duncan visits his hospital room. Without exonerating him, she reports her son Brett's dream in which Kait forgives Dung. When Duncan faces Dung at the police station, he denies knowing anything about the crime. On July 23, he travels to Kansas City to recuperate, allegedly under the care of his brother-in-law and sister, who reportedly own an import shop. Police later confirm that Dung has no sister.

8. Arquette residence, Albuquerque, New Mexico

A month later, Duncan retrieves letters Dung wrote in Vietnamese. They carry Orange County postmarks. Duncan takes the letters to the police for translation as possible clues. Steve Gallegos believes the shooting was random.

9. Cape Cod, Massachusetts

On August 19, Duncan receives *Many Lives, Many Masters* (1988), a treatise on psychic phenomena. She reads it the day before journeying to Craigville, Massachusetts, to attend a Cape Cod writers' conference beginning August 22. The Atlantic Coast setting is well suited to authors, who visit the seaside resort for mutual support and further development of their work. In early November, Duncan speaks at a workshop in Santa Fe northeast of Albuquerque.

10. Betty Muench's residence

After learning that a truck driver, Eugene Lindquist, saw Kait trying to flee Mexican stalkers in a gold Camaro, Robin insists that her mother visit Betty Muench. The psychic discloses that Kait knew she was set up and wants her killers exposed. Someone informs the police anonymously of Muench's findings.

11. Asian ghetto, Albuquerque, New Mexico

On January 4, 1990, Duncan retrieves Kait's watch and day planner from her purse. Against her husband's objections, Duncan begins circulating flyers requesting information about the killing and offering a $5,000 reward. Around Christmas, men driving a Plymouth menace her and Robin while they post handbills in an Asian ghetto of Albuquerque.

12. Orange County, California
Duncan confers with Susan Smith on the map that she drew for Kait. Smith reports that Kait was excited about the car-wreck scam, which she observed in March in Orange County south of Los Angeles, California.

13. Albuquerque, New Mexico
To discover why police are not cooperating, Duncan calls reporter Mike Gallagher of the *Albuquerque Journal,* located at 7777 Jefferson Street Northeast. On January 18, Bernalillo County District Attorney Robert Schwartz holds a press conference to announce the arrest of Miguel Garcia, Dennis "Marty" Martinez, and Juvenal "Juve" Escobedo from Martineztown, a city barrio that Kait described as "creepy" on the night of her murder. Police locate the alleged killers' Camaro and rely on information from Robert Garcia, who claims to have accompanied the three the night they shot Kait.

On January 22, the police case crumbles after they learn that Robert Garcia was incarcerated the night of the shooting. On January 29, newspapers report that the police have dropped charges in the case and released the suspects. Sergeant Ruth Lowe concludes that Kait must have died by random shooting.

14. Costa Mesa, California
In February, Duncan learns from Betty Muench that Kait saw "R & J" on the vehicle door. On a visit to the branch library, Duncan locates R & J Car Leasing in Costa Mesa, California. She discovers from Kait's bank statement that she received money after the trip and deposited $1,490 in her account in April 1989. The time coincides with her move out of the Arquette residence to Alvarado Square Apartments.

15. Albuquerque, New Mexico
Sergeant Lowe promises to investigate the car rental in California. After Deputy District Attorney Susan Riedel charges Juve Escobedo and Miguel Garcia with murder, Escobedo flees. Gallagher reports on the suspect activities of Van Hong Phuc of Santa Ana. Betty Muench informs Duncan that the Vietnamese used the Mexicans as hit men. Duncan tells her husband that much of her novel *Don't Look Behind You* was prophetic of Kait's murder.

16. Rio Grande southwest of Albuquerque, New Mexico
Betty Muench reports that Juve Escobedo is alive and in Albuquerque, possibly sequestered in the grease pit of a garage. Duncan searches the Valley section of town west of the Rio Grande and locates a vacated garage but can't break in. She mentally chastises herself for taking chances on investigations best left to professionals.

17. Albuquerque, New Mexico
Kerry gets information on the wreck involving Kait and Dung on March 28, 1989. Kerry insists that Kait was not in the car when Dung rear-ended Bob Manh Bui's vehicle. At a meeting with police, Duncan reports that Kait was going to reveal the scam. The police stop speaking to the Arquettes.

In January 1990, Mike Gallagher publishes a news story on inconsistencies in the murder case. Dung admits he introduced Kait to Bao Tran, An Le's cousin, who masterminded the scam. Betty advises Robin that Bao Tran's check to Kait is damaging evidence that may have precipitated the hit. Duncan hires Paul Becht as a private detective, who engages another detective in San Diego, California. Duncan discovers that Marty Martinez had bragged about killing another person and not getting caught.

18. Psychical Research Foundation, Gainesville, Florida
Dr. William G. Roll, director of the Psychical Research Foundation, explains to Duncan the workings of precognition, an awareness of events before they happen. Her childhood friend, Dr. Marcello Truzzo, parapsychologist at the Department of Sociology, Eastern Michigan University at Ypsilanti, gives her the names of three psychic detectives. Noreen Renier of Maitland, Florida, replies immediately to Duncan's letter and agrees to work with a police artist on a drawing of the killer.

19. Desert Castle
Noreen Renier also relives Kait's meeting with Rod, a former boyfriend, at Coronado Center, Albuquerque's largest shopping mall, and their drive to the northeast to Desert Castle twelve miles away. Kait apparently witnessed an argument over interstate trafficking and hurriedly left the residence. Duncan searches for the castle in the Sandia Mountains northeast of the city in Sandoval County.

20. Greensburg, Pennsylvania
That same day, Nancy Czetli, a psychic living in Greensburg west of Pittsburgh, Pennsylvania, assures Duncan that Kait witnessed a drug deal. Barbara Cantwell warns Duncan to stay away from interstate traffickers. Czetli discerns that Kait knew she was being stalked and considered informing on Dung. Czetli identifies Miguel Garcia as the shooter and tells Duncan that she found the wrong desert house. The psychic explains the drug setup, for which Hispanics acted as transporters. She reports that Kait met her grandfather after death and warns of another murder.

21. Arquette residence, Albuquerque, New Mexico
In February, Duncan pieces together Kait's lies covering her trip to California with Dung.

22. El Paso, Texas
Duncan researches reports on drug trafficking from south of the border through El Paso, Texas, due south of Albuquerque on the New Mexico border.

23. Albuquerque, New Mexico
Police arrest Miguel Garcia on March 5. After the case is postponed, Susan Riedel asks Duncan not to talk with the media. The police release Garcia on April 24. In July, Marty Martinez admits to murder-for-hire, then withdraws his confession.

24. Oklahoma
As the psychic predicted, An Le commits a similar drive-by murder in Oklahoma.

25. Orange County, California
On August 5, authorities arrest lawyers and doctors in Orange County southeast of Los Angeles, California, for insurance fraud stemming from phony car accidents. On January 13, 1993, a crackdown in California nets forty arrests for scams.

26. Albuquerque, New Mexico

The search for clues grows muddled. Tanya Hicks, a private investigator for the defense, obtains a video of Dung selling drugs. Steve Gallegos admits that he didn't investigate clues in California and didn't translate Dung's Vietnamese letters. Gary Miller reports that the FBI stayed out of the investigation at police request. In despair of ever learning the whole truth, Duncan intends to end the investigation on September 18, 1991, Kait's twenty-first birthday.

27. East Coast

In 1994, after Duncan published *Who Killed My Daughter?*, the family reopened the case and organized a team of detectives, crime scene specialists, forensics analysts, insurance claims investigators, and experts on organized Vietnamese crime. Don Arquette retired from his job as electrical engineer at Sandia Laboratories and moved his family from New Mexico to an undisclosed site on the East Coast. With proceeds from the film version of Duncan's book *I Know What You Did Last Summer,* the author founded National Investigations Agency of New Mexico, a nonprofit private investigative agency offering free service to victims of violent crime who gain no satisfaction from law enforcement agencies. Duncan coauthored *Psychic Connections: A Journey into the Mysterious World of Psi* (2000) with William Roll.

The family continued to post a detailed follow-up of the unsolved crime on the Internet, including photos of Kait and a message board for reader write-in. Since 1997, the site received more than 100,000 hits. A decade after the murder, the Arquettes offered a $25,000 reward for new information leading to the killers' arrest and conviction. Meanwhile, Duncan began *The Tally Keeper,* a sequel to *Who Killed My Daughter?*

Further Reading

"Censorship Roundup," *School Library Journal* (April 2001).

"Children of Eve: The Lois Duncan Fan Club," http://www.geocities.com/Athens/Parthenon/8033/ld.html.

Cloud, John, "In Silent Testimony." *Time* (January 25, 1999).

"Interview with Lois Duncan," http://www.travers.com/educ/erms/EighthGrade.html.

Kies, Cosette. *Presenting Lois Duncan.* New York: Twayne, 1994.

"A Letter from Author Lois Duncan," http://www.cynthialeitichsmith.com/LoisDuncan.htm.

"Duncan Arquette and Tom Arriola Interview," http://www.courttv.com/talk/chat_transcripts/Duncan-arriola.html.

"Lois Duncan," http://www.iag.net/~barq/Duncan.html.

"The Murder of Miss Kaitlyn C. Arquette," http://www.netzone.com/~holmes/wall/kca.html.

"Office of Enforcement Operations," http://www.usdoj.gov/criminal/oeo.html.

Overstreet, Deborah Wilson, "Help! Help! An Analysis of Female Victims in the Novels of Lois Duncan." *ALAN Review* (Spring 1994).

"Reach Out and Touch an Author," http://www.cyberbee.com/author.html.

"Real Crimes," http://www.realcrimes.com/.

Sandlin, Scott, "Mom Writes On about Daughter's Slaying." *Albuquerque Journal* (October 18, 2001).

Sutton, Roger, "A Conversation with Lois Duncan." *School Library Journal* (June 1992).

"Who Killed Kait Arquette?," http://www.iag.net/~barq/kait.html.

"Who Killed My Daughter?" *People Weekly* (November 24, 1997).
   See also *Don't Look Behind You* entry, this volume.

The Yearling

By Marjorie Kinnan Rawlings

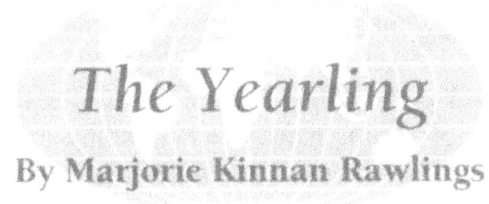

Classic historical fiction, 1938

Geographical Summary

The unforgiving environment of central Florida swampland was a familiar milieu to fiction writer and memoirist Marjorie Kinnan Rawlings. She lived from 1928 to 1941 in a humble cottage at Cross Creek near the 383,088-acre Ocala National Forest, established as part of the U.S. park service in 1908. During her residency, she wrote about regional development, wildlife, and local people, whom she befriended. In *The Yearling,* she expresses the Baxter family's struggle on the uplands to grow crops, hunt game, and fish for enough food to eat and to trade for shoes and overalls, axes, rope, and medicines. The land controls action and character development and tends to overshadow human will with a blind unpredictability.

Isolated at Baxters' Island, Jody Baxter learns obedience from give and take with his parents and neighbors and with nature and weather. Penny, his father, demonstrates how to move prudently among rattlesnakes and alligators near the sinkhole, a lime sink or cave-in where water has dissolved vast underground deposits of limestone, causing collapse of the thin upper crust. He also gives Jody lessons in the interdependence of nature and survivalism so his son can empathize with bears emerging from hibernation, deer reaching the end of a normal life span, and wolves starving for meat.

Hunting in the backcountry prepares Jody for manhood. From Penny and the neighboring Forresters, he learns to keep still and listen to hunting dogs while tracking bear, wildcats, and deer. On his own, he studies small animals, plants, water, and sky for signs of changes in weather or seasonal alterations in animal behavior. From hunting with his father after a nor'easter, he discerns that nature can alter the balance for all creatures and in the process, can jeopardize human survival by overflowing creeks and rivers, polluting groundwater, driving animals from their lairs, leveling sugar cane and corn stalks, and rotting yams and cow peas. In Penny's words, if the storm continues beyond the seventh day, "We jest as good quit fightin' and lay down and die."

Most difficult for Jody is a yearning for a pet to relieve his solitude while the family survives a devastating year. Rawlings emphasizes that Jody embraces Flag, his fawn, to fill the void left by his friend Fodder-wing's death. To the adult Baxters, the timid fawn grows into a pest that nibbles or tramples the sweet potatoes and corn that will nourish them and their livestock during the coming winter. The boy accepts the hard edge of survival in the wild by killing his wounded pet.

While running away from home, Jody experiences threats his parents have fought. In hopes of reaching Boston to be with his beloved Grandma Hutto, he copes with thirst, hunger, fatigue, and natural predators as he paddles a dilapidated canoe northeast up the St. Johns River, the state's largest river, which flows from Melbourne and is navigable for two hundred miles inland from the Atlantic Ocean. The hardships of swamp travel quickly compromise so ambitious a journey. Returning to the Baxter farm, Jody becomes man of the house during his father's recovery from overexertion. No longer interested in flutter-mills, Jody helps dig a well, one of the mundane tasks that will ease his mother's daily labors and ensure the family's comfort.

Detailed Itinerary

1. Upland Florida near Lake George

Around 1872 west of the Ocklawaha River and south of Lake George, the story begins on Florida's central highland, a stretch of high country topped with evergreens, the habitat of wild mammals, amphibians, and birds. Near the St. Johns River, a major watercourse in northeastern Florida, and northeast of the town of Volusia in Volusia County on the state's lower east coast, Ora and Ezra Ezekiel "Penny" Baxter live with their only surviving child, thirteen-year-old son Jody. They occupy a humble cabin with stick-and-clay chimney on an isolated rise covered in scrub they clear and farm.

In the serenity of an island of long-leaf pines, moss-draped live oak, red bay, wild cherry, gum, hickory, holly, and magnolia, Penny chooses a peaceful semitropical farmstead far from town and surrounded by arid forest. Living apart from neighbors and village intrusion, he recovers from the trauma he suffered during the Civil War, particularly at the battle of Bull Run, the name of battles fought in Virginia west of Washington, D.C., on July 21, 1861, and August 29–30, 1862. Unlike the Forresters, who kill and torment animals when they choose, Penny and his son rely on farming and kill only what is necessary for sustenance.

Rawlings emphasizes the abundance of underground rivers and of artesian springs that produce creeks and runs. Unfortunately for the family, the Baxters lack a well in land where the water level lies deep. Their only choice is to haul fresh supplies from the sinkhole on the tract's western boundary. While hunting, Penny leads his son into a red bay thicket, a seemingly impenetrable stand of cover for game.

2. Grahamsville, Florida

Not all of farm life is grim or laborious. In April, Jody abandons his hoe while Penny takes Julia, the family's hunting hound, in the wagon to Grahamsville in north-central Florida.

3. Silver Glen, Florida

The boy follows Silver Glen Road. Carefree as he departs the farm, he chases wild bees and erects a flutter mill in the palmetto at the creek, which joins Lake George and the St. Johns River. Silver Glen is a pleasant pool that lies in semitropical forest at the base of the sand hills. Bubbling 750,000 gallons of water to the surface daily, it is the largest of twenty-five deep, freshwater springs in the United States, seventeen of which lie in Florida.

4. Forresters' Island in upland Florida

One morning old Julia barks at the remains of the sow, black Betsy, killed by Old Slewfoot, a giant black bear. The dogs pursue his scent, but Penny fails to kill the predator because his muzzle-loader misfires. Penny has little choice but to trade with the Forresters for a better weapon.

5. Dragoon Trail across Florida

Jody and Penny ride north on their plow horse, Old Caesar, to Forresters' Island to swap their feisty dog for a double-barrel English shotgun. On the way, Penny points out blazes the Spanish left when they explored the area in the sixteenth century. Ponce de León, a Spanish adventurer who landed at the St. John's River delta and gave the state its name, was the first to arrive on April 3, 1513. He preceded by fifteen years the exploits of Pánfilo de Narváez, another conquistador who came in search of gold. In 1539, Hernando de Soto, the famed Spanish expeditioner, explored the area from Tampa to the Mississippi River.

Jody and his father continue along the old Spanish trail, which extends to Tampa on the west coast to Fort Butler, a log stockade and barracks established in 1838 to supervise river traffic at Astor in Lake County on the opposite shore of the St. Johns River from Volusia. After dinner, Penny works up a trade with Lem, Gabby, Arch, Pack, Buck, and Mill-wheel Forrester.

6. New Smyrna on the Indian River

At the sinkhole the next day, Penny regrets not finishing the digging of the family's well. Jody recovers from fever and fishes by moonlight with his father. He spies the mysterious Minorcans carrying sacks of gophers. Penny tells him of the people's hand-to-mouth existence after their arrival from the west Mediterranean island of Minorca, the second largest of the Spanish Balearic Islands, which resembles Florida with its long coastline, rugged uplands, and balmy climate.

7. Volusia, Florida

After killing a buck, Penny and Jody cross Juniper Creek and take the main road southeast to Volusia. They sell venison to Captain McDonald, who lives near Fort Butler. They take the ferry—a hewn log raft—over the St. Johns River and purchase goods from Mr. Boyles. Down a lane of oleanders past magnolias in bloom, they visit the cottage and garden of Grandma Hutto, a family friend who sheltered Jody and Ora while Penny was in the army. Jody swims in the deep, dark river, which sweeps past Volusia Bar toward Lake George.

At dawn on Saturday, Grandma's son Oliver arrives on the freight and passenger steamer with gifts. Buck, Lem, and Mill-wheel attack Oliver for courting Twink Weatherby, whom Lem claims. At Boyles's store, Penny joins Oliver's side in the uneven battle. After Lem knocks Jody unconscious, he awakens at Grandma's house. Jody carries a message to Twink that Oliver will meet her on Tuesday at dusk. The two Baxters ride home on Boyles's mare. Jody scribbles a note to Oliver that Twink has gone upriver to Sanford.

8. Upland Florida near Lake George

In mid-June, a rattlesnake strikes Penny while he trails his lost hogs. He shoots a doe and uses the liver and a piece of the heart to extract the venom. Buck and Mill-wheel take Penny home, where Doc Wilson treats the bite. Buck begins clearing two acres near the sinkhole for Sea Island cotton and robs honey from a beehive in a dead pine. Against Ora's objections, Penny allows Jody to adopt the doe's orphaned fawn.

9. Forresters' Island, Florida

When Jody next visits the Forresters, he learns that Fodder-wing died at dawn. Penny builds a pine coffin and nails on a cover. Because Penny comes from a Christian background, he speaks a farewell. The setting of the boy's grave is pleasant—a south hammock, a fertile spot near Fodder-wing's grapevine swing under a live oak, a tall, stout tree that doesn't shed its leaves in fall.

10. Upland Florida near Lake George

At summer's end, Jody sees a ghostly Spaniard near the sinkhole, which is sixty feet deep and rounded like a great bowl. The spot is milky from the loads of wash that Ora brings to pound on a block with her paddle. Late in September, the family's luck changes after an unnatural seven-day rain rots their crops, levels the sugar cane, and forces swamp animals to flee rising water. The torrents wash the flat sand road into a ravine, uproot pines, and heap rubbish in low-growing scrub. As the water recedes, dead animals lie by the dozens on the ground.

The Baxters, Buck, and Mill-wheel set out toward Silver Glen and take the southeastern road to check on Doc Wilson. After Buck directs them to Sellers Bear Hole and Squaw Pone Bear Hole, they bag a lynx, buck, and panther. The next morning, Jody kills a bear, which they haul home through Juniper Prairie in the heart of the Ocala Forest.

11. Jacksonville, Florida, to Boston, Massachusetts

Buck learns that Oliver shipped out from Jacksonville. Lem is angry that Twink followed Oliver to Boston. To earn cash, Penny proposes selling ten bear cubs on the Atlantic coast at St. Augustine, America's oldest city, which Don Pedro Menéndez de Avilés founded in 1565. Because Lem intends to wreak vengeance on Oliver for stealing Twink, the Forresters opt for Jacksonville.

12. Upland Florida near Lake George

Penny returns home to the south via the old Spanish trail through a hammock to Juniper Spring, which is clear, blue, and bubbly as it emerges from a subterranean cavern. He kills an eight-foot alligator and removes the tail meat, then nets a deer west of Sweetwater Spring, a natural cooling pool near Juniper Prairie, Silver Springs, and the Ocala National Forest.

13. Jacksonville, Florida

Meanwhile, the Forresters set out with the cubs, traveling north past the sinkhole through Hopkins Prairie. They intend to pass Salt Springs on the way north to Palatka, where they will cross the St. Johns River. While they are gone, Jody and Penny shoot curlews on Mullet Prairie. After trading for the cubs in Jacksonville, Buck fills Ora's shopping list.

14. Volusia, Florida

Penny sets aside money for cottonseed and designates the rest to buy Christmas items. He shoots a buck to give him more meat to trade for goods. The Baxters travel over the river by ferry, where Jody tries to befriend a haughty boy. While Jody and Penny shop at Boyles's store in Volusia, Ora squabbles with Grandma Hutto. After Penny intercedes, Grandma serves lunch and invites them for Christmas.

15. Upland Florida near Lake George

Four days before the holiday, Buck reports that Old Slewfoot killed a boar hog. Penny tracks the bear, which also savaged a newborn calf. The bear leads Penny's hound northwest around Hopkins Prairie. On Christmas Eve, Penny follows his dogs to Salt Springs Run and shoots Slewfoot beyond the widow Nellie Ginright's cabin between Bear Spring and the St. Johns River.

16. Fort Gates, Florida

To manage the huge carcass, Penny and Jody head out two miles west in search of help at Fort Gates. They take a sandy road beyond swamp and scrub. Unexpectedly, they encounter the Forresters on the way to spend Christmas at Fort Gates north of the Ocala Forest in Putnam County. The rough men trade for half the bear meat in exchange for shipping the carcass to Volusia. Penny dreads taking his rowdy neighbors into polite company on a holiday.

17. Volusia, Florida

At Volusia, both Grandma and Ora complain about the Forresters' bad behavior. When Oliver arrives with his new wife Twink, the six brothers burn his mother's home. Rather than rebuild, Grandma chooses to move to Boston, the Massachusetts port from which Oliver's ship regularly embarks.

18. Upland Florida near Lake George

The next morning, the Baxters return home for the winter. They see nothing of the Forresters, who appear to avoid more trouble by doing business at Fort Gates. It is clear to Jody that his father is no longer able to manage alone on the farm. Worsening the family's predicament is Flag, who wastes peas and eats half the tobacco sets. Jody's parents insist that the boy shoot his pet.

19. Forresters' Island

Jody runs to Pa Forrester and learns that the six brothers are trading horses in Kentucky. Pa refuses to take Jody's side in the matter of shooting the yearling. Sadly, Jody returns home to face his responsibility.

20. Upland Florida near Lake George

After Flag eats more corn and peas, Ora wounds the deer, which Jody must put out of its torment with a second shot. He faints by his dead pet.

21. Volusia, Florida

Betrayed and grieving, Jody runs north up the Fort Gates road. He intends to cross the river by ferry and travel northeast to Jacksonville and up the Atlantic coast to Boston to live with Grandma Hutto. He wanders the swamps to Salt Springs Run near Nellie Ginright's cabin and maneuvers a half-sunk canoe with a piece of a paddle upriver toward Jacksonville. Hunger overcomes Jody, who yearns for his home and family. A mail boat crew rescues him and carries him to Volusia. He heads out for Silver Glen, destroys his flutter-mill, and runs home.

Further Reading

"Florida Archeology," http://dhr.dos.state.fl.us/bar/fap/.

"The Florida Black Bear: A Threatened Species," http://hammock.ifas.ufl.edu/txt/fairs/17072.

"Historical Timeline," http://www.florida.com.

Kleinberg, Eliot, "Claimants Grasp at 'Yearling' Author's Manuscripts." *Charlotte Observer* (September 23, 1990): 19A.

"The Land Cover of Florida," http://fcn.state.fl.us/gfc/viewing/landcovers/lndcov.html.

Lieb, Patricia, "Rawlings House Is a Visit to a Past Era," http://www.writeonmag.com/rawlings.html.

"Marjorie Kinnan Rawlings," http://karamelik.eastlib.ufl.edu/html.

"Marjorie Kinnan Rawlings Society," http://www.clas.ufl.edu/english/Rawlings.Society/rawlings.html.

"Ocala National Forest," http://www.gorp.com/dow/southern/ocalinfo.htm.

"Okefenokee Swamp," http://home.att.net./~cochrans/okefen01.htm.

Rawlings, Marjorie Kinnan. *Cross Creek*. Atlanta, Ga.: Mockingbird Books, 1942.

Sammons, Sandra Wallus, and Nina McGuire. *Marjorie Kinnan Rawlings and the Florida Crackers*. Lake Buena Vista, Fla.: Tailored Tours, 1995.

Snodgrass, Mary Ellen. *Encyclopedia of Southern Literature*. Santa Barbara, Calif.: ABC-Clio, 1997.

Tarr, Roger L. *Marjorie Kinnan Rawlings: A Descriptive Bibliography*. Pittsburgh, Penn.: University of Pittsburgh Press, 1996.

"The Virtual Swamp Resource Page," http://www.florida-everglades.com/. Bellman, Samuel I.

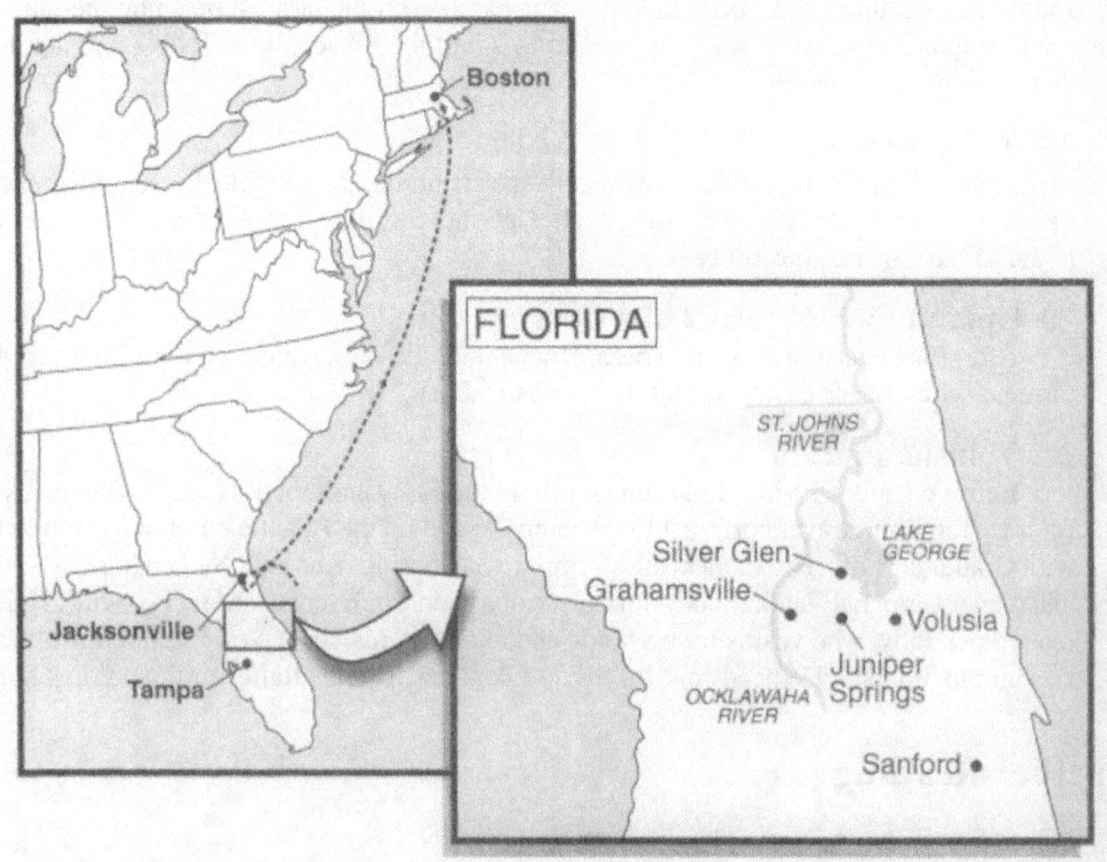

Filmography

Anne Frank Remembered, Jon Blair Film Company, 1995

Cross Creek, biography of Marjorie Kinnan Rawlings, EMI, 1983

The Diary of Anne Frank, TCF, 1959

Great Expectations, Universal, 1934

Great Expectations, Cineguild, 1946

Great Expectations, TCF, 1998

I Know What You Did Last Summer, Mandalay, 1997

The Joy Luck Club, Buena Vista, 1993

Julius Caesar, Metro-Goldwyn-Mayer, 1953

Julius Caesar, Commonwealth United, 1969

A Lesson Before Dying, Home Box Office, 1999

Macbeth, Republic/Mercury, 1948

Macbeth, Caliban, 1972

Macbeth, Lamancha/Grampian, 1997

The Miracle Worker, United Artists, 1962

The Miracle Worker, Disney Productions, 2000

Moby Dick, Warner, 1930

Moby Dick, Warner, 1956

Moby Dick, Hallmark Hall of Fame, 1998

Simon Birch, loosely based on *A Prayer for Owen Meany*, Hollywood Pictures, 1998

Snow Falling on Cedars, Universal, 2000

The Yearling, Metro-Goldwin-Mayer, 1946

General Bibliography

Africana. New York: Civitas Books, 1999.

Ahlstrom, Sydney E. *A Religious History of the American People*. New Haven, Conn.: Yale University Press, 1972.

American Decades (CD-ROM). Detroit: Gale Group, 1998.

Ashby, Thomas. *A Topographical Dictionary of Ancient Rome*. London: Oxford University Press, 1929.

Biography Resource Center (database). Farmington Hills, Mich.: Gale Group, 2000.

Blain, Virginia, et al. *The Feminist Companion to Literature in English*. New Haven, Conn.: Yale University Press, 1990.

Bloom, Harold. *Asian-American Women Writers*. New York: Chelsea House, 1997.

Buck, Claire, ed. *The Bloomsbury Guide to Women's Literature*. New York: Prentice-Hall Press, 1992.

Bradbury, Malcolm, ed. *The Atlas of Literature*. London: De Agostini Editions, 1996.

Bunson, Matthew. *A Dictionary of the Roman Empire*. New York: Oxford University Press, 1991.

_____. *Encyclopedia of the Middle Ages*. New York: Facts on File, 1995.

Chaliand, Gérard, and Jean-Pierre Rageau. *The Penguin Atlas of Diasporas*. New York: Viking, 1995.

Contemporary Authors (CD-ROM). Detroit: Gale Research, 1994.

Dictionary of Hispanic Biography. Detroit: Gale Research, 1996.

"Directory of Royal Genealogical Data," http://www.dcs.hull.ac.uk/public/genealogy/royal/.

DISCovering Authors on CD (CD-ROM). Detroit: Gale Research, 1995.

DISCovering Multicultural America, http://galenet.gale.com:8888.

Drabble, Margaret, ed. *The Oxford Companion to English Literature*. New York: Oxford University Press, 1985.

Eaglen, Audrey. *Twentieth-Century Children's Writers*. New York: St. James Press, 1989.

East, W. G. *An Historical Geography of Europe*. London: Methuen, 1966.

Eerdmans' Handbook to the World's Religions. Grand Rapids, Mich.: William B. Eerdmans, 1982.

Encyclopedia Americana (CD-ROM). Danbury, Conn.: Grolier, 1999.

Encyclopedia Britannica (online). Chicago: Britannica, 2002.

Encyclopedia of World Biography. Detroit: Gale Research, 1998.

Gentz, William H., gen. ed. *The Dictionary of Bible and Religion*. Nashville, Tenn.: Abingdon Press, 1973.

Goring, Rosemary, ed. *Larousse Dictionary of Writers*. New York: LarousseKingfisher Chambers, 1994.

Graves, William, ed. *Historical Atlas of the United States*. Washington, D.C.: National Geographic Society, 1993.

Hispanic Writers. Detroit: Gale Research, 1993.

Lattin, Vernon E. *Contemporary Chicano Fiction: A Critical Survey*. Binghamton, N.Y.: Bilingual/Editorial Bilingue, 1986.

Mackay, Angus, and David Ditchburn, eds. *Atlas of Medieval Europe*. London: Routledge, 1997.

Manguel, Alberto, and Gianni Guadalupi. *The Dictionary of Imaginary Places*. San Diego, Calif.: Harcourt Brace Jovanovich, 1980.

New Catholic Encyclopedia. Washington, D.C.: Catholic University of America, 1967.

Nicholls, C. S., ed. *Encyclopedia of Biography*. Oxford: Helicon, 1996.

Peck, David. *American Ethnic Writers*. Hackensack, N.J.: Salem Press, 2000.

Ploski, Harry A., and James Williams, eds. *The Negro Almanac*. Detroit: Gale Research, 1989.

The Reader's Companion to American History. Boston: Houghton Mifflin, 1991.

Ridge, Martin. *Rand McNally Atlas of American Frontiers*. Chicago: Rand McNally, 1993.

Rollyson, Carl, ed. *Notable American Novelists*. Hackensack, N.J.: Salem Press, 1999.

Sherr, Lynn, and Jurate Kazickas. *Susan B. Anthony Slept Here: A Guide to American Women's Landmarks*. New York: Random House, 1994.

Smith, Huston. *The Illustrated World's Religions*. San Francisco: HarperCollins, 1994.

Snodgrass, Mary Ellen, ed. *Black History Month Resource Book*. 2nd ed. Farmington Hills, Mich.: Gale Group, 1998.

———. *The Encyclopedia of Satirical Literature*. Santa Barbara, Calif.: ABC-Clio, 1996.

———. *Religious Sites in America*. Santa Barbara, Calif.: ABC-Clio, 2000.

———. *Who's Who in the Middle Ages*. Jefferson, N.C.: McFarland, 2001.

Stephens, Robert O. *The Family Saga in the South: Generations and Destinies*. Baton Rouge: Louisiana State University Press, 1995.

St. James Guide to Young Adult Writers. 2nd ed. Detroit: St. James Press, 1999.

"Terms and Definitions," http://www.ussorca.org/term.htm.

The Ultimate Road Atlas & Vacation Guide. New York: Rand McNally, 2000.

Waldman, Carl. *Atlas of the North American Indian*. New York: Facts on File, 1985.

Walker, John, ed. *Halliwell's Film & Video Guide*. New York: HarperPerennial, 1999.

Webster's New Geographical Dictionary. Springfield, Mass.: Merriam-Webster, 1988.

Wexler, Alan. *Atlas of Westward Expansion*. New York: Facts on File, 1995.

Wheal, Elizabeth-Anne, Stephen Pope, and James Tayloe. *Encyclopedia of the Second World War*. Edison, N.J.: Castle Books, 1989.

Worrell, Judith, ed. *Encyclopedia of Women and Gender*. San Diego, Calif.: Academic Press, 2001.

Index

Afghanistan, 153, 155, 159
African Americans, xiii, 39–43, 83–88, 89–94, 131–135, 143–145, 173–176
Al Qaeda, xii
Alabama, xi, 119–124, 174
Alaska, 140, 142
Albuquerque Journal, 189, 190
Albuquerque, New Mexico, xi, xii, 14, 187–93
Albuquerque Police Department, 188, 189, 190, 191
Algonquian, ix, 125, 126
Allies, 1, 4, 5, 6
Altadena, California, 83–87, 88
American Civil Liberties Union, x, 58, 123
American Foundation for the Blind, 123
American Mercury, The, 59
American Revolution, 86
Amsterdam, ix, 1–8, 9, 21
Anagnos, Michael, 119
Anaya, Rudolfo, x, 11–18
Ann Arbor, Michigan, 140
Anne Frank Foundation, 7
Anne Frank: The Diary of a Young Girl, xii, 1–9
Apennine Mountains, 76–77
Appalachia, ix, 35, 57
Arabian Sea, 155, 156, 159
Arizona, 147, 150, 152
Army Air Corps, 101
Arquette, Kait, xi, 33, 187–93
Asian Americans, x, 65–72, 167–166, 187–192
Atlantic Ocean, ix, 28, 31, 125, 127, 147, 149, 196
Audio Earphones Award, 131
Auschwitz-Berkenau, 6, 9
Australia, xii, 46, 49, 55
Azores Islands, 126, 127, 130
Aztec, 13

Baldwin, James, xii, 39–42
Baltimore Herald, 58, 59

Baltimore, Maryland, 57, 59, 60, 63, 83, 85, 87, 88
Baltimore Sun, 59
Baltimore/Washington International Airport, 29
Baluchistan, 153, 154, 159
Bangkok, 181, 186
Barbarella, 184
Batangan Peninsula, 179, 180, 182, 186
Baton Rouge, Louisiana, 91, 92, 93, 95
Bayonne, Louisiana, 89, 91–92, 95
BBC (British Broadcasting Company), 2, 4, 5
Bell, Alexander Graham, 121, 122
Bergen-Belsen, Germany, ix, 6–7, 9
Bible Belt, x, 57
bicentennial, U.S., x, 83, 87
Bill of Rights, 58
biographical drama, 119–124
Birkenhead, England, 113, 114–15, 117
Birmingham, Alabama, 175
Bless Me, Ultima, x, xiii, 11–18
Bohemia, 139
Bonaparte, Napolean, 127
Boston & Maine Railroad, 148
Boston, Massachusettes, xi, xiii, 27, 28, 29, 31, 86, 88, 119, 121, 122, 147, 148, 149, 152, 180, 196, 199, 200
Botany Bay, 46, 55
Brave New World, ix, x, xii, 19–25
Bridgeport, Maryland, 27, 28, 31
British Columbia, 167
Broadway (New York), 42
Brooklyn (New York), 44
Brown University, 179
Brutus, 75, 76–80
Bryan, William Jennings, x, 58–59, 60, 61
Buffalo, New York, 103
Bull Run, Battle of, 98, 196
Butler Act, x, 58, 62
Butler, Octavia, x, 83–87

Cairo, Egypt, 53, 54
California, x, xii, 11, 12, 14, 65, 66, 67–68, 69, 70, 83–87, 88, 140, 168, 169, 172, 187, 190, 191, 193
Cambridge, Massachusetts, 123, 147, 149, 180
Cambridge School for Young Ladies, 123
Camp Leonard Wood (Missouri), 97, 101–102, 103
Canada, 139, 140, 147, 150, 151, 152, 161, 166, 180, 186
Cape Cod, Massachusetts, 28, 31, 126, 189
Cape de Verdes, 127
Cape of Good Hope, 127, 130
Capitol, Roman, 77, 78, 81
Capone, Al, 97
Caribbean Sea, 133, 135, 149
Carnegie, Andrew, 123
Carrol Ground, 127
Cather, Willa, x, 137–142
Cawdor, 105, 106–107, 111
Central Intelligence Division, 181
Central Park, 40, 44
Chesapeake Bay, 27, 28, 31, 83, 84, 88, 174
Chester, England, 113, 116, 117
Chicago, x, 39, 41, 58, 63, 97–98, 99, 100, 101–102, 103, 122, 138, 142, 144
Chicago Fire, 100
Chicago Loop, 97, 99
China, 65, 66–67, 70–71
Chinatown, ix, 67–68, 69, 73
Chinese Americans, xii, 65–72
Cholistan Desert, 153, 154–157, 159
Christianity, 40
Christmas Carol, A, 149
Chu Lai, Vietnam, 179, 181, 186
Chungking (China), 65, 66, 69, 70
Churchill, Winston, 2, 5
Civic Biology, A, 58
Civil War, American, 91, 98, 101, 122, 180, 196
civil war, Roman, 75, 76, 78
Clarksdale, Mississippi, 144
classic literary fiction, 39–42, 45–55, 125–130, 137–142
Cleveland, Ohio, 181
Colmekill, 108, 111
Colossus of Rhodes, 76
Columbia Exposition, 122
Commoner, The, 58
concentration camp, ix, xii, 2, 6–7
Confederacy, 98

confessional journal, 1–8
conquistadores, 12
contemporary mainstream fiction, 27–31, 65–73, 131–35, 167–72
Coolidge, Calvin, 99
Cornwall, England, 115, 117
Covent Garden, 46, 55
creationism, x, 57–62
Crisfield, Maryland, 27, 28, 29
Crozetts, 127, 130
Cu Chi tunnels, 179, 186
Culpeper, Virginia, 174, 177
curandera, x, xiii, 13
Cushman, Karen, x, 113–17
Czechoslovakia, 139

D-Day, 1, 5, 9
Danang, Vietnam, 150, 180,181
Danville, Pennsylvania, 173, 174, 175, 177
Darrow, Clarence, 59–60, 61
Darwin, Charles, x, 57, 58, 61
Dawson, Canada, 140
Dearborn Station (Illinois), 97, 98, 101–102
death camp *see* concentration camp
death penalty, 53, 89–94, 131, 134
Decatur, Illinois, 97, 100
Del Rio, Texas, 90, 93, 95
Delaware, 27, 30, 31, 83, 86
Demilitarized Zone, 180
Derawar Fort (Pakistan), 154–55, 156, 159
de Soto, Hernando, 197
Dicey's Song, xii, xiii, 27–31
Dickens, Charles, xii, 45–54
Dillinger, John, 97, 100
Dingarh, Pakistan, 154, 157, 159
Dingwall Castle, 105, 107, 111
disabilities, 119–123
Don't Look Behind You, xi, xii, 33–38, 190
Dorchester, Maryland, 86, 88
Douglas, Stephen A., 97, 101
Douglass, Frederick, 85
Dubliners, 92
Duke University, 35, 36
Duncan I of Scotland, 105, 106
Duncan, Lois, xi, 33–37, 187–193
Dunsinane, 106, 109–110, 111
Durham, North Carolina, 35, 38

Easton, Maryland, 29, 83, 84, 86, 88
Edward I, 113, 115

Edinburgh, Scotland, 106, 108
Eisenhower, Dwight D., 5
Elbe valley, 139
Elizabeth I, 108
England, 19–21, 23–24, 25, 45–55, 107, 108, 109, 113–17
English Channel, 19, 21, 79
Epperson v. Arkansas, 62
Equator, 125, 128
Erith, Kent, England, 52, 55
exorcism, xii, 145

Falkland Islands, 23, 25
Fascism, 4
FBI, xii, 34, 192
Federal Witness Security Program, xi, 33, 35
Fen River, 67, 73
Fife, 105, 106, 108, 109, 111
Fifth Avenue, 40
First Amendment, x, 58
Florida, xi, xiii, 33, 35–36, 38, 195–200
Fonda, Jane, xi, 184
Formosa, 125, 130
Forres, 106–107, 108, 109, 111
Fort Abbas (Pakistan), 153, 159
Fort Huachuca (Arizona), 147, 150, 152
Fort Sheridan (Illinois), 97, 101, 103
Forum, Roman, 78
France, 1, 5, 7, 41, 79, 168
Frank, Anne, ix, 1–8
Frank, Margot, 2, 3, 6–7
Frank, Otto, ix, 1, 2, 3, 4, 7
Frankfort-on-Main, 2, 9
French Indochina, 180
Frost, Robert, 149

Gaines, Ernest, vii, xii, 89–94
Garden Grove, California, 188
Genesis, 58, 59
Georgian Bay, Canada, 151, 152
Germany, 1, 2, 5, 6–7
Gestapo, ix
Gibson, William, 119–124
Gies, Miep, 1, 3, 4, 5, 6
Go Tell It on the Mountain, xii, xiii, 39–43
Gold Rush of 1849, 66
Gottland, 140, 142
Grahamsville, Florida, 196, 200
Grant, Ulysses S., 98, 122
Gravesend, England, 45, 46, 53, 55

Gravesend, New Hampshire, 147, 148, 150, 151, 152
Great Depression, x, 97, 99
Great Divide, the, 138
Great Expectations, xii, 45–55
Green Haven Prison, 134–35
Greenwich Village, New York, 44, 133
Gudu Barrage (Pakistan), 153, 155, 159
Gulf of Tonkin, 180, 186
Guterson, David, x, 167–172

Hakra River (Pakistan), 156, 159
Hammersmith, 45, 49, 50, 55
Hanoi, Vietnam, 180, 186
Hardy, Thomas, 148
Harlem, New York, 39, 40, 41–42, 44, 131–35, 174
Harvard University, 123, 180
Hastings, Nebraska, 137, 139, 142
Hawaii, x, 70, 101
Helen Keller Endowment Fund, 123
Helen Keller International, 123
Het Achterhuis (*The Annex*), 7
Himalaya Mountains, 155
Hispanic Americans, 11–18, 187, 188, 190, 191
historical drama, 57–63, 75–80, 105–111
historical fiction, 97–102, 113–17, 161–66, 173–77, 179–88, 195–200
Hitler, Adolf, 1–6
Ho Chi Minh City. *See* Saigon
Holland. *See* Netherlands
Homecoming, 27
Hong Kong, 69, 70, 73
Hoover, Herbert, 99
Horace Mann School for the Deaf, 122
Hunter, G. W., 58
Huxley, Aldous, ix, x, 19–24
Hyde Park, 21

Iceland, 21, 23, 25
Illinois, x, 39, 41, 58, 63, 97–98, 99, 100, 101–102, 103, 138, 142, 144
In a Solitary Blue, 27
India, 153, 154, 156, 159
Indian Ocean, ix, 125, 127, 128, 130
Indus River, 153, 154, 155, 159
Inherit the Wind, xii, 57–63
Inverness, Scotland, 105, 107, 108, 111
Ireland, 107, 111, 114
Iroquois, 162

Irving, John, xi, 147–152
Israel, 2
Italy, 4–5
Ivy Green (Alabama), 119–123

Jacksonville, Florida, 198, 199, 200
Japan, ix, 66, 67, 125, 128, 130, 168, 169
Japanese Americans, x, 167–166
Japanese Sea, 128, 130
Java, 125, 130
Java Sea, 128
Jefferson, Thomas, 99
Jim Crow South, 40, 41, 144
Johnson, Lyndon B., 150, 180
Joy Luck Club, The, xii, 65–73
Joyce, James, 92
Judaism, xii, 1–8
Julius Caesar, x, 75–81
Juniper Springs, 198, 200

Kansas City, Kansas, 144
Karachi, Pakistan, 155, 159
Kashmir, 159
Keller, Helen, xi, 119–124
Kennedy, John F., xi, 149
Kent, England, 46–47, 48, 50–51, 52, 55
Khanpur irrigation canal (Pakistan), 153, 154, 159
Kindred, x, 83–88
Kutch (India), 156, 159
Kweilin, 65, 66, 71, 73
Ky, Nguyen Cao, 150

Lake George, 196-199, 200
Lake Huron, 151
Lake Michigan, 97, 98, 99, 101, 103, 138
Lake Superior, 173
Las Vegas, New Mexico, 14, 18
Lawrence, Jerome, 57–62
Leavenworth (San Francisco, California), 66, 69, 70
Lee, Robert E., 57–62
Lee, Robert E. (Captain), 101
Lenox Avenue, 39, 40, 42, 44, 132
Leopold, Nathan, 60
Lesson Before Dying, A, xii, xiii, 89–95
Life magazine, 68
Light in My Darkness, 123
Lincoln, England, 115, 117
Lincoln, Nebraska, 137, 139, 141, 142

Lincoln, Abraham, 97, 101
Lincoln, Mary Todd, 101
Lincoln-Douglas debates, 97, 101
Lindbergh, Colonel Charles A., 98
Little, Malcolm. *See* Malcolm X
llaneros, 11
Loeb, Richard, 60
Logan Airport (Boston), 29
London, x, xii, 4, 19–21, 23-24, 25, 45, 49–40, 46, 51, 52, 53, 55, 57, 111, 116
London Bridge, 49, 52, 5355
Long Way from Chicago, A, x, xiii, 97–102
López de Santa Ana, Antonio, 101
Los Angeles, California, 83, 84, 188, 189, 190
Louis, Joe, 92
Louisiana, 89–95
Louisiana State University, 90–91, 92

Macbeth, ix, xiii, 105–111
mah jong, 66
Maine, ix, 83, 86, 148, 161–66
Malcolm X, 132, 174
Malcolm X Boulevard, 132, 135
Malpais, x, 20, 22–23, 25
Man Who Never Was, The, 184
Manhattan, New York, 40, 42, 44, 126. *See also* New York City
Manhattan Detention Center, 131–132, 133, 135
Many Lives, Many Masters, 189
Manzanar, 168, 169, 172
Marble Mountains, 179
Marines, U.S., 150
Mark Antony, ix, 75, 77, 78–80
Maryland, x, xii, 27, 28, 29, 30, 31, 39, 41, 83, 84–87, 88, 174
Maryland Historical Society, 83, 87
Massachusetts xi, xiii, 27, 28–29, 31, 119, 120–121, 161, 162, 180, 182, 182
Massachusetts Bay Colony, 148, 162, 165, 166
Maya, 13
Mayflower, 162
McCarthy era, 57
McKinley, William, 58
Mecca, 156
Mehrabpur (Pakistan), 154, 156–57, 159
Melville, Herman, 125–130
Mencken, H. L., 59, 61
Menéndez de Avilés, Don Pedro, 198
Mengele, Dr. Josef, 7
Metropolitan Museum of Art, 41, 44

Mexican War, 97, 101
Mexico, 101
Mexico City, 139, 140, 142
Michael L. Printz Award for Excellence in Young Adult Literature, 131
Middle Ages, x, 105, 113–117
Midwest, x, xiii, 137–42
Midwife's Apprentice, The, x, xiii, 113–17
midwifery, 113–17
Military Police, 181
Minorca, 197
Miracle Worker, The, xiii, 119–124
Miracle Worker, The (theatrical production), 123
Mississippi, 122, 143, 144–145, 146, 145, 168, 174
Mississippi River, 89, 91, 98, 197
Missouri River, 137
Moby Dick, ix, xiii, 125–130
Mojave Desert, 168, 169, 172
Monster, xii, xiii, 131–135
Moray Firth, 105, 106, 107, 111
Morgan, Howard, 60
Morrison, Toni, xi, 173–76
multicultural contemporary fiction, 11–24, 89–95, 143–146, 153–159
Museum of Natural History (New York), 41, 44
Mussolini, Benito, 4
My Khe, Vietnam, 179, 180, 182, 184, 186
My Lai massacre, 184
Myers, Walter Dean, xii, 131–135
mystery/suspense fiction, 33–38

Nantucket, 126, 127, 128, 129, 130
Nashville, Tennessee, 90, 93, 95, 98
Nation of Islam, 132, 174
Nazi, ix, 1–8
Nebraska, x, 58, 132, 137–141, 142
Nervii, 79, 81
Netherlands, The, ix, 1–8, 9, 21
New Bedford, Massachusetts, 125, 126, 130
New College of Florida, 36
New England, ix, x, xiii, 86, 125, 126, 128, 130, 165
New Hampshire, 147–151, 152
New Mexico, x, xi, 11–17, 18, 19, 20, 22–23, 187–93
New Orleans, 19, 22, 25, 91
New Smyrna, Florida, 197, 200
New South Wales, xii, 46, 51, 55

New York City, 39, 40, 41–42, 44, 57, 58, 131–134, 139, 142
New York Stock Exchange, 42
New York University Law School, 133
Newbery Medal, 27
Newgate Prison, 50, 51, 54, 55
Ningpo, 66, 73
nonfiction, 1–8, 187–193
Norsemen, 105, 107
North Africa, 4, 75
North Carolina, 35, 86
North Sea, 2, 3, 105, 106

O Pioneers!, x, xiii, 137–42
O'Brien, Tim, xi, 179–85
Oakland, California, 68, 73
Oberlin College (Ohio), 60
Ocala National Forest (Florida), 195, 198, 199
Ocklawaha River, 196, 200
Of Human Bondage, 40
Oklahoma, 191
Omaha, Nebraska, 97, 132, 137, 139, 140, 141, 142
On the Origin of Species, 59, 61
Optimism, 123
Orange County, California, 187, 189, 190
Orlando, Florida, 38
Out of the Dark, 123
Oxford, England, 114, 116, 117

Pacific Ocean, 66, 125, 127, 150, 180
Pakistan, xi, 153–159
Palestine, 2
Palmer House Hotel, 97, 100
Palmyra, Illinois, 97, 100, 101, 103
Pánfilo de Narváez, 197
Pearl Harbor, x, 101, 168
Peck, Richard, x, 97–102
Pecos River, 12, 13, 15, 18
Peking, 73
Penobscot Indians, 161–65
Penobscot River, 161, 162, 163–65, 166
Pentecostalism, 40
Peoria, Illinois, 97, 103, 98
Pequod, ix, xiii, 125–129
Pequot, 125
Perkins Institute for the Blind, 119, 121
Petersburg, Virginia, 38, 86
Philadelphia, Pennsylvania, 85, 88
Philippi, 75, 79–80, 81

Philippines, 70, 128
Phillips Exeter Academy, 147
Phoenix Sky Harbor (Arizona), 150
Piano Lesson, The, xii, xiii, 143–146
Piatt County, Illinois, 97, 98–99, 100, 101
Pilgrims, 162
Pittsburgh, Pennsylvania, 35, 38, 143–144, 146
Platte River, 137, 142
Plymouth, Massachusetts, 28–29
Plymouth Colony, 28
Poland, 6
Pompey the Great, 75, 76, 77
Ponce de León, 197
Prayer for Owen Meany, A, xi, xii, 147–152
Proverbs (Book of), 61
Provincetown, 27, 31
Psychic Connections: A Journey into the Mysterious World of Psi, 33
psychic phenomenon, 33, 187, 189, 191, 192
Puget Sound, 167–72
Punjabi Plains (Pakistan), 153, 159

Quang Ngai City, 179, 181, 183, 184, 186
Quang Ngai Province, 179, 182
Queens, New York, 44, 133, 135
Quincy, Massachusetts, 161, 166

racism, xiii, 40, 41, 90, 91
Rahimyar Khan (Pakistan), 153, 154, 155, 159
Ramadan, 125, 156
Rawlings, Marjorie Kinnan, xi, 195–200
regicide, 105–110
Republican River, 137
Richmond, Virginia, 33, 34, 38, 50
Richmond-upon-Thames, 46, 50, 51, 55
Riker's Island, 132, 135
Rio de la Plata, 127, 130
Rio Grande, 14, 18, 188, 190
Robinson Crusoe, 162, 163, 164
Robinson, Jackie, 92
Roman Empire, 2, 75
Roman Republic, ix, 75–80, 81
Romeo and Juliet, 23
Roosevelt, Eleanor, 123
ROTC, 147, 149, 183
Russia, 6

Sag Harbor, 126, 130
Saigon, 181, 182, 183
Saint Sebastian, 179

Salisbury, England, 116, 117
Salisbury, Maryland, 27, 28, 29, 31
San Diego, California, 14, 191
San Francisco, California, ix, 14, 65, 66, 67–68, 69, 70, 73
San Francisco Exposition, 123
Sandia Mountains, 191, 193
Sanford, Florida, 197, 198, 200
Santa Ana, 188
Santa Fe, 14, 16, 18, 19, 20, 22–23, 25, 33, 189
Santa Fe Railway, 13, 98
Sarasota, Florida, 36, 38
Sarasota-Bradenton Airport, 35
Sardis, 75, 79, 81
Scenes from Childhood, 68
Schumann, Robert, 68
science fiction, x, 19–24, 83–88
Scone, ix, 106, 108, 111
Scopes Monkey Trial, 57–62
Scopes, John Thomas, ix, x, 58, 60, 61
Scotland, ix, xiii, 105–111, 115
Scott, Winfield, 101
Seattle, Washington, 139, 142, 167
Senate, Roman, 78–79
Seventeen Against the Dealer, 27
Shabanu, Daughter of the Wind, xi, xii
Shakespeare, William, ix, xi, 22, 23, 75–80, 105–111, 123
Shanghai, xii, 66, 67, 69, 71, 73
Shansi Province, 67, 73
Shiloh, Battle of, 98
Sibi, 155, 159
Sign of the Beaver, The, x, xiii, 161–66
Silver Glen, Florida, 196, 198, 199
Sixteenth Street Baptist Church (Birmingham, Alabama), 175
slavery, 77, 83–87, 133, 149
Snow Falling on Cedars, x, xiii, 167–172
Soho (London), 50, 55
Song of Solomon, xi, xiii, 173–77
Song of the Stone Wall, The, 123
Song Tra Bong River, 179, 181, 183, 186
Sons from Afar, 27
South America, 23, 25, 34, 127, 130
South Carolina, 36, 169
South China Sea, 150, 179, 180, 181, 184, 186
South Sea, 128
Southeast Asia, xii, 147
Southern Pacific Railroad, 12, 13

Southwest, American, xii, xiii, 11–18, 19, 20, 22, 150, 187–193
Spain, 77
Spanish-American War, 58
Speare, Elizabeth George, x, 161-66
Springfield, Illinois, 97, 103
St. Augustine, Florida, 36, 38, 198, 200
St. Johns River, 196, 197, 198, 199, 200
St. Kitts, 133, 135
St. Louis, Missouri, 97, 98, 99, 100, 103, 138, 139, 142
St. Paul's Cathedral, 49
St. Raphael Parish, Louisiana, 90, 91, 92–93, 95
St. Valentine's Day Massacre, 97, 98
stalking, xi, xii
Staples, Suzanne Fisher, x, 153–158
Story of My Life, The (Helen Keller), 121
Straight of Sundra, 128, 130
Stuyvesant High School, 131, 132, 135
Sulaiman Range (Pakistan), 155, 159
Sullivan, Annie, xi, 119–124
Sumatra, 125, 127, 130
Sunflower, Mississippi, 144, 146
Supreme Court, U.S., 62
Surrey, 19, 25, 50
suspense novel, 33–38
Susquehanna River, 174, 177
Sweden, 138, 140, 142
Swedish Americans, 137–141

Tacoma, Washington, 169
Taiyuan, 67, 73
Tan, Amy, xii, 65–72
Tarquinius Superbus, 77
Tempest, The, 22
Tennessee, xiii, 57–63, 90, 93, 95, 98
Texas, 12, 13, 19, 90, 93, 95
Thailand, 181
Thames River, xii, 46, 49, 51, 52
Than Khe, 179–80
Thasos, 79, 81
Thieu, Nguyen Van, 150
Things They Carried, The, xi, xii, 179–86
Third Reich, 2
Tiber River, xi, 76, 77, 79, 81
Tientsin, 67, 70, 73
Till, Emmett, 174
Tombs, the, 39, 42, 131
Tonkin Gulf Resolution, 150, 180
Toronto, Canada, 147, 150, 152

Tra Bong, Vietnam, 179, 181
Tra Khuc River, 181
Tri Binh, Vietnam, 183
True Crime, 187–193
Tubman, Harriet Ross, 85–86
Turner, Nat, 86
Tuscumbia, Alabama, 119–23, 124
typhus, ix

U.S.S. *Maddox,* 180
U.S. War Relocation Authority, 169
Underground Railroad, 85
Union army, 98, 122
United Nations, 2
University of California at Berkeley, 68
University of California at Los Angeles, 84
University of California at San Francisco, 68, 73
University of Chicago, x, 60, 61
University of Nebraska, 137, 139
University of New Hampshire, 148, 149
University of New Mexico Hospital, 187, 188193
University of Southern California, 83
Valparaíso, Chile, 162
vaqueros, 11, 12
Vicksburg, Mississippi, 98, 122, 124
Vietcong, 150, 182, 183
Vietnam, xi, xii, 70, 147–50, 179–86
Vietnam War, xi, xii, 147–48, 149–50, 179–86
Voigt, Cynthia, xii, 27–31
Volusia, 197, 198, 199, 200

Wabash Railroad, 97, 98, 99, 100, 101, 103
Wall Street, 42, 139
War of 1812, 126
Washington, x, 139, 142, 167–72
Washington, D.C., 33, 34, 38, 57, 58, 62, 98, 149, 196
Washington, George, 86
West Virginia, 131, 143, 146
Westerbork, 4, 6, 9
Westminster Abbey, 21, 49, 55
WGN Radio, 58, 61
whaling, ix, 125–130
White Mountains, 148–149, 152, 180
Who Killed My Daughter?: The True Story of a Mother's Search for HerDaughter's Murderer, xi, xii, 33, 187–193
Wilhelmina, Queen, 2, 5
Williamsburg, Virginia, 33, 35, 38

Wilmington, Delaware, 27, 30, 31
Wilson, August, xii, 143–46
Winnipeg, 180, 186
witchcraft, x, 13, 14–16
Woodside, 69, 70, 73
World I Live In, The, 123
World War I, 41, 97, 99, 101, 123, 170, 174
World War II, ix, x, xii, 11, 12, 65, 66, 67, 69, 97, 167–71, 179, 184
Worthington, Minnesota, 179, 180, 182, 183, 184, 186
Wright-Humason Oral School, 123

Writing Vietnam Conference, 179
Wuchang-Canton railway, 66
Wushi, 70, 73

Xavier College, 92

Yazoo Basin, Mississippi, 144
Yearling, The, xi, xiii, 195–200
Yellow Dog, 144, 145
Yukon Territory, 137, 139, 140

Zionism, 2
Zuñi, x, 19, 22, 20

www.ingramcontent.com/pod-product-compliance
Lightning Source LLC
Chambersburg PA
CBHW080538300426
44111CB00017B/2786